THE LIFE AND DEATH
OF AN UNKNOWN CELEBRITY

The Life and Death
of an Unknown Celebrity

Darren Cockle

JANUS PUBLISHING COMPANY LTD
London, England

First published in Great Britain 2012
by Janus Publishing Company Ltd,
93–95 Gloucester Place,
London W1U 6JQ

www.januspublishing.co.uk

British Library Cataloguing-in-Publication Data
A catalogue record for this book is available from the British Library

ISBN 978-1-85756-779-3

Cover Design: Darren Cockle

Graphic Design: Baker
www.jackets.moonfruit.com

Printed and bound in Great Britain

This book is dedicated to Sarah, Samuel and Olivia.

Sarah Ruth Louise Cockle

Acknowledgements

Thank you to Carla Breslin. This book would not have got past the first chapter without your encouragement, kind words of support and your love. You are a truly remarkable lady and make me smile every day.

My mum and dad for being the most loving and supportive parents a son could ever wish for. They have guided me through the darkness and loved my children as their own. Tracy, my sister, for listening to endless chapters on a weekly basis and her overuse of the word 'Wow'.

I would like to thank Leeanne Vinson and Ben Gale for believing in me and for your continuing help and support. To Ruth Mclellan, Cathy Rand, Dominic Stevens, James Jordan, Jenny Jones and Anthia Davy for being such wonderful friends and for putting up with me.

Miranda Rock Smith for being a good friend, reading my manuscript and giving invaluable feedback.

Aidan Breslin for setting up my website and enabling me to write a weekly blog.

The staff of Teddies Nursery, Southampton, for your personal involvement in mine and my children's lives, giving us so much support in our time of need.

All the staff at the Bedruthan Steps Hotel for providing a relaxing environment to enjoy a holiday regardless of my state of mind.

Claire Pickering and Jeannie Leung for your professional touch in turning my manuscript into a book and making it available to the public.

Sarah's employer BDO Stoy Hayward for their support, which far exceeded all expectations any of us have as an employee.

Starbucks and John Lewis for letting me sit and write in your coffee shop for six hours with only one drink purchase.

All of my Twitter followers for building my confidence with all the kind words and retweets – especially Carla Breslin, Cinta Garcia, Ben Hatch, Elaine Pantling and Nicole Cody.

Simon Says child bereavement charity for their unlimited support. I will be giving them a yearly donation from the sales of my book so they can continue to help others.

Terry Bown for his genuine warmth, honesty and experienced guidance in the midst of my grief.

My children, Samuel and Olivia, for giving me peace to talk on the telephone when they craved my attention. I love you both very much and cannot thank God enough for having you in my life.

Prologue

Beautiful green eyes, thick, shoulder-length dark brown hair and a very warm, cheeky smile. I could begin to describe Sarah like this. I could say she was 5 foot 8, which she always claimed was tall for a girl. She had lovely soft skin covering her perfect figure. Sarah used to say that her breasts were her best assets as they were the perfect size. They were to her what Baby Bear's porridge was to Goldilocks: just right. She had killer pins, too. Though her feet were a bit hobbit-looking, which meant she had to wear ugly shoes during her childhood as her feet were too wide for fashionable ones at the time. I still loved her even with this slight imperfection.

Now if I were to say beautiful green eyes, bald head, one breast, a large scar across her stomach, small scars on the back of her hands from too many injections, puffy complexion, swollen fingers resulting in the removal of her wedding ring, I would be painting a completely different picture – but she is still perfect. She is still my Sarah, my wife and mother of our two children and she is still very much alive. Did I mention her wide feet and how much I love them?

I should have said Sarah was selfless, brave, thoughtful, caring, funny and intelligent because no matter how one looks, these qualities remain consistent. This is what makes somebody your soulmate. You need to get under the shell. Sadly the shell dies, whereas the soul cannot. It becomes part of the person they chose to share it with.

In 2006, a week away from Sarah's thirty-third birthday, a lump discovered in her right breast a month earlier turned out not to be a blocked milk duct as first thought but devastating, life-changing news in the form of breast cancer. This day also happened to be our daughter's first birthday. Our son had recently turned four. I had been busy preparing my wife's birthday present, which was a CD titled *The Best Thirty-third Birthday Album in the World Ever*. Talk about ironic! This was to include our wedding song by Moloko called "The Time is Now" and many other favourite songs of ours from our thirteen years together.

Many people do survive cancer. Indeed, many people spend their lives fighting it, but others have to say goodbye too soon. On 20 March 2009, my worry about becoming a single father of two became a reality as I had to say goodbye to my wife, best friend and soulmate. Just two days later Jade Goody's family were doing the same. Jade was made famous after appearing on a reality TV show. Sarah was celebrated by me but was unknown to the public. Jade's story overshadowed ours and was also a constant reminder that heightened my grief. Unfortunately people are dying of cancer every day, leaving husbands, wives, parents, siblings and children to cope with their loss.

My individual loss is monumental. My whole future was immediately altered and a long list of dreams was shattered. I cannot begin to explain what I have lost and the enormity of it. What I can do is explain what I have gained and learned from my loss and how I have dealt with it and remained positive. Not only was Sarah very much prepared for her death, but she also prepared me for my life after her death. I couldn't begin to be a successful single father without her and whilst I *am* without her, she is never far away. Sarah is the unknown celebrity.

Crisps are Good for You

I wish I could say that we met in an art gallery, or during a storm at the top of the Eiffel Tower, or as a result of being in a minor road accident. True-love stories generally require this kind of introduction for people to say, 'Oh! that's lovely', or 'Pass me a bucket'. I dare say the latter could be the case if our first meeting was owing to a minor road accident, especially one involving blood or twisted limbs.

But meeting that special person doesn't usually involve crisps. Well, Spicy Nik Naks to be exact. I had been drinking all afternoon and according to my friends, I couldn't even string a sentence together. Maybe if I hadn't been drinking I would not have needed some food to satisfy my hunger, so maybe some things are for a reason. Pubs have a limited food choice approaching midnight, so on this occasion a packet of spicy crisps had to suffice. This was to be the first and last time that I would throw crisps at a girl to get her attention. I also helped myself to her drink. Knowing what I now know about Sarah, I am surprised that she didn't shoo me away.

I remember sobering up and as I started talking to her my words became clearer and more confident. Not much time passed before I blurted out, 'Will you take me home with you tonight?' Sarah's reply was that she couldn't because she would never hear from me again once morning arrived. I finally persuaded her to take me home, silently promising myself that I would definitely call and see her again if I stayed over. We only kissed and talked that night. Sarah was far too much of a lady to let anything else happen. She teased me for years about kissing her feet, but I don't recall doing that. Neither do I remember thinking, those are really wide feet.

I am aware that this was not the most romantic encounter and I am highly surprised it turned out to be the start of something beautiful. Sarah was twenty and I was twenty-five.

During our thirteen years together before cancer came along we lived a normal, happy life. We went on many holidays abroad, had weekends away in hotels and we ate out to the point where eating in became a treat. We had the same sense of humour and taste in music and films. My happiest memories are basic ones, though. I loved arriving home from work at the same time and then chatting about our day over a glass of wine. Many evenings we would relax on separate sofas, her sofa and mine, feeling content with each other, regardless of conversation or silence. We were comfortable in each other's presence, sharing thoughts and funny stories, sharing laughter and a smile.

If I had my time over again, I would visit the same pub and live it all over again.

Into the Darkness

In September of 2006, Sarah told me not to fuss when she discovered a lump while she was breastfeeding our daughter of ten months. I made the appointment for her to see a doctor the following day, which was unusual as I normally left all decisions to her. I think the reason for this was so I wouldn't incriminate myself and I wanted an easy life.

Sarah saw a female doctor, who assured her that there was nothing to worry about. It was Sarah's decision as to whether or not she had a mammogram, but she opted for an appointment to put everybody's mind at rest. The doctor reassured us that she wasn't concerned as it looked like it was a blocked milk duct although a mammogram was a good idea as a formality.

As the hospital appointment neared my mum told me that Sarah may have to have an injection if she had a cyst. Knowing how needle phobic she was, as I had often seen her covering her eyes during hospital dramas, I decided to go with her to the hospital. One in nine women having mammograms at the time was told that they had some form of cancer. I didn't think for one second that Sarah would be given bad news and be the unlucky statistic. If one in nine got a prize, I would have been feeling confident. The odds of winning the jackpot in the national lottery were fourteen million to one and I believed I could win that. I could be that one lucky person in a life-changing draw.

I was feeling very relaxed as I waited for Sarah to have her mammogram which was, after all, just a formality. I was sitting playing a game on my phone, when Sarah came back into the waiting room and told me that she didn't have a blocked milk duct or a cyst. I put my phone away and stared at the floor. If fear was visible then I would have seen it grip my ankles and start to climb.

The mammogram was closely followed by a biopsy. Sarah looked away at the same time as I did when a needle was inserted into her right breast. As I sat by her side I knew things didn't look good. The three nurses' facial expressions worried me. I mustered up some courage to ask a question.

'What do you think it is?' I said to the nurse who was inflicting pain with a needle.

She looked directly into my eyes and spoke clearly. 'I am not going to lie to you. I am concerned because it doesn't look good,' she said.

Just twenty minutes later, which was an hour after we arrived, the oncologist told us in the way only cancer specialists can that, 'It does look like cancer.'

We asked how certain he was and were told that there was a slight chance that it could be something disguising itself as cancer. Who or what disguises itself as cancer? Surely that was wrong, but it was the only hope we had until our next appointment, which was more than a week away.

On leaving the hospital we drove to the nearest pub for a stiff drink and a shameful cigarette. We had not had one for a very long time. We had given up when we decided to have children. I remember screaming and swearing at other drivers en route to get out of the way. Sarah turned to me and told me not to take it out on anybody else as it wasn't their fault.

My hands were trembling as I clutched my pint of beer. I was holding it so tight I am surprised that it didn't shatter. I looked out of the window and stared at nothing in particular. The rain was falling hard, which was quite fitting with how I felt at the time. Sitting across the pub table from each other holding hands, we managed to convince one another that it was not cancer. There was still hope. We were of course putting on a brave front and underneath we were both terrified.

We hardly spoke to the children when we collected them from nursery later that day. We got them into bed early and showed no interest when reading their stories. We went to bed early too, but we didn't sleep. I had so many thoughts entering my mind that it was impossible for sleep to come naturally. My positive thinking was trying hard to combat the onslaught of negative thoughts and questions. Did Sarah really have cancer? Would we be growing old together? Surely it was all a big mistake!

In eight days' time a light was going to go out.

Thursday, 26 October 2006 was our daughter's first birthday. Her day should have been filled with happiness and cake. But Olivia didn't seem to notice; neither did she acknowledge the lack of input on her special day. She was too young to know what birthdays were. Samuel was four, though, and would probably have sensed that something was wrong.

Heading to the hospital on the day of the results, hope was in our hearts. We were both positive people and hope was all we had.

'It will be okay, Piggy,' said Sarah quite confidently as I pulled into a parking space.

I don't know why her pet name for me was Piggy, but what I do know is that my life was about to be surrounded by a whole pile of shit and become a bit of a pigsty.

It is really hard to explain how you feel when told that the person you have devoted your life to has breast cancer. I wanted to cover my ears but it was too late. I wanted to make a run for the door but I don't think my legs would have been strong enough. I can see clearly in my mind the two of us sitting there, paralysed by shock and fear. I can still hear the words, 'It's bad news; you do have cancer.' That moment will always be with me. It's like an emotional tattoo, which hopefully will fade a little in time.

I looked out of the window at an ugly tower block of flats. Dark clouds surrounded it and they were coming for me. I could have been staring out of a window that had the best possible views and I would have seen nothing. It could have been a clear blue sky above a shimmering calm sea. A waterfall could have been gushing down into a river surrounded by an array of beautiful flowers and wildlife. The sun shining through the splashing water could have been creating a rainbow begging to be photographed.

All beauty had temporarily vanished. Future dreams had also ceased. Dark clouds surrounded me and filled my senses. The numbness from the shock of being told your wife has breast cancer is debilitating. It is like a deep pain that descends that has no obvious location. It fills your stomach, your heart, your head, your back, your shoulders and even your face can feel it. All it took was a moment to change everything .To piss all over our plans. To dim the lights in our life. To make us truly appreciate one another.

We had only been married five years. I loved her so much but I don't think I really knew how much until that moment. I also realised how much I loved our children. We were a family and I was such a lucky man.

They found three lumps in Sarah's right breast and I assumed that they would just remove them. I had not expected to be told that her breast would be removed within a week. I thought back to a programme on the BBC Sarah and I had watched some weeks earlier before she had discovered the lump. We were just channel-hopping while relaxing on different sofas, when Sarah settled for a documentary about ladies who have had mastectomies. I sat through the whole programme, which was unusual as I would normally complain about it being too morbid. The ladies were being interviewed about their surgery and how it had affected their lives from two years on to twenty in one lady's case.

I remember saying to Sarah how terrible it must be for a girl to lose a breast, but surely losing a leg is worse and I haven't seen a programme about that. Sarah agreed that losing a leg would be worse, but only a woman would know what it's really like to lose a breast. I didn't know what was going through Sarah's mind at that moment when she was told that a mastectomy was the only option, but I was devastated and speechless. The breast cancer diagnosis had shocked me but hearing that Sarah was to have a breast removed disturbed and depressed me more than anything. There was hope that the cancer could be cured, but there was no hope that her breast could be replaced.

My thoughts were interrupted by the word chemotherapy. It was explained to us that as soon as Sarah had recovered from having a mastectomy, chemotherapy treatment was advisable. We were told that treatment would reduce further risk of cancer and that Sarah would lose her hair. The oncologist informed us that if Sarah refused to have chemotherapy then her cancer had a 50 per cent chance of returning. By having the treatment it would reduce these odds to below 10 per cent. I wanted to swap places with Sarah. I wasn't needle phobic and I didn't have a breast to lose. Men can also get away with a bald head. I was too stunned to think about anything else.

Sarah asked if she could have reconstructive plastic surgery at the same time as her mastectomy. Neither of us got the answer that we wanted. Reconstruction would have to wait until after all of the treatments. We were then told that radiotherapy would be necessary after chemotherapy to treat the affected area directly. The skin gets damaged by this process and would need to heal before reconstruction could be possible and effective. Sarah would be without a breast for at least ten months.

We desperately wanted to get the children to bed early that night. I was so upset reading Sam stories at bedtime that night that I don't know how I got through them. Sarah and I were obviously very frightened and were heading for another sleepless night. I was feeling numb with the shock – two pillows were not enough for the heaviness of my head. I tried to imagine Sarah with only one breast and without hair. There were no positive thoughts this time. I was staring at the ceiling in the dark. My world was filled with darkness.

Saturday, 4 November was a special treat. We were staying at a nearby hotel without the children as a late birthday celebration for Sarah. We were both tired owing to many troubled sleeps over the past week and therefore welcomed the short distance to travel. Whether the hotel was a kilometre from our house or on the other side of the world, it really was unimportant. We just wanted to be together and celebrate the life we had shared. This was to be the end of our normal life as we knew it: everyday life where you argue, go to work, moan about that elusive parking space or having to go food shopping with the children.

We had such a wonderful time. We drank champagne, dined, laughed, loved, listened to *The Best Thirty-third Birthday Album in the World Ever* and decided that nothing was going to ruin our life or our happiness. Sarah was still asleep at 7.00 a.m. and wasn't aware that I was staring at her as I lay next to her in the hotel bed. I was on my side and could feel the springs of the mattress digging into my elbow as I rested my head in the palm of my hand. I was looking at every hair on her head and praying that chemotherapy wouldn't claim it. I thought about the three lumps in her breast and wondered if it was really necessary to remove the whole breast. I would have removed the lumps if it was up to me, but I was an engineer and not a doctor. Sarah probably sensed that she was being spied on and started to stir, so I collapsed onto my back. It would have freaked her out to see me staring at her. My eyes were closed but I could still see every hair and every curve. In three days' time my mental picture would be a lot different from the reality that surgery would create.

The evening before Sarah had surgery she bared her breasts to me for the last time and said, 'You had better take a good look, because you won't be seeing these babies for a very long time.' She was referring to reconstruction and the possibility of feeling whole again once her course of treatments came to an end.

On 8 November 2006, the day of Sarah's surgery arrived and all I could think about was my wife undergoing a barbaric mutilation of her body. Sarah was really short-tempered with me as she got out of the car and I told her I was going through it, too. She must have thought I was having an attempt at humour as she glared at me. I couldn't imagine what she was going through and probably never will. I was too numb and stressed to understand fully what was going on.

My mind was filled with so many images, a mixture of past, present and future. I was thinking how perfect she was and how much I didn't want this. How would this affect our future in general and our sex life? How big would Sarah's chest scar be after this, not to mention how big would her mental scar be? I had this recurring image of her breast being cut off with a big knife and callously thrown into a bin. Happy memories also flooded my mind of her flaunting her breasts at me. Memories of mammary glands are an oddity. It's strange thinking back to how I felt and my thoughts of bra-shopping and how I enjoyed buying them for her, making birthday and Christmas shopping easy. I was also thinking of her sense of fun when she was pregnant with Olivia and out of curiosity had weighed her breasts on our kitchen scales. I could share this with you but it is very rude to discuss a lady's weight. We used to have a lot of dinner parties at the time so I would like to apologise for the misuse of our kitchen equipment.

I realise now how selfish I was. Sarah was alive. I should have been thankful for that. I guess I wasn't ready to count my blessings just yet.

I have never liked waiting but I don't remember much about the four hours I waited for Sarah to have her surgery. The operation didn't take long but she had to spend a long time in recovery before being taken back to the ward. People have blackouts when they have consumed too much alcohol and have been known to lose their memory and have little recollection of the evening. I think the shock and fear combined caused a similar blackout in me. I recall going home for a short while because Sarah's mum, Jacqueline, was staying to help out with the children and provide aftercare for her daughter. I didn't even get through the front door before I broke down.

I went back to the hospital at midday. I was so desperate to see Sarah that I couldn't sit still. I kept circling the hospital and pacing up and down corridors waiting for her to come out of recovery. I must have asked the nurse on the ward at least six times if Sarah was there before she eventually nodded her head. She told me that Sarah had lost a lot of blood and was very weak. This was the first time I had ever heard the word weak and Sarah in the same sentence. As desperate as I was to see her, I didn't run to her bed because I was anxious and unsure of what to say. I walked slowly to her side as if I was walking into a strong wind. Sarah was very pale and drowsy. I looked around at the other beds and they were all empty. She was the only patient on the ward.

'Are you okay, darling?' I said.

I didn't know if she was going to answer me or scream at me. I didn't know if having her breast removed would break her strong spirit, consume her with self-pity or make her depressed or constantly angry.

'I'm so cold,' she said faintly as she started to shiver. Her teeth were chattering, creating the only sound on an empty ward.

I found the nurse and returned with a blanket. I covered her over, kissed her on the cheek and told her I would return in the evening. I cried along every corridor and along every road as I headed home.

Once the children were in bed that evening, I headed to our favourite restaurant, The King and I, to get Sarah a Thai mixed starter – she always used to say that the chicken satay was to die for!

Walking into the hospital reminded me of the film *The Shining*. It was deserted and many of the lights had been turned off. I only passed about two people on the way to Sarah's ward. Sarah was awake but still very pale. I showed her the food but she felt too sick to eat anything. She loved the fact that I'd brought it, though. In fact, she loved me. We were born to be together but I didn't know if it would be forever. Sarah's health and her survival was a growing concern. I was so worried that if fear was cancerous it would have spread throughout my whole body and killed me instantly.

I stayed for about an hour, making sure she had everything she needed, but she hated it when I fussed. She told me that I would make a good nurse and maybe I should consider a career change. But I wouldn't be able to stick a needle in a human being, so becoming a nurse was out of the question. I thought long and hard about what I could do if I left the world of engineering. My mind was blank for a moment until it went back to worrying about Sarah.

I came back the following morning and Sarah was talking to a breast nurse. The nurse was showing her some breast pads which came in different sizes to match the remaining breast. It was to be placed in the empty bra cup so that clothes could hide all traces of the mastectomy and not draw attention to it.

Seeing Sarah sitting there at that moment was one of my most upsetting and heart-warming moments combined. She was so depleted, her head hanging limp and her bottom lip sticking out momentarily before the tears came. I felt so helpless and completely traumatised yet filled with so much love for her at the same time. There was less of her now but I loved her more.

We left the hospital together just twenty-four hours after her operation. She had a tube coming out of the wound on her chest which worked as a drain and was attached to a bag .This bag had to be emptied daily or before it filled with blood, whichever happened sooner. Sarah had to carry this around for a week and sleep with it next to the bed. There was a selection of colourful wool bags with handles to choose from at the hospital to place the blood bag into. They think of everything, don't they! She also had a dressing covering her wound which had to be changed daily.

The first night at home was a real worry. Sarah was distraught after having had her breast removed and she was weak from blood loss. She was also unable to get comfortable or relax enough to sleep and insisted on going into the spare room so that she wouldn't disturb me. She looked so unwell that I lay awake too, covering my sobs. I remember thinking: my wife is going to die, please don't let it be tonight. If it has to happen at least let the children become independent adults and grow up with a mum.

It was a huge relief to me that my mother-in-law stayed for most of the week. She cooked for us, changed her daughter's dressing and emptied the blood bag when necessary. After five days Jacqueline went home. I was back at work so Sarah got Sam to empty the blood bag because she disliked looking at it. He was only four but fascinated by this and enjoyed helping.

In the days that followed surgery, Sarah wore a nightshirt to bed, which she always put on in the bathroom. Samuel was the only person to have seen her scar because he had asked to see it. Sarah said he winced and commented on how much it must have hurt. I didn't ask to see the scar and neither did Sarah offer to show me. I was not brave enough to ask as I was worried my facial expression would disappoint and hurt her. I never questioned Sarah's need to get changed in the bathroom and I didn't mention her missing breast. I wanted to pretend that it never happened. Sarah didn't discuss her mastectomy much but she did mention her scar and how ironic it was that it looked like a smiley mouth. It was typical of Sarah to see the funny side!

Chemotherapy

Chemotherapy was to begin in December and I had to warn Sam that his mummy was about to have some medicine that would make her hair fall out. He cried and asked if it would grow back the same. After reassuring him that it would he cried some more and then said, 'But I want it to grow back red and spiky.' If only we could live our lives with the same outlook as our children, only knowing what you need to know. Children need to be protected, though, and rightly so. He didn't know what cancer was. He didn't know that death was a possibility.

I, on the other hand, knew full well what the possibilities were. Cancer had already taken the life of Sarah's stepfather, Mike, a few months after our wedding in 2001. We had witnessed the rapid change from a healthy man, so full of life and so important to those around him, to a man who needed a wheelchair in his final days. He was only 51 years of age. To watch a loved one deteriorate so quickly is very disturbing. To stand by feeling helpless as the cancer spreads through the body, causing it to die, is heartbreaking. Obviously this isn't always the case. A lot of cancers are treated and never return.

I used to sit downstairs on our sofa listening to music every night before going to bed, trying to find meaningful songs for my mood, similar to the way in which you might listen to melancholic songs after a break-up. As hard as I tried not to let these thoughts enter my mind, I was also thinking about funeral songs. I didn't know at this point that Sarah was going to die from cancer. What I did know was that while she was alive it would be a constant concern and the feeling would never leave us.

Christmas was only a week away when the day arrived to start chemotherapy. It was 9.30 a.m. and Sarah was complaining that the half of a Lorazepam tablet she had taken an hour earlier wasn't working as we queued up at the signing-in desk. She had taken this to relax her because of her needle phobia. Dr Last had recommended that Sarah start with half and increase to one tablet on her second visit if necessary.

'I knew I shouldn't have listened to that oncologist when he suggested I only take half,' she said. 'The children's Tixylix cough medicine would have probably made me drowsier,' she added as she reached the front of the queue.

The waiting room held about sixty chairs. With tears in her eyes, Sarah pointed out that these were filled with elderly ladies. It is true that breast cancer is more common in ladies over fifty and so Sarah did stand out. Here she was aged 33 and the mother of two children under five, about to join these ladies in the chemo queue. Apparently not everybody using the same chemo drug suffers from hair loss. I whispered to Sarah that it looked positive, as only a few ladies were wearing headscarves and the majority had hair. She laughed out loud at this and called me a wally for not noticing the wigs!

Sarah was asked to take a numbered ticket which would be called out when the nurse was ready to take some blood. It was the same as a deli-counter system apart from being busier. There were about twenty ladies in front of Sarah but she was in no rush to offer up her arm. I was feeling stressed for two. I couldn't stop sighing and my chest was really tight. After thirty minutes I followed Sarah through a gap in a curtain to hold her hand while the nurse inserted a needle and took some blood. The nurse told Sarah to relax her arm because she had her hand clenched into a fist. I expect that Sarah wanted to punch her for not being very sympathetic or patient after we had both explained the needle phobia in depth. Sarah kept her eyes on me and relaxed her arm as best she could until the needle was removed. All traces of colour had drained from her face as if the blood had been taken directly from there. She attempted to stand up but fell back down onto the chair. After a couple of minutes, the dizziness subsided and Sarah removed her hands from her face. She stood up and I followed her to the waiting room.

'That nurse is a right bloody butcher. I am definitely taking one and a half tablets next time,' she said.

A couple of hours after a blood test a doctor would make a decision as to whether or not treatment would go ahead depending on your blood count. If it was low then treatment would be postponed. As this was Sarah's first treatment, her blood count was fine and therefore treatment went ahead. A large bag of drugs, including antibiotics and steroids, was prescribed to combat the side-effects.

On seeing the steroids Sarah said, 'Great! Not only do I have to walk around with one breast and a bald head, but I am also going to be fat as well. It doesn't get much better than this!'

After the doctor had given the go-ahead, we had to wait for Sarah's name to be called. This could be anything from a two- to six-hour wait. It was strange sitting there hearing cheers when a lady's name was called. Everybody reacted as if they had won the bingo and yet they were about to have a drug injected into their bloodstream that would make them feel very sick and tired. It's hardly surprising cheers followed names, though, as it was such a relief to be on the final hurdle.

Sarah's name was called out at eleven thirty and we followed a nurse through some double doors and entered the chemo ward. There were about eight green armchairs evenly spaced around the ward. Only one of them was vacant and that one was for Sarah. I looked at the ladies occupying the other chairs. They were all at least fifty years of age and they were all reading magazines. The chairs looked even older than the ladies sitting in them. The chair that Sarah was sitting in looked like one my grandmother used to own. The arms were bare and the dust was still circling the air long after her sitting down. Next to every chair was a hatstand on wheels, on which was a see-through plastic bag filled with the chemotherapy drug. A tube carried the liquid from the bag to a needle that was either inscrted into a hand or a chest. Sarah didn't have a bag next to her chair because her specific drug mixture hadn't been made up yet.

In an attempt to keep her hair, Sarah had opted for the freezing cap. This was red and looked like a jockey's hat. It is attached to a freezing machine, where your scalp is frozen for two hours prior to treatment. This apparently works by freezing the cells in your scalp, stopping the chemotherapy from killing them off. At the best of times Sarah wasn't a fan of the cold and she hated this. When the cap was removed, pieces of ice were stuck in her hair. Sarah was shivering and she cried for the second time that day.

'I would rather lose my hair than sit through that again,' she said.

I have never met anyone who has kept their hair by using this device. The wig lady at the hospital told us it only really delays the inevitable. It also delays your treatment by two hours, which is a very long time when all you want to do is get out of there as soon as possible.

With remnants of the ice still in Sarah's hair, a nurse arrived with the drug. The magic, calming drug that Sarah took at 8.00 a.m. had long worn off and she was really fed up as the nurse fumbled around trying to find a vein that was desperately trying to hide. It was quite distressing watching the nurse make six attempts to find a vein in Sarah's apparently veinless arms. Indeed, she certainly was the least "vain" person I have ever known. We were told that the bag would take about an hour to empty and fill her body with the drug.

Chemo Thursday, as we called it, was to be fortnightly. It should have been three-weekly, but Sarah agreed to take part in trials to aid the experts in finding out which method of treatment was most effective. The entire day of the treatment was pretty much written off, regardless of whether or not you had your head frozen. A total of twelve treatment days were scheduled and couldn't be avoided, so it was best to get them over with as soon as possible.

It was both depressing and draining sitting in a chemotherapy ward all day. If treatment finished early we would go for a nice relaxing lunch in the best restaurant Southampton had to offer. We had worked up quite a hunger sitting in a waiting room since 9.00 a.m. as all we had eaten was a handful of sweets. These were necessary because they disguised the taste of the drug entering her bloodstream. It's quite common for ladies to describe a metallic taste during treatment which can make you sick. A sick bowl was placed with the magazines on every table, next to every chair.

Sarah's first treatment was over. It was 3.00 p.m. when we left the hospital and very late in the day to be going for lunch.

On 23 December 2006, we took a family holiday to France. Sarah's entire family was coming with us, so we had booked a huge farmhouse in a very remote place. I wanted to cancel as the oncologist had advised us against travelling. Sarah had only just had her first treatment and it was impossible to tell how it would affect her. Finding insurance cover that was below £1,000 was difficult. These extortionate prices worried me and I assumed the insurance companies knew something that I didn't. In the end we found one for about £400. The concern was that her blood count could drop and she could get an infection of some kind. If this happened then an airlift to hospital could be required.

After a car journey followed by a ferry trip and another long drive, we finally arrived at our Christmas destination. I was panicking because we didn't have any bottled water and started ranting at everyone that Sarah couldn't drink out of the tap as it might make her ill. Her aunt put her arms around me and told me to chill out. I wept uncontrollably into the shoulder of her coat and was handed a glass of whisky to calm me. I drank a whole bottle of whisky that evening in front of a roaring log fire, next to which was a Christmas tree that all the children helped to decorate. Of course once they were in bed we made the tree more presentable. We also bought a star for the top of the tree in a local department store. Probably a complete fire hazard but when plugged in it lit up displaying a beautiful array of colours. The star was cheap and tacky but Sarah fell in love with it and asked if she could be the one to take it home. Having recently being diagnosed with cancer, nobody was going to deny Sarah anything.

On Christmas Eve I left the dinner table in a strop because I couldn't cope with the constant demands of the children. I walked a couple of hundred yards to the main road and sat on a bench near a deserted bus stop, remembering all the good times while slowly freezing and wondering how long Sarah would be in our lives. I sat there for an hour and during that time only three cars passed me. I wondered if the drivers could see my pain, because I certainly wanted them to.

On Boxing Day Sarah took the children out for some fresh air and a walk in the small local village. She passed through a cemetery and read some of the gravestones to the children, already processing the possibility of an unhappy ending. She explained what death was and her idea of Heaven. She told Sam that Heaven was whatever you wanted it to be. In her case it was bed and chocolate, as these were her favourite things. She would repeat this to Sam many times, but we never told the children that Sarah might die. We wanted to protect them as much as we could.

France was soon part of our past and New Year's Eve was only a day away. We had invited our close friends Dave and Sian around as the four of us always celebrated it together. Year after year we had enjoyed entertaining each other until the early hours and we had taken many holidays and weekends away together at various hotels throughout the years. Dave is a very funny man who always used to bring out the funny side in me. On this occasion it would prove impossible. Sarah wasn't able to stomach alcohol as a result of her chemotherapy treatment and was understandably not in a party mood. It was very sweet of our friends to spend the evening with us. I am sure it wasn't easy for them, either, or much fun. Sarah went to bed at 11.00 p.m., which was quite a few hours earlier than previous years.

Dave and Sian kissed as Jools Holland completed his 2006 countdown on his live TV show while I sat with my head in my hands. I was remembering all the fun times of years gone by. Every year while drinking and chatting we used to try to predict which celebrity would pass away in the year ahead. This year there was a possibility it could be someone a lot closer to us. I don't know if it was just me having this thought but I am assuming not, as neither of us suggested who was going to die that evening.

Sarah really did enjoy that Christmas in France, as did I, and even now I can recall all the good times from our holiday in France: the children waking up at 4.00 a.m. and proceeding to open their presents; Olivia taking her first few steps on Christmas Day without the aid of a sofa or table for support; fifteen of us sitting at a huge farmhouse table enjoying obscene amounts of food – indeed, all of us trying to enjoy simple family life.

Most people pass through life without realising that they are blessed with special moments every day. I didn't realise how many treasured memories I would later recall from France as I was blinded by fear. At the time Sarah's hair was already starting to fall out, giving her the opportunity to point out that the freezing cap was crap and a waste of valuable time. I was also worried that Sarah would fall ill. All this combined to stop me from appreciating our valuable time together as a family. But I can still feel the intense cold when I cast my mind back to Christmas that year and it has left me with many memories, even if I didn't realise it at the time.

New Year saw a new calendar on the wall. The first half was already filled with dates for chemotherapy and radiotherapy and the second half would be spent awaiting a date for reconstruction. Having two children probably stopped us from looking ahead too much, so thankfully we mainly focused on each day as it arrived and the needs of our children. There was a strong possibility that chemo would make Sarah infertile. We had talked about having another child as I had always imagined us having three children, but I was now thankful we had at least managed to have two before cancer had entered our lives.

In 2001, not long after we got married, Sarah asked me if she could get a kitten. I answered with a definitive 'No', as I would never let an animal stop me from going on holiday. 'Can we have children, then?' were her next words. I had walked right into that one and a new chapter in our lives.

Not long after, Sarah became pregnant with our first child. Sarah wasn't a massive fan of being pregnant, but she liked the fact that she had an excuse to put on weight and eat what she liked; she even had a hidden stash of biscuits in her drawer at work. We attended antenatal classes together and perhaps learned too much. Does anyone carrying a baby really need to have a demonstration with a replica womb or to be shown what 10 cm in diameter looks like? I swear the doll used in the demonstration was about 7 kg and most definitely obese! At this point most of the ladies in the room were crossing their legs. Surely this is not a good time to show them some frightening-looking instruments, which looked like they may have been used in the days when bad people were hung, drawn and quartered. Ignorance is bliss sometimes, don't you think?

It was 6.00 a.m. one day when Sarah's waters broke and she was very laid-back about the whole thing. TV programmes, especially soaps and hospital dramas, generally have a scary portrayal of this occurrence. They lead you to believe that as soon as the waters have broken you have to go into panic mode. In reality, all that has happened is that the womb "door" has opened and the baby is on its way down the vaginal slide, out of the darkness and into the light. If you haven't already packed a bag then you will have to do without. Instead of this "call me an ambulance now" moment, we did a crossword. Following breakfast and three hours of gardening, we had some lunch and greeted Jacqueline at our door. Her mum is a midwife and she told us we should go to the hospital, but it was 4.00 p.m. before Sarah reluctantly agreed to go. I am aware that labour is different for everyone and horrendous for some. It certainly isn't something I would relish and it therefore pleases me that I am a man.

I was pretty useless at the hospital. Sarah didn't expect anything from me as fussing would have made things more stressful for her. She was already annoyed at being talked into going to hospital earlier than she thought necessary. We had discussed a birth plan which involved only gas and air and agreed that I would leave the birthing room when the birth was imminent. This was because Sarah wanted to maintain her dignity. She didn't want me witnessing potential splits or messy accidents. She also thought the intimacy between us would be affected if I was a spectator.

I headed for the waiting room as midnight approached. At 12.20 a.m. I was half-asleep but heard footsteps. These were not the patter of tiny feet of a very advanced baby but those of my mother-in-law, who was standing in front of me asking me to go with her. I walked into the room and Sarah was clutching our baby to her chest. She had such a big smile on her face. I said, 'That's an ugly girl,' as I was convinced we were having a girl. We had chosen the name Olivia. I had been calling her The Bump, Olivia, for months and reading stories to her. We had a boy's name prepared, though, and Sarah introduced me to Samuel. I compared the birth to being sat in a restaurant waiting for food to arrive, then nipping to the toilet and your meal waiting for you on your return. I wonder why a lot of us men joke in such important, life-changing moments. Maybe it's just me. But I am glad that we shared the same sense of humour and I could always make Sarah laugh.

Sarah was incredibly brave about the birth and only when asked replied, 'It smarts a bit.' She was equally brave when it came to having our second child, whom she gave birth to at home in our dining room. Not on our dining-room table, I might add, for the sake of clarity for any of our dinner guests we've had since then.

At 8.00 a.m. I had to drop Samuel off at nursery. I swear that Sarah controlled her contractions until I was out of the door, as ten minutes after I left she gave birth to Olivia. I was only gone for thirty minutes, but a 4.5 kg daughter was waiting for me on my return. Sarah's only pain relief was two paracetamol. At 5.00 a.m. when she'd asked me for them, I had somehow panicked and took them myself. They happened to be the last two in the packet, but thankfully I managed to find some more and avoided the wrath of my wife nearing the final throes of labour. Her bravery and positive approach, as well as her inability to complain, made my life so uncomplicated and relaxed. Sarah took this same approach with cancer. I think she knew that if she fell apart then I probably would.

*　　*　　*

At the start of 2007 on 4 January, Sarah had her second treatment of chemotherapy. At 8.00 a.m. she swallowed one and half Lorazepam tablets. We dropped the children off at school and nursery and arrived at the hospital at 9.20 a.m. Sarah staggered out of the car and couldn't walk in a straight line. She was giggling and holding my arm for support. Having her bloods done was a lot less stressful this time but by no means easier as no veins were visible. However, Sarah didn't seem to mind and neither did she get annoyed when I showed her my arm to point out the huge blue veins that covered it like a road map. It took three nurses about five attempts to get any blood. A vampire would have been very disappointed. Sarah nearly fell over as she stood up, but not because of the needle. Her magic drug was doing exactly what she wanted.

'I had better stick to taking one of those pills next time,' she said as we found the only two seats next to each other in a crowded waiting room.

Sarah's name was called at midday, which meant that we would be out in good time for lunch because Sarah had chosen to stay away from the freezing cap this time.

The following week Lynne, a hairdresser and close friend of Sarah's, came to our house to shave her head. Her hair had been coming out in handfuls after just two chemo treatments. Jenny, another close friend of Sarah's, had already bought her a wig on eBay. It came from Hong Kong and cost £1.00. It was a reddish colour and in the style of a bob. This was to be her favourite wig. Lynne found cutting Sarah's hair very upsetting and could only bring herself to use scissors, cutting it as short as she could.

When Lynne had gone home, Sarah asked me to get the clippers and shave her head completely. The clippers belonged to Jenny and again faced with a stressful situation, I joked that Jenny probably did her bikini line with them. Without hair she was still beautiful, her green eyes shining even more. She wore her wigs in public, though. It was too cold not to and she never liked to draw attention to herself. I did offer to shave my head too, but she thought this was a mad suggestion, knowing how vain I was. If she had agreed I still don't know if I would have. Maybe it was just an empty gesture, one that was born out of frustration and helplessness.

The accumulation of chemotherapy was taking its toll, though we still went for our lunch date on Chemo Thursday if we got out early enough. The day after chemo was usually OK, but the Saturdays were hard, when extreme nausea and tiredness kicked in. This was the day that Sarah would be at her lowest. She refused my request for her to stay in bed. Tears and apologies may have been uttered but complaints never were, despite the side-effects. She often apologised for not being strong enough to help fully with the children, tearfully saying, 'I am sorry for being a useless sack of shit.' I hugged her and made her go back to bed. I would like to point out here that Sarah was never useless throughout her whole life. Maybe at singing, but it didn't stop me enjoying hearing her. By Wednesday she was back to her old self. This meant we had just over a week of normality before the next round of treatment.

To try to lift Sarah's mood I suggested clothes shopping. She was very enthusiastic about this. We had always loved shopping together, especially if there was a lunch stop in the middle of it. Shopping in the past, which we called our "old life", was difficult enough, often visiting the same shops over and over again until a decision was made. This was based on either elimination, boredom or an argument. But buying clothes when you have one breast isn't easy. Now it was a case of finding tops or dresses that had a higher neckline. If a dress had a neck that was too low then we had to find a cardigan to match, to hide her temporary fake breast pad. Sarah tried on loads of clothes and I thought she looked fantastic in all of them and we went home with about four bags of clothes that day.

The following morning I walked into our bedroom and found Sarah sitting on our bed crying. She told me all of the clothes were going back as there seemed little point in keeping them. She then said, 'I'm a freak.' I told her how beautiful I thought she looked. That it made no difference to our life and that it didn't change a thing. We had each other and the children and as long as we had that, we had all we needed.

At this point I still had not seen or asked to see her scar. But the longer you leave something like that the harder and more of a bigger deal it becomes. Sarah ended up keeping most of the clothes, remaining positive and thinking about the end of her treatments, dreaming about an end to this temporary break in living a normal life. She was looking towards her reconstruction surgery that would hopefully happen six months down the road. She was planning on choosing the best option available, which involved having fat taken from her stomach to build a breast. She often joked that she was going to get a tummy tuck and perfect boobs for a career in modelling.

As the weeks passed and chemo continued, we received lots of help from family and friends. Sarah's sister, Claire, would fly down from Leeds on some of the weekends after treatment. She would cook for us and fill our freezer with meals for the weeks ahead. This was such a great help and much appreciated. Having someone else staying with us eased my worries and relieved a lot of the pressure. Sarah and I both had reservations about asking for help, but a few friends didn't wait to be asked. They just took the initiative to cook or take the children out for a few hours.

Sarah's taste buds had been seriously affected by chemotherapy. She had to double the amount of coffee to be able to taste it. Maybe it also helped keep her awake a little longer on certain days. Her sense of smell was heightened, though, and windscreen wash was to be avoided, as she would feel very sick seconds after I sprayed it. Long journeys were a bit fraught, as I could barely see through the dirty windscreen. A small risk worth taking to keep the car sick-free! Especially if the smell of sick makes you sick. Vinaigrette dressing was also a trigger, as were beef-flavoured Hula Hoops. Sarah loved her food and was very adventurous with it. I was always jealous when we ate out as she would invariably try something new on the menu and I would sit there wishing I had chosen the same dish. While she was frustrated about the disappearance of her taste buds, I said that this might be a blessing as I was doing the lion's share of the cooking now; though my cooking had improved since we first met.

Back then my culinary skills were bordering on dangerous and completely unhealthy and dull. My weekly meals would mainly consist of beans on toast, cheese on toast or Toast Toppers on toast. If you haven't heard of Toast Toppers then I am pleased for you. They come in the form of different-flavoured soup-like sauces that come in a tin. All you have to do is pour the contents onto the bread and grill; though it does resemble sick. The texture when cooked is somewhere between dried chewing gum and porridge. Probably a full week's worth of salt in one portion. It was a quick meal, though, and certainly an advantage if you had lost your sense of taste or couldn't cook. I had once got quite sick after having pork chops and mash. I only realised why when my mum pointed out that you need to defrost the meat before placing it in the frying pan.

My cooking was often the subject of Sarah's dinner-party stories and a favourite of hers. I had cooked her a roast dinner quite early on in our relationship. It was about the only meal I could cook and I wanted to impress. She had opened the oven to check on the chicken because the smoke alarm was going crazy and what she found were luminous blue potatoes surrounding a chicken with a very black bottom. After close inspection she realised that I had left the blue plastic packaging underneath that was attached to the chicken. On one occasion I tried to impress Sarah by serving up a plate of pizza and mash. Once she had finished laughing, she advised me that the two dishes should never be put together.

Years later, just before we were married, Sarah suggested that I sign up for a cookery course. This was mainly because she was fed up with cooking the majority of our meals. She was also fed up with my continuous annoying questions. How do you want your carrots chopped? How much water shall I put into the pan? What colour do you want your potatoes? I am so pleased that Sarah suggested this. The course ran for ten weeks and it was called Cooking from Around the World. Every week I would cook a meal from a different country. Sarah loved the different culinary delights I brought home every Monday night. I swear that if it wasn't for that cookery course I would have got through much more bread when it was my turn to cook.

Sarah was a great cook, having learned a lot from her mother. These days I am also very good in the kitchen and I have Sarah to thank for that. She only baked with Samuel on a few occasions, but he still wears the Mummy's Little Helper apron she bought him. And while Samuel and Olivia will never learn how to cook under their mother's guidance, they will definitely learn how to as a result of her influence.

I think the loss of her taste buds bothered Sarah as much as the disappearance of her hair. However, she managed to point out that hair loss had its advantages. She always looked on the bright side! There was no more having to wash it; wigs could be left to soak for an hour without her head needing to be there. Her legs were smooth so shaving was unnecessary. Neither did she have to worry about her bikini line. Not that she was going to be wearing a bikini any time soon. We had been discussing a holiday, though. Sarah's life cover included critical illness protection and we expected it to pay out fairly soon. Treatments were to finish in July and I thought it would be a good idea to have something positive on the calendar to look forward to. I searched the Internet for days before finding the perfect place. It was a hotel in

Cornwall overlooking a beach with spectacular views. It was simply perfect for families. It was very expensive but I booked it immediately.

At the same time we were well aware that it might have to be cancelled, though, because if Sarah developed an infection or her blood count was too low then treatment would be delayed. If she missed even one treatment then the holiday wouldn't be possible. But we were both feeling positive that the holiday would go ahead. I had subtly mentioned cancer when booking and asked if I would lose our deposit if we had to undergo extended, unavoidable chemo. The kind lady taking our booking not only promised a full refund, but she also knocked a few hundred pounds off the total cost of the holiday. A friend of mine from work asked if we were spending our cancer winnings before they had even been paid out. Sarah thought this was very amusing and hoped that the money would be forthcoming.

The life cover Sarah had taken out would only pay out on notification of a critical illness which was invasive. As Sarah had had a mastectomy then it met the criteria. I was at work when Sarah phoned me. Just two days had passed since booking our holiday. She told me she had just got a balance from a cash point and our new balance was £75,000 plus a few hundred pounds which was already in our account. The insurance company had paid out in full and not found an excuse to avoid doing so. Once the money had cleared we went to our building society to clear our mortgage. We sat at the desk without a smile and without emotion. I was thinking £75,000 for a breast and mortgage-free as a result – but it didn't sit well with us. The transfer was made and the mortgage was paid. The lady dealing with us spoke through the silence and said, 'You are so lucky to have paid off your mortgage.' She then asked us how we felt. Neither of us could muster up any enthusiasm to answer.

When we stepped outside it was raining. The weather seemed to be morphing with our mood again. I asked Sarah if she felt as flat as I did. Most people are overjoyed when their mortgage is finally paid off. They probably celebrate with a glass of champagne or a meal or both. I couldn't think past how our mortgage had been paid. Over the coming weeks a few people, including friends, told us how lucky we were to own our own house. Lucky! Sarah was being treated for a very aggressive cancer, though we didn't know how aggressive at the time. All she had left was a scar for a breast and I remember thinking how bloody unlucky we were. Treatment had made Sarah feel very ill at times and extremely fatigued. The veins on the back of her hand had collapsed, making the chemotherapy ordeal much worse. In fact, we were desperately searching *for* luck. Our whole life had changed and as a result, cancer would always be in our lives. A day could never pass without a reminder or the feeling of worry over our heads. Questions and thoughts ran riot in my head. Will treatment be successful? If so, then I would feel lucky? Having your house paid for is a bonus – but it was a bonus in a really crap situation.

Chemotherapy continued and as a result of Sarah's veins collapsing and her phobia of needles, she dreaded having blood tests. She managed to make this easier, though. She was told by a lady also having chemo that bloods could be taken the day before treatment at your own doctor's surgery. This made such a difference and she would wear a glove for an hour beforehand – more helpful advice from ladies experiencing the same problem. The glove keeps the hand warm and makes a vein more accessible. At the surgery, the nurse was so gentle and unhurried compared to the hospital staff.

The six sessions involving Docetaxel were eventually over and a new drug was introduced. Sarah's hair would now start to grow back as hair loss this time was not one of the side-effects. It was the start of another six sessions, this time three weeks apart. If all went well then chemo would be over in fifteen weeks.

The new drug made Sarah more tired and run-down. She was only run-down for a few days though and she always managed to pick herself up and smile again. Her strong mental attitude never failed her; neither did her sense of humour.

I was at work one day thinking about how Sarah was coping with the children. It was half term and very cold outside. She had decided to take them to the park for an hour or so. Being cooped up in the house with two young children was far worse than facing the cold. I am not talking Arctic temperatures here, but the wigs that Sarah wore were not as warm as her own thick hair. It was also a week after treatment and she wasn't exactly bursting with energy. I sent her a text asking how she was feeling. 'I am freezing my tit off,' was her reply. She knew that would put a smile on my face. I laughed longer and louder than I had in ages.

On school days I would get the children dressed and ready for school and nursery and take them before work. On one occasion Sarah commented on an outfit I had chosen for Olivia. She told me that she looked bonkers. She followed this up with the words, 'If anything does happen to me then God help Olivia.'

Not only was Sarah very witty about our situation, but she was also was very good at taking advantage of it. She would send me into town to the biggest department stores with instructions to go to the perfume and make-up counters for beauty products. I told them my wife was having chemotherapy and that her skin had become sensitive to many products. I asked in my most charming voice if they could possibly let me have some samples to try. I loved seeing her joy when I came home with a whole bag full of goodies.

The end of chemo was upon us and our holiday was getting closer. Radiotherapy was all that was left of treatments to get through, involving three weeks of travelling to the hospital every day. We were already sick of the sight of the damned place. The radiotherapy sessions were only five minutes long but would take up a big chunk of the day. They were painless apart from the fact that they were financially painful! Parking was extortionate. A nurse told me that the average cancer patient can spend around £200 on parking fees. This expense on top of all the money that is spent on prescriptions adds up to a small fortune. Sarah was switched on enough to get a year's prescription card which must have saved us around £300.

Radiotherapy could cause sickness but it didn't with Sarah; unless you can include being sick of the sight of the hospital. Although radiotherapy is painless when administered, it does eventually burn the skin and resemble a cooking burn. Obviously it could never be mistaken for this considering that it was on her chest. Well, I suppose if you were carrying a hot dish from one room to another while topless it might be possible. Maybe plausible if something had fallen down the back of the oven. But then of course you would have to be really stupid to lean over a red-hot hob with no top. Anyway, Sarah was left with a burn mark on her chest that could just about be seen above the line of her clothing.

Her hair was growing back nicely, though. It was about an inch long and very thick. All treatments had gone to plan. No more weekly visits to the hospital. Hopefully now we could return to some kind of normality and start living again. Sarah really needed to have breast reconstruction before she could feel whole again, of course, and to start living again and be able to move on. She also wanted to be able to put her wedding and engagement rings back on. These still wouldn't fit owing to swelling from the multiple injections.

With treatments behind us a family holiday was extremely welcomed. We longed for the relaxation after a very stressful six months. Other factors had caused stress, too. Strangers had added to our already difficult time when a man had called the house when I was at work one day. He had an Irish accent, if he wasn't faking it. He told Sarah that I was fooling around with his 15-year-old daughter and that she had to put a stop to it otherwise he would call the police. Sarah was quite shocked by this and asked me about it when I got home. My first thought was to think whom I had upset enough to make something up like that. I told Sarah that if it was true the police would already have been to our door. I also said that any father would also be beating the door down if there was any truth in it.

While she never believed it, she later got upset in February when a Valentine's card was hand-delivered. The words inside read: I can't wait to see you again, Big Boy. Happy Valentine's Day. This was a few days after treatment and Sarah was already feeling low. We never did do the whole Valentine's Day thing. We felt it was much better if we chose when we wanted to be romantic and go for a meal. Neither did we ever find out who sent the Valentine's card or made the accusatory phone call. What I do know is that for somebody to do that, they must have a pretty pathetic existence and can't be very happy.

Sarah and I had enjoyed one particular Valentine's Day some years earlier before children or BC as we referred to it. We had been to London shopping and arrived back in Southampton at around 8.00 p.m. We were hungry and decided to go for a meal but couldn't understand why all the restaurants were full. Sarah finally realised and said, 'It's bloody Valentine's Day.' We ended up going to a very run-down pub full of old men who were very drunk singing love songs around a table. I suppose it was kind of romantic in an odd kind of way.

Other factors causing us stress at the time included identity theft. Someone from Wolverhampton had got hold of my details and was enjoying a very good spending spree at the bank's expense. He had taken out three mobile phone contracts and was cheeky enough to opt for insurance.

There was also a problem with a Polish neighbour who was new to our area. We had just spent £1,500 having our kerb dropped and a white line painted. I was fed up with carrying a baby and ten shopping bags past every house in our road just to get to our front door. This way, we could finally park outside our own house. He obviously thought the same and I asked him politely on many occasions not to park there, but he ignored me and continued to do so. With my stress levels so high I called the police. They told me it wasn't a priority as it wasn't a life or death situation. I explained what I had been through and how angry I was. I then added that it soon would be a life or death situation as I would deal with it myself.

Anyway, the next time he parked there I was waiting. Sarah was out somewhere with Sam and I was at home with our 1-year-old daughter, Olivia. I am aware that I was silly to take such a risk and leave her in the house alone, but I couldn't help it. I had never been so angry in my whole life. The inconsiderate parking offender was just getting out of his car with a friend when I caught them. They were both well over 6 feet tall and obviously worked out. I ran out of my house and charged at them like a rhino. They froze when they saw me. They didn't get a chance to speak as I grabbed the guy whom I had tried to reason with on so many occasions and screamed at him, telling him that my wife was ill with cancer, needing to take every bit of my anger out on him. Thankfully I didn't and it was the last I saw of him. Looking back it was such a pathetic thing to get angry about. But I know now that it wasn't that that I was really angry about. It was just a situation and I had anger within that needed to come out somehow.

Into the Light and the Sun

Setting off in the car to Cornwall I could feel my stress levels going down with the levels on the fuel gauge. I had chosen Cornwall because travelling abroad could have caused problems. Insurance was still hugely expensive and in some cases not possible. The heat from a sunny climate would also irritate the delicate skin on Sarah's chest, possibly causing permanent damage, so we still had to be careful.

One added bonus of the hotel was that every room had a listening-in monitor which was linked to reception. This enabled parents to leave their children in the room and have a relaxing evening. We had concerns about this as big in the news at the time was the story about a girl who had disappeared from her hotel room while on holiday. She was never found. A few friends and family were also concerned about this set-up. The hotel had employed extra security as a result of the missing girl and a security guard was posted on every floor stairwell. Staff were also employed to sit at the monitor in reception and alert parents of any noises from rooms.

Leaving the children in the room while we went to dinner on the first night was quite nerve-racking. We were surrounded by couples who all had the same flashing and vibrating device placed on their tables. Every now and again a parent would rush back to their room to check on crying or fighting children. I did the random checks between courses, but our children always were good sleepers. We soon relaxed and felt secure about their safety. In fact, we started to feel very relaxed about everything.

The restaurant had huge windows that overlooked the beach, providing a panoramic view of one of the best beaches I have ever seen. Even my appreciation of beauty was returning. My eyes were opening again. They seemed to have been closed for such a very long time. Darkness was giving way to light even on days when the sun had not shone. As far as we were concerned the cancer had gone. Sarah was looking healthy again and her hair was getting thicker. Her taste buds were improving and so were our lives. While soaking up spectacular views we ate some of the finest meals ever placed in front of us, washed down with champagne. We were celebrating our freedom. Our freedom from the children and from a timetable of hospital dates. Reconstruction was the final hurdle, but first Sarah had to wait about six months for her radiotherapy burn to heal before this very complex surgery could go ahead.

All four of us loved that holiday. I always think of it as the place where our new life began. Everything would get better now. We were really appreciating both life and each other. Sitting in the car park after packing up to go home I cried. I told Sarah that I had had the time of my life and I didn't want the feeling to end. I thought if we went home I would lose these feelings that had made me smile all week. I was aware that cancer would never leave us and Sarah had already voiced her concerns, telling me that she thought we hadn't seen the last of the cancer. And deep down I felt the same, but I kept the thoughts as deep as I could. I used to pray for a decent amount of time. I asked for twenty years, thinking that if I had to lose Sarah then I could cope if it happened after twenty years when the children were grown-ups.

It was with this thought about cancer returning that I decided it was best to think of a career change. I was a precision engineer and worked fairly long hours. I needed a job that would enable me to look after the children if Sarah was to be taken from us. I woke up one morning with the solution: I would train to become a teaching assistant and work in a primary school. I signed up for a NVQ level 3 course at our local college. One of the requirements for the course was to work a day a week on a voluntary basis in a school and fortunately, my engineering employer agreed for me to work four days a week to make this possible. I was earning £30k a year at the time and friends and colleagues thought I was crazy making a career change that would only pay me about £10k. But I had a very strong feeling that I was doing the right thing. I told myself that if Sarah died then I would be able to work and look after the children. If she didn't then I would be fortunate to spend all the school holidays with her. It was the right thing to do. Primary schools are very much a woman's world and on the first night at college I found myself among fifteen women. Sarah thought this was highly amusing and used to tease me about it.

Sarah returned to work at her accountancy firm. They had been very supportive and kept her on full pay throughout her treatments. For the first time a kind of normality was returning, though I still hadn't seen her scar as she got changed in the bathroom and wore a top in bed. I really wanted to see it but was still afraid to ask. Over a year had passed but Sarah was never without her top on in my presence.

February came round and it was time for another trip away. We decided to take the children to London for the weekend, so I booked a hotel apartment which was very close to the Natural History Museum. We even enjoyed milkshakes in Harrods; Sarah wanted to take us there because she had happy memories of going herself as a child. We also took the children to Hamleys the toy shop to let them spend £20 each. What were we thinking? Christmas had only just passed and they had very much been in Santa's good books and obviously spoilt by his sympathy. We learned a valuable lesson: always try to avoid letting children loose in a toy shop. The search for the perfect toy took nearly three hours.

During our first day in London and only a couple of hours into it, Sarah and I had a row. This was our first argument since she was first diagnosed. It was trivial and based on my indecisiveness regarding lunch, though it didn't last long. I put it down to Sarah being tired and my dislike of overcrowded places. I only found out when we arrived home that Sarah was preoccupied at the time. She was worried because she thought she had found another lump. I had really enjoyed the weekend – Sarah had wanted me to – and she had kept it to herself about a potential lump in her remaining breast. An appointment was made very quickly and fear immediately replaced the calmness.

Waiting to go in for an appointment was horrible and thoughts of secondary cancer were fighting to get to the front of our minds. In fact, sitting in a waiting room, minutes away from extremes of good and bad emotions, is way beyond horrible. I sat there holding my breath, praying to God for a false alarm; indeed, praying for the existence of God. Every time the door opened I would take a deep breath in anticipation. When Sarah finally walked through the door, which felt like an eternity, she smiled and I knew all was well. I wept with relief in her arms. Was this how life was going to be from now on? Would the fear ever go away? Although we would probably be on tenterhooks with every headache or suspected lump, we had to remain positive. Every day that came and went would be a blessing.

Sarah was looking better than she had ever looked. Her hair was all new hair and had come back very thick and shiny. Calmness had returned. We had hope for a future as a family. Being mortgage-free had begun to sink in – our children would always have a roof over their heads. Dealing with financial pressure on top of health pressures would have been too much to deal with. A lot of cancer patients end up losing their homes as a result of being unable to work and not having critical insurance cover.

A date in May for reconstruction had arrived in the post. Sarah saw this as the end of a tough journey. She could move on after this. She told me she desperately wanted to feel in proportion again. Having reconstruction would make her feel balanced and feminine as she had before. Sarah had opted for what the plastic surgeon had described as the "Rolls-Royce" in reconstruction. There would be no implant. Her new breast would be made entirely from skin and fat taken from her stomach. Sarah would have another scar, where a long cut would be made across her stomach. This procedure would involve taking a strip of skin not much bigger than a postage stamp from the stomach and stretching it over fat also taken from her stomach. This was a very complex operation which would take about eight hours. Only two months to wait.

I booked another holiday to make the wait more bearable. These days I didn't need much of an excuse for a holiday. I consider them a necessity as they create so many wonderful memories. Memories are priceless. This time we headed off to Dorset to a cottage with a swimming pool. A week surrounded by the beautiful countryside away from daily chores always has a calming effect. And spending valuable time with the closest people in my world always warmed my heart. We had arguments like everyone else. What holiday is complete without them? But generally they were silly arguments about the lack of help with packing or about a forgotten corkscrew. The children always play their part in these family dramas, too.

Back home and now exceptionally relaxed, Sarah received a phone call from Salisbury Hospital. Her operation had been cancelled owing to an emergency. I have never seen Sarah so disappointed. She was inconsolable. We had to wait for another date. She desperately wanted this over. Our lives were pretty much in limbo until it was. Sarah also desperately wanted to go out and replace all of her bras with new ones.

Very soon after, another date was fixed for June. Sarah had to have a routine medical a week before the operation so the surgeon could establish whether or not she was healthy enough for it to go ahead. If Sarah had been a smoker then the operation would not have been possible because of all the blood vessels involved. Despite being a non-smoker and appearing fit and healthy, Sarah failed the medical. It was bad news again. A nurse called and informed her that she was carrying the MRSA bug. Her long-overdue operation had to be cancelled again. This time Sarah was extremely angry. She screamed and ran off to our bedroom in a rage. I was too shocked to know what to do. I wanted to admit defeat. How could I make my wife feel better? What comforting words could I offer? I am a man and find myself naturally wanting to fix things. I feel completely lost and helpless when I can't. I waited for a short while before offering comfort. Sarah always had the ability to refocus and smile.

The cancellation turned out to be a blessing in disguise. A few days later Samuel walked into our bedroom clutching his stomach. I took him to a walk-in medical centre, where the nurse evaluating him told me she thought he had appendicitis. At least we knew the way to the hospital.

Later that day I dropped Sarah and Sam at the hospital with a suitcase. I had hoped that they would only be staying one night, but Samuel ended up staying for a week. It took them that long to establish the problem. Sarah slept on a fold-down bed next to Sam, while I was at home and responsible for Olivia. I thought she looked pretty good going into nursery in stripy pink trousers and a red spotted top. I would then spend my day going to and from the hospital with clean and dirty clothes. I would take food, too. I would sit there for as long as I could chatting and playing to help relieve their boredom. If Sarah's operation had not been cancelled I would have been staying with Sam while Sarah was in Salisbury. That would have been tough and dangerously stressful as it is a forty-five minute drive.

The doctors continued to conduct tests on Sam throughout the week. They kept telling us that he wasn't ill enough to have a problem with his appendix. Sam was getting really fed up with needles. I expect he picked up on his mum's utter dislike of them. On one of the days when I was there he had to have a blood test. Sam had refused because he said it hurt too much. The nurse tried her best to persuade him with talk of magic cream that numbs the hand. "You won't feel a thing" is probably the most overused statement in hospital history. In the end I had to hold him down so that the nurse could do it. Tears ran down my cheeks as I did so. It felt like a form of abuse.

Sam had been put on the list for theatre about three times and then taken off again owing to uncertainty. I remember feeling relieved. I didn't want them to cut open my boy. Sarah on the other hand was despairing. Hospital was becoming the bane of her life. By the end of the week she had had enough. She insisted that Sam should go to theatre to find out what the problem was. They didn't argue. It was 9.00 p.m. on Friday when my phone bleeped. It was a text from Sarah which read: It's done. All is okay. She had told me earlier that Sam was on the list but not that he was in theatre. She knew that I couldn't do anything and I would be climbing the walls with worry. She faced it alone. It turned out that Samuel's appendix had burst and was clinging to the bladder wall. Thankfully, with a course of strong antibiotics, he was back to good health very quickly. All of the week's events had taken Sarah's mind off the cancelled reconstruction. She was actually relieved it turned out the way it did.

Reconstruction

Reconstruction was now arranged for 11 July 2006. The night beforehand I asked to see Sarah's scar. I told her that I had wanted to for a long time but kept putting it off. Sarah told me that she didn't think I wanted to see it. I cannot believe I had waited so long. In November it would be two years since her mastectomy. I am ashamed about this. Although it never really affected us intimately, I am aware it should have been dealt with sooner. I especially thought this on seeing it. There was no shock reaction. There were no tears of sympathy. I was very relieved and elated to be facing something that I had stupidly ignored for so long. I was filled with a sense of calm. Suddenly I blurted out that I didn't want Sarah to have reconstruction. I said I was sorry for being so selfish. She told me she was having reconstruction for her. It was something she had to go through.

I drove Sarah and her suitcase to Salisbury the next morning. The sun was shining down from a clear blue sky. Our positive mood reflected well with the good weather. Sarah was given a large private room which she was very pleased about. As I said goodbye I told her she looked radiant. I said she looked more beautiful than ever before. I can still see her sitting there in a large chair next to her bed. She had her boots on that she had bought during the month that her cancer was first diagnosed. They had been reduced in an advertising campaign to promote breast cancer awareness month. She had a large smile on her face as I looked back towards her and I kept looking back until I exited the ward. I was taking a mental photograph for the worst-case scenario. I was so proud of her. She was so brave. I was so lucky and thankful that she had chosen me to be her husband.

The children were being looked after by my mum and dad, so I drove there from hospital to collect them and take them home. I hadn't paid much attention when Sarah said she had forgotten something that morning requiring her to go back inside our house. She had left a chocolate lolly on each of our beds. There was a postcard next to each one and a personal message. She had done this in case she never made it out of surgery. On mine she wrote: Thank you for being a brilliant husband. I love you loads. She wrote similar messages on the children's cards, but all they could see was chocolate.

The following day was a very long one. Sarah often said in a tongue-in-cheek kind of way, 'What doesn't kill us only makes us stronger.' We were certainly finding out the hard way. Sarah went into theatre at 8.00 a.m. I spent most of the day in a daze, wandering around aimlessly while she was in the hands of the surgeons. I had been calling the ward constantly from 4.00 p.m. I kept being informed that she was in recovery but all was thought to be well. At 9.00 p.m. Sarah was back on the ward. Once I heard this I could collapse into bed to sleep.

I spoke to her in the morning and she sounded pretty good considering her ordeal. She was very tired but relieved that it was all over. The op had been a success. I arrived at lunchtime, having been to the supermarket and bought Sarah her favourite Thai chicken soup. I heated it up before I left and bought some crusty bread to go with it. When I arrived, she was thrilled. I think she was more excited to see the soup than she was to see me. She told me she was dreaming about the soup all morning.

She had another drain attached to her chest, which she wasn't best pleased about. This time it only had to be in place for a few days. The surgeon said that the procedure went very well and that she should expect to stay in hospital for about five days. Once again I was in charge of the house and the endless amount of jobs this entailed. I don't know why, but I found it incredibly stressful searching for clothes for Olivia in her wardrobe. It always took me an age to choose an outfit for her. Nearly as long as it took her to find a toy in Hamleys. Everything I chose for her she would say, 'I don't like that.'

Only three days had passed when Sarah rang me to tell me she could come home. We were both overjoyed. Sarah felt whole again. This was a new beginning. She was moaning to me in the car about the lack of visitors during her days in hospital. Children always seem to listen in on adult conversations and they seem to pick up on every word. Constant reminders instructing them to pick up clothes from the floor are forgotten within minutes, yet they never forget swear words or gossip. We were to be reminded of this a few days later, having been oblivious to little ears listening in at the time.

Samuel was at a friend's party on the Sunday after Sarah came back from hospital. One of the mums at the party called me to one side and told me that Sam was banging on the bathroom door. A few children were in there and he was getting impatient. I was horrified when she told me what he had said: 'Hurry up, you bunch of bastards.' My immediate thought was that he must be hanging around with the wrong crowd. It didn't take me long, with the help of a flashback, to remember where he had heard it. A week earlier Sarah, while we were on the way back from Salisbury Hospital, had said, 'They're all a bunch of bastards,' when referring to her lack of visitors. Realising that Samuel was very good at eavesdropping on our conversations, we would have to be more cautious in future. I wondered how much he had learned about Sarah's illness this way.

I was going to be forty in a few weeks, so Sarah had booked a table at Gordon Ramsay's at Claridges in London. She told me about it before booking to ensure it was what I wanted. I was very excited and we decided to book a room in the hotel for the night, too. I always hoped that life would begin at forty. Surely everything was going to be good for us from now on.

Sarah got an infection in her wound two days before we were due to celebrate my birthday. The wound where the drain had been attached hadn't healed properly. We had been told that this might be a possibility, but it involved Sarah going back into hospital to be treated. Sarah was still quite weak from her eight-hour operation and this procedure, resulting in the eradication of her infection, would take a couple of hours in theatre. Sarah had been coughing a lot lately having first started just before her reconstructive operation. The annoying thing about coughs is that they take forever to go away sometimes. I called Claridges and moved our celebration to October.

Sarah was back home in a couple of days. Hopefully for the last time. We really wanted to see the back of hospitals. On 17 August we went to a local hotel for a meal to celebrate my birthday. It was a Sunday and there were about four people in there including ourselves. I was selfishly thinking how I wished we were celebrating in Claridges. Sarah shouldn't have been there really – she wasn't feeling that great after her recent spell in theatre. She should have been in bed resting but insisted on a celebratory meal to wish me a happy fortieth birthday.

A Caravan Holiday in Heaven

The school summer holidays were coming to an end. We both felt a bit guilty that Samuel would go back to school and have very little to talk or write about. Most of the time had been spent travelling to and from the hospital and resting at home, so Sarah suggested that we should take them away for a surprise weekend. Most of my happy childhood memories, that make me smile from deep within, involve a caravan. A white plastic box that through a child's eyes is like stepping into a Tardis. Why sleep in a tent when you can have the luxury of caravan camping? I booked one in Dorset for the last weekend of the summer holidays on a site owned by a famous holiday chain that promised Disneyland-type thrills on a budget. Surely there can't be much difference between someone earning minimum wage dressed as Mickey Mouse or Pluto and another dressed as a bear or a tiger.

We packed the car the evening before setting off so that the children wouldn't suspect a thing. They were very excited when we informed them we were taking them to a theme park for the day. We spent the day at the park making the most of the rides and soft-play areas. I always work out how to get our money's worth by dividing how many rides we needed to go on to justify the entrance fee. I came out sweating after crawling through endless dusty tunnels in the soft-play zone and my trousers were covered in paw prints from holding the animals in the petting area. My knees hurt from all the crawling around and I needed regular puffs on my inhaler as my asthma was playing up. I did really enjoy myself, though, and I realised this was our second chance. I felt like we were a family again. Hair loss, one breast and cancer formed our past and an appreciation and enjoyment of life was our future.

The children didn't notice when I ignored the signs for home and drove in the opposite direction towards the caravan site. But they stared out of the window with a mixture of disbelief and excitement as I exceeded the 5 mph speed limit into caravan Heaven. I told them we were staying for the weekend and in return they told us that we were the best mum and dad in the world. As an adult, caravan holidays are not and shouldn't be the first choice for a family holiday. They are freezing cold at night and as hot as a greenhouse by day. Heavy rain at night is enough to scare the children out of their skins. The boot of your car is always completely full and excess luggage rammed against the back window rules out the reverse manoeuvre. Endless unloading of shopping bags with enough food for a month which is ingeniously shared between one small cupboard and the world's smallest fridge.

Self-catering holidays are tiring but such a joy for a child. The children amused themselves running up and down the caravan and jumping on every bed. I cracked open a bottle of wine with a spoon as much to Sarah's dismay, I had yet again forgotten to pack the corkscrew. I threw the children outside, put on some music and the two of us sat together and relaxed. Meanwhile, our two were circling the caravan banging on every window and side. It sounded a bit like heavy rain. All I wanted was right here by my side and I knew I would feel even better once we had put the kids to bed.

Just after midnight and after a glass or two of red wine, the only sound that could be heard was a wheeze coming from my chest. I had only started to suffer from asthma when Sarah developed cancer. My inhaler is usually sufficient to keep it at bay, but a day of crawling through tunnels and handling rabbits, followed by too much wine, had made my asthma impossible to control. At around 2.30 a.m. Sarah told me I needed to go to the hospital. Hospitals were becoming a regular feature in our life.

Moments later I was driving through the caravan park, feeling anxious and short of breath. I noticed a police car at the entrance to the caravan site, so I pulled up alongside and explained my predicament. Unbelievably they gave me directions to the nearest hospital, which was about 10 km away, instead of offering to assist. My chest was so tight and I was thinking about how worried Sarah was.

I was about to drive away when I spotted a doorman standing at the club entrance. As luck would have it he was only there that late owing to a big fight breaking out between some dads. He called an ambulance and within ten minutes I was being treated in the back of it. The paramedic told me it was very wise to call them as I might not have made the journey to the hospital. I was put on a nebuliser for about thirty minutes and given some steroids to take away with me. Within an hour my asthma had completely subsided and I went back to join Sarah.

It dawned on me that I had a responsibility to look after myself. We didn't need any more stress or upset. Surely we had been dealt our fair share. Sarah was relieved to see me back so soon and we hugged and slept soundlessly.

The sun was shining the next morning. Thoughts from the night before about packing up and going home were all gone. After an unhealthy fry-up I took the children swimming. Sarah could only watch us because her wound under her arm still needed to heal.

I climbed into a freezing cold outdoor pool with Sam and Olivia while Sarah positioned herself by the poolside. All the sunloungers were taken and she had to stand. She was surrounded by smokers who thought nothing of dropping cigarette butts onto the floor that children walked on barefoot. I'm pretty sure that doesn't happen in Disneyland. I had become such an anti-smoker since Sarah had become ill. I was addicted for about fifteen years and of course now that I had managed to break the habit, I climbed way up on my high horse. I thoroughly enjoyed chasing the children around the swimming pool, pretending to be a shark one moment and a polar bear the next. It was very hard coming up with sea life sound effects, though.

The main reason for my enjoyment was the simple fact that Sarah was watching us. I could see how much it made her smile to witness us having fun. I was making her laugh by poking fun at the other mums and dads around us. I ended up chasing about six children around while their parents smoked cigarettes or drank beer. Children were taking turns to choose a sea creature for me to impersonate. I said I shouldn't be a whale as it might offend too many people and give them a complex. I was showing off, but Sarah was the only audience I needed.

We continued to have a stress-free and enjoyable weekend without a single argument. A weekend without a row is always a bonus for any family. Arguments were quite rare in the midst of a cancer diagnosis and treatment, though. The whole weekend was heavenly. My feelings were somewhere between enlightenment and peace. Did cancer have to come along for me to realise fully that the grass is not greener elsewhere? To understand that true happiness was right under my nose, in the present, unfolding in real time of the here and now. Holding Sarah's hand and kissing her now felt different. She was part of me. I didn't just feel her in a physical sense. Every one of my senses appreciated and acknowledged her presence. I couldn't stop myself from touching her or looking at her. Every time I did so I wanted to thank her for being in my life and also to tell her how unique she was. Without trying to sound too sickly and bring about red-faced embarrassment, I felt I had been given a taste of Heaven, a place where beauty isn't just seen but felt, a place where the search for contentment is over. I had found my piece of Heaven on a caravan site in Dorset. What are the chances of that? I wonder if I would have found my piece of Heaven if cancer had not taken over our lives.

The children were due to return to school, which meant that the wait for our birthday celebration at Claridges was nearly over. I certainly didn't want to wish time to pass quickly but I was really looking forward to it.

October came around and we headed to London for our meal and a night in the hotel. Sarah was going to be thirty-five in a few weeks so it was a double celebration. Since her operation, Sarah had been a dress size 10. She loved telling as many people as she could about this. She said she had dreamed about being this size after having two children. Although it had left her with a very large scar across her slim stomach. When she showed it to people she often joked that it was a shark bite.

Claridges, combined with a seven-course meal at Ramsay's, was bloody expensive! £720 to be exact. I would like to point out that breakfast was included. It was more expensive than my first ever car. I am sure that we could have had just as enjoyable an evening at home. Perhaps sitting on our own sofa washing down Minstrels with a glass of wine or two. We never regretted it, though. It certainly was a unique experience. The food was exceptional but the hotel could have done with a lick of paint. The air-conditioning unit in our room also needed to be quietened. I am aware that the amount of money we spent could feed quite a large number of families in the Third World. I am also now aware that certain hotels and restaurants are ridiculously overpriced. But I know for sure that quality time together can never be overpriced or regretted.

I had finished my teaching assistant assignments and by some miracle had been rewarded with an A grade, though I continued to work on a voluntary basis at my chosen school as I enjoyed it too much to give it up. I had applied for two jobs without much success. However, at least I had managed to get to the interview stage, which was good experience. Hopefully this would help me with another one that was approaching, for which Sarah took me shopping to choose a shirt and tie that couldn't fail to get me the job, aware how much I wanted recognition for my hard work.

A Darker Place

Sarah's cough was still a concern, so she made an appointment to have it checked out. Owing to her history she was referred to the hospital for a chest X-ray. Olivia's birthday was fast approaching and memories of two years previously flooded my mind. I had to convince myself it was just a common cough. We were a family of four so everything would have to be okay. Then I received a letter in the post asking me to attend an interview for the teaching assistant position I had applied for at the same time Sarah had a letter detailing a date and time for her X-ray. Confirmation of both appointments arrived on the same day for the same day and the same time.

I found myself attending my third interview five days before Olivia's third birthday. A few people at the school had complimented me on my choice of shirt and tie. By lunchtime, I was employed as a teaching assistant and Sarah was back home after having her X-ray. She was so proud of me for getting the job. Indeed, she was so thrilled and happier than I had seen her for a long time. We now had to wait for the X-ray results.

A week passed but we managed to keep busy organising Olivia's birthday party. I also resigned from my post in engineering. I had worked as a precision engineer for twenty-five years and wondered if life would begin at forty. It was certainly going to change, but would it be for better or for worse?

Not a great deal was determined from the X-ray results. Something had shown up but it was unclear as to what it might be, so Sarah was booked in to have a CT scan. This was a sophisticated X-ray machine that showed areas of the body in more detail. We endured a two-week wait and during this time Sarah's cough wasn't going away. If anything it seemed to be getting louder. I wasn't sure if this was the case or whether I was becoming more aware of what it could mean for us all. Exactly two years to the very day and time we were at the very same hospital where Sarah had had her mastectomy.

The CT scan was painless but we were both very frightened. Sarah had to drink an aniseed-flavoured liquid forty-five minutes before having the scan while I went for a coffee in the uninviting hospital cafeteria. I stared into my cup as if looking for answers in there, thinking that a doctor or a nurse was close by looking at a screen that would be giving them answers. As I sat there I spotted a friend who is a nurse. She was on duty. She knew us both very well and our situation. I couldn't hide my emotions and wept openly as I told her I had a very bad feeling about the outcome. I fought with my negative emotions and managed to bring the positive ones to the fore by the time Sarah returned from the scan. We drove home and before Sarah could take her coat off, she hugged me and said, 'I don't think I'm going to make it this time around.' I held her tight as we cried together. At that moment I felt like we were the only two people in the whole world.

Meanwhile, I tried my best to enjoy my new job. It was very challenging and made even more difficult by another week of waiting for the hospital appointment with the consultant to confirm results. Sarah was due to return to work on 25 November 2008. I actually didn't mind the waiting. I figured that as long as I was waiting I was also avoiding hearing bad news.

It was bad news but still inconclusive. The lymph nodes in Sarah's chest had become enlarged. The consultant couldn't at this point say for sure if the cancer had returned, but there was a chance it could be something else. This "chance" gave us something to cling on to. Any uncertainty brought hope for us. A biopsy would provide all the information we would need. This was scheduled for a week's time; four weeks after Sarah had had her initial X-ray. The biopsy would leave another scar, this time at the top of her chest.

We were told that there were three possible outcomes. The worst news would be for it to be secondary cancer. This could be treated but never cured. Sarcoidosis would be the best news, as this can also cause the lymph nodes to be enlarged but is fully treatable. Another possibility was a cancer called lymphoma. This was more favourable than the secondary type as it can also be cured in a high percentage of cases.

On 18 November 2008 Sarah went into hospital for her biopsy. She had to stay in for two days. Her awaited return to work was only a week away, having been signed off since her reconstruction in July. Sarah did return to work on 25 November, which helped distract her mind somewhat. Christmas was also approaching fast, offering another distraction.

Our appointment at the hospital where the final test results were waiting finally arrived. The morning of 2 December 2008 was like many others. Olivia was spending the day at nursery and Samuel was spending his day at school. They were oblivious to how important the day was to us and to our future as a family.

I desperately wanted the appointment to be over. Indeed, I desperately wanted to avoid it altogether. Many students receive their exam results in the post after a long wait and some find themselves staring at the envelope for hours, not wanting to look inside, too afraid to open it in case it brings bad news and upset, for their future depends on a pass. If the envelope stays closed they can avoid knowing about a possible fail. It felt a bit like that for me while sitting in the hospital waiting room, in which the door we had to walk through was my envelope. The big difference – apart from the obvious that one is a door and the other an envelope – was that instead of a pass or fail, Sarah's test results would mean live or die. Once the door was opened there was no going back. I couldn't run away from this unavoidable moment. I sat staring at every nurse and doctor who passed. I was trying to make eye contact, hoping to learn something from them. Maybe their body language would tell me something in the same way I look at air stewards on a flight during turbulence. Surely if they are calm and smiling, then all must be well. I was searching for hope in my own turbulent mind.

The nurse eventually called out Sarah's name and my chest tightened. I tried to feel hopeful as we opened the door and closed it behind us, where three female members of staff sat behind a desk. We sat down. I knew two of them. One was an oncologist I had met at chemotherapy sessions. The other was a breast care nurse who was also in charge of chemotherapy trials. I should have realised that she was there to talk to Sarah about chemotherapy trials again, once the bad news had been delivered. Sarah was way ahead of me and although she had worked it out, she waited patiently to be informed about the results.

'I'm afraid that it is bad news,' were the first words that came from the oncologist's lips.

In a trembling voice she told us that Sarah had secondary cancer. Quite a number of the lymph nodes were affected and considerably enlarged. The next person to speak was Sarah. I was frozen to my seat, unable to speak. Sarah bluntly and directly asked how much time she had left. We were told that the best-case scenario was to be a small number of years. I immediately processed this and decided to interpret it as three or four years. The worst-case would be just a few months. The moment these words found their way into my ears, they attacked every nerve ending in my body. I recalled a saying from my childhood. Something about sticks and stones may hurt my bones, but words can never hurt me. Such a ridiculous saying. At that moment I would have gladly been lined up and pelted with sticks and stones of all sizes rather than this. The cuts and bruises would have healed and been forgotten about soon enough. However, the power of words may heal eventually, but they can never be forgotten or taken back. You can of course remember times when you have experienced physical pain, but remembering it does not cause you to feel it over again. Remembering spoken words responsible for such heartbreak and upset can be felt so deeply many times over, regardless of the passing of time.

Sarah gave a large sigh, looked towards the breast care nurse and said, 'I knew it was bad news as soon as I saw you sitting there.'

I was unable to move. The little colour I had left drained away from my face. I felt as if I was ten times heavier, weighed down by so many thoughts about a depressing future without my Sarah, without my best friend and the one person who knew me better than I knew myself.

Eventually I spoke and said, 'What about our children? They are only six and three and they need their mum.'

Sympathetic looks bored into my eyes during the split second that eye contact was manageable. I squeezed Sarah's hand hard and never wanted to let go. I knew my words were pointless and but a helpless plea, as these three ladies were unable to offer us a pardon, for they could not change the inevitable. All beauty had faded when Sarah was diagnosed two years previously. As the days had passed, though, we had managed to pick ourselves up and had grown even closer together, fully appreciating all things beautiful. We had stopped taking each other and the children for granted, realising how much we were blessed. Now, all hope was gone. My eyes were open but they may as well have been closed. I felt like I had been thrown into a cold, dark prison cell and the key had been callously broken and thrown away. Words had just hit me harder than any sledgehammer ever could. I was momentarily paralysed by the blow. My heart shattered, my stomach shrank and every part of me was too traumatised to function. Even the tears would not come. They were of course building momentum and would very soon flow from my eyes in a tidal wave of emotion.

Chemotherapy was scheduled to start in a week's time. The same drug as before would be used and Sarah would lose her beautiful hair once again. It had grown back so vibrant but it would be gone within a month. The oncologist told us that they would do everything they could to prolong Sarah's life. Hopefully the chemotherapy would shrink the cancer and stop it from spreading further. To ease some of the anxiety, Sarah asked for a central line to be attached to her chest. Her veins were still a problem and she still had scars as a result of past treatments. The central line would enable blood to be taken and all drugs to be administered painlessly and relatively stress-free.

Walking from the room I was in a daze and couldn't speak. It was all I could do to put one foot in front of the other. We walked at a quick pace back to the car, desperate to leave the hospital grounds. As soon as we sat in the car and the doors closed, I was overwhelmed by emotion. We leaned across and held each other. Sarah was first to speak and uttered the selfless words, 'I am so sorry, baby.' Minutes after receiving the most tragic news and she was thinking about me. Love is so easy to understand when facing such trauma. I wish I could have swapped places with her. I believe that all children need their mothers more than they do fathers if given a choice. I told her that she shouldn't be sorry as she had nothing to be sorry about. I realise now that she was feeling sympathetic towards me, knowing I would have to bring up the children alone, without her. She was also saying sorry because she understood how much pain I would feel being without the one person whom I both loved and needed.

We drove home and Sarah joked that we should get a cup of tea. I think this is very much a British thing – a cup of tea will make you feel better in a crisis. I remember being in a car accident with my family as a child. Nobody was hurt but we were all shaken. I remember my mum saying two things. The first was to ask my dad why he went through a red light and the second was to suggest the miracle cure of a cuppa. I think it actually worked on that occasion. Probably because a cup of tea was such a rare treat for a 7-year-old. It kind of made me feel like one of the grown-ups.

On this occasion, standing in our kitchen, I thought the only thing that could possibly make me feel better would be a sedative. I was struggling to think of anything positive to say. Every thought I had depressed me some more. My thoughts were about telling the children and about bringing them up alone. Images of Sarah's last breath and her funeral flickered unwanted through my mind.

I turned to her in desperation and said, 'I feel like putting us all in a car and gassing it.'

Sarah was so upset by this and told me not to feel that way and pleaded with me never to say it again. She told me that she was going to have the treatment. She also told me that she had no intention of going anywhere just yet. Olivia would be starting school two years' time and Sarah was adamant that she would be there to take her in on her first day. I believed every word and my negativity started to subside. I didn't want to spend the next couple of years too depressed to enjoy our last moments. I decided it was important to enjoy every day as much as possible. If I didn't I might live to regret it. Sarah's positivity and ability to pick herself up inspired me to do the same. I was suddenly feeling more hopeful, more optimistic. Some may argue that it had something to do with the tea!

Before we picked the children up from the childminder we decided that we couldn't and wouldn't tell them. Sarah might survive for a good few years and we wanted to protect the children as much as possible and save them from worry and upset. I went to work the following morning as normal. I had hardly slept and was extremely tired. Sarah also went into work to inform them that she would be taking time off again. My morning at work was a real struggle. I don't know why I decided to go in. I should have been told to go home, as I wasn't in the best mental state to be dealing with children in a very challenging school.

At lunch time I drove the 2 km to our city centre to meet Sarah for a coffee. From the moment I got in the car until I parked I wept uncontrollably. I was not aware of the tears as they made quite a regular appearance these days. The sound I was making was alien to me, though. Like a wounded animal. It was as if my hearing belonged to somebody else. By the time I parked the car at the shopping centre I had regained my composure. I was on time and I wanted to greet Sarah with a smile.

I took the lift up to the clothes store where I was to meet Sarah. I would like to point out that this makes me a bit of a hypocrite. I used to get very angry and moan at able-bodied people when we had our babies in prams and there was no room in the lifts. I even used to ask if they had a problem with their legs, much to Sarah's embarrassment. In my defence, the lift was empty and I just wanted to reach Sarah as quickly as possible. It had been a very long morning and I felt as if I was seeing Sarah for the first time in months.

We noticed each other at the same time, walking for the first few steps before quickening our pace to embrace. We had both managed a smile from a distance, but once in each other's arms we cried into each other's shoulder. I held on tight and didn't want to let go. I had a feeling that if I did then she would fall into an abyss and be lost forever. Maybe a cup of tea would be a better idea than a coffee.

Last Christmas?

Christmas was only three weeks away and provided us with a good distraction and an opportunity to spoil our children with gifts and happy memories.

Every night we read stories to our children and have done so since birth. Early evening is actually more accurate as we always have them asleep by 7.00 p.m. Bedtime in our house is like a military operation. Racing around to get them washed and dressed for bed and lights out to enable adult time and peace was a daily occurrence. I find stories a chore sometimes and tend to speed read. I can do *Jack and the Beanstalk* in under a minute. I was now realising how important these shared moments were. In the days that followed our dreadful news I paid more attention to everyday routines. I would sit halfway down the stairs in silence, listening to Sarah read to the children in turn. I would stifle my cries, knowing for certain that one day I would be doing them alone. A time when the sound of her voice would no longer be heard in our house. When I would only be able to hear her read in my mind. What I didn't know was how long she would share these simple, yet important moments with us.

Sometimes I would creep unheard until I was outside the children's rooms. I would then record Sarah reading stories, having conversations and saying goodnight. I didn't tell her that I was doing this as she didn't like the sound of her own voice. Recordings of her singing nursery rhymes are priceless. One reason for this is that nobody would ever buy them and another is that they wouldn't ever be for sale.

Sarah decided she wanted to create some memories for her children. She thought about doing a memory box after watching a programme on TV about some ladies in the same situation. She decided to wait because she was convinced that she had at least two years to put one together.

The first chemotherapy session was less stressful this time around because we knew what to expect and Sarah was relaxed as a result of not having to be injected. The oncologist told us that the best indication of chemo being successful would be her cough subsiding. The drug caused the same tiredness and sickness as before, lasting about three days. We could then make plans to create some lasting memories.

One of the first things we did was buy some expensive tickets for a train ride on the Watercress Line. This was a very popular thing to do at Christmas and included an hour's comfort on a steam train, which travelled for half an hour in one direction before heading back after a glass of mulled wine and a mince pie. The children would get to meet Father Christmas and receive a gift to suit their age group. The children loved this and I took some photographs of Sarah sitting with them both. We appeared to be a normal family on an afternoon out. Other parents were taking photos too, but theirs were of Santa sitting with their children. I was thinking that if I had been given the shock news that Sarah had died suddenly then I wouldn't have many photos of her and the children together. We always took a lot of photographs of our children to look at in years to come. Taking pictures as a family just in case one family member dies is not something one usually thinks about.

My mind was filled with sadness and guilt because the children were so happy. Sad because this could be their last Christmas spent with their mum and guilty for keeping it to myself and pretending that everything was okay. Samuel offered to take a picture of the two of us. I wondered if he knew much about the seriousness of his mum's illness from overheard conversations. Looking at the photographs later that day I thought how well Sarah looked. Sarah pointed out that I was the one who looked like I was dying of cancer. The stress and worry was really starting to show, not in Sarah's looks but in mine. Pregnant ladies are often told they are glowing, radiant and healthy. Happiness and pleasant thoughts of a new life ahead obviously playing a big part. I, on the other hand, was withdrawn and struggling to shine or have pleasant thoughts because a life was being destroyed in our case, not created. I was really trying to be upbeat, especially as it was Christmas, and I had to stay as strong for Sarah as she was for me.

On Christmas Day I was surprised how much we enjoyed ourselves. I have always loved Christmas and the overindulgence that comes with it. Sarah wasn't really a fan and would quite happily have put the tree up on Christmas Eve and taken it down on Boxing Day. Watching our children run around filled with excitement and appreciation made it impossible to stay miserable.

After a tiring day and with the children in bed, we relaxed and enjoyed a quiet house together. Sarah was on the phone to her sister, Claire, so I decided to record some of the conversation as Sarah was in good spirits and laughing. She was telling Claire about how after reconstruction everything was supposed to return to normal and how we should have been able to draw a line under it. I listened as she told Claire what a joke that was and while laughing she said, 'Just throw me in the dustbin.'

Claire must have asked if she had cried much during the day. Sarah told her that she tried not to but got upset a few times. The first time was when the children were opening their stockings and again when opening the presents under the tree. I laughed when she said, 'If I'm not here next year will Darren get the presents right? I can't quite see him sitting bloody wrapping up all the bastard stocking presents like I did.'

By New Years Eve Sarah's hair was very patchy. She was thoroughly depressed about this. The first time it fell out she took it in her stride and just accepted it. This time around she wondered if her life would end before it grew back. We managed to enjoy the year's end and moved into 2009 with every intention of seeing in 2010 together.

After three chemotherapy sessions, which took us into late January, we went to the hospital to get the first update on how Sarah was responding to her treatment. Her cough had practically gone away so we were very hopeful of good news for a change.

My optimism that the cancer had shrunk to microscopic proportions was short-lived.

The doctor told us that chemotherapy had been unsuccessful. Her enlarged lymph nodes were unchanged. We were so shocked to hear this as her cough had disappeared and so we couldn't understand it. We were told that the improvement with her cough was down to the steroids she was taking, as was the weight gain. This meant that they would need to try another type of drug right away. After at least a three-hour wait, of course.

I sat in the waiting room trying not to be too negative. I told Sarah that at least the chemo she'd had over last month had stopped her cancer from getting worse. I remember saying that if this new drug didn't work then we could return to the first one and at least keep the cancer at bay. What kind of existence would that be for anyone, though? And what about any potential different side-effects to deal with from the new treatment?

A loud bang was heard coming from the bathroom three days later while Sarah was taking a shower. I was lying on our bed in the next room at the time. I sat up and listened intently. I could hear the sound of running water and I then heard Sarah moving around and a cough. Not much time had passed when suddenly there was another very loud thud. Sarah had definitely fallen over. I ran to the bathroom door and called her name. She answered in a low, muffled voice and told me that she was okay. The door opened inwards, which isn't the most sensible of designs. I tried opening it, but Sarah was lying on the floor behind it, stopping me from doing so. She eventually managed to move and let me in. I helped her up and supported her until she could lie down on the bed. She had lost a cap from one of her front teeth and there was blood coming from her ear.

Sarah had had a similar occurrence seven years previously. After a night out drinking she was taking a shower when suddenly she blacked out. She was alone in the house but called me on my mobile at work to tell me what had happened. At the end of our hallway, leaning against the wall was a glass mirror. Sarah remembered taking a shower and then the next moment she woke up on the floor with thousands of pieces of jagged glass beneath her. She must have staggered out of the shower at speed and fallen unconsciousness into the mirror. There were long, triangular pieces of glass that could have come from a horror film and yet she didn't have a single scratch. I felt that God must have been looking out for her and was thankful. It obviously wasn't her time to leave us yet. At the time I just hoped that the next seven years were not filled with bad luck owing to a silly superstition regarding broken mirrors.

With blood coming from Sarah's ear from this latest fall, I thought it was a good idea to go to the hospital. I called the chemotherapy emergency line I had been given if I was concerned or if there were any problems owing to treatment and I was assured that someone would answer regardless of the time. The phone rang for thirty minutes and went unanswered. I suggested going to the Accident and Emergency Department, which wasn't well received by Sarah. She assured me she was fine and didn't need to go to hospital, but I finally managed to persuade her.

It was a Sunday afternoon and it was no surprise to us to see it full of people suffering from drink-related problems and sports injuries, or a combination of both. I signed her in and mentioned that I'd had no success with the emergency line. Sarah finally got to see the evaluation nurse and explained what had happened. We thought it would be straightforward and Sarah would be taken straight to the chemo ward, but the nurse told Sarah that she was now a casualty patient and would have to wait in line. This could take all afternoon. In a very abrupt manner Sarah told the nurse that she was going home. She pointed out that she had little time left as it was and that she wasn't going to waste it in an A & E waiting room. The nurse did all she could to persuade Sarah to stay because of concerns about the blood in her ear, but realising that Sarah wasn't about to listen, she put her at the front of the queue. It turned out that Sarah was right and that it didn't need a trip to the hospital or indeed any treatment. It was just a small cut on the inside of her ear. Sarah took delight in telling me I should listen to her as she is always right. We put the shower incident down to the effects of the new drug in her system.

The following afternoon we took the children to a river near our house to feed the ducks – a walk we had done many times with them and which was always a very peaceful family outing. They started out on their bikes but by the time the wheels had completed a revolution I ended up carrying them. On the way back to our house I was watching Sarah and the children walking hand in hand in front of me. It was such a wonderful and precious sight to behold. I thought about the future and imagined how it would look watching the children walk without her. I thought about ghosts and their existence or otherwise and wondered if it was possible that Sarah might return as a ghost and walk unseen by their side. Would we feel her presence? I felt very alone. Please, God, let this new drug work ...

During this stressful time we still had arguments and disagreements like any other married couple. Sarah was prone to moments of frustration and anger. This wasn't just a cancer thing, though. She had always had volcanic moments over the years, but I found these moments increasingly harder to deal with now because it's very difficult to be mean or to win an argument with someone who is terminally ill.

Arguments change over the years. Early arguments in our relationship were probably all down to lack of communication. And arguments after having children can get out of hand owing to sleep deprivation. Most of our arguments were about my lack of help around the house as Sarah cooked and cleaned most of the time. She would leave items belonging to me on the stairs for me to put away and I would step over them time and time again. They were invisible to me. This would infuriate Sarah and she would be frosty towards me. Not long after having children Sarah was in the kitchen mashing potato and I had been pleading with her to tell me what was wrong with her. I was constantly asking her to just bloody well tell me what I had done wrong rather than snap at me for no reason. She started hammering the masher down onto the potato in fury in response to my question, sending potato flying everywhere. Then she screamed at me and said, 'Mash your own fucking potato!' and fled to our bedroom. I waited a few minutes before going to see how she was and to apologise for anything I may, or may not, have done to upset her. I climbed the stairs, carefully stepping over my slippers, headphones and books on the fourth step, unaware that these items were at the heart of the problem.

We still had moments like these but they were more about the severity of our situation. Most of the time we coped well, but we definitely had our off-days. One such day I was telling her off because she was shouting at the children and suggested that she take some time out. I had learned this from her because she had told me the same thing on many occasions. She was chopping up some raw chicken in the kitchen with the largest knife she could find, having worked herself up into a rage because she had no control over her future. She was lifting the knife over her head and slamming it down again and again. I was scared and told her to put the knife down. She told me she didn't want to and that what she really wanted was to shove it deep into her stomach.

I couldn't always find the right words of comfort. I would stand there helpless, staring at her and wishing it was all just a horrible dream. Sometimes I would speak and then wish I hadn't when I said the wrong thing in a moment of anger or upset. Sarah was terminally ill and on this occasion I had upset her so much that moments later she was packing a suitcase intending to leave. She never did, of course; she didn't need to because she was going to be taken away from us anyway – to a place where she wouldn't need a suitcase or her clothes ...

February

In early February 2009 I was standing at the bottom of the stairs, when Sarah told me she had double vision and that everything looked strange. I said that it could have something to do with her falling in the shower when she had hit her head as that was less than a week ago. I made an appointment for her to see the oncologist and also suggested we make one at the eye hospital. We saw the oncologist first and Sarah was told that she would need to have a brain scan. Apparently, although quite rare, cancer sometimes spreads to the meninges – the lining of the spinal cord and the brain. I wanted to dismiss this as we had been given enough bad news already, so I asked Sarah to get a second opinion at the eye hospital. She said we might as well wait to see what the scan showed up.

I was getting desperate and that evening I searched online for herbal remedies that may help. I found one that had such rave reviews that I couldn't resist and so I bought three bottles. Sarah agreed to take them and referred to them as horse tablets because they were so big; however, she also pleaded with me not to get my hopes up. She said that I needed to accept that she was going to die.

I had booked our favourite hotel in Cornwall for June, aware that it might be our last chance for a holiday together as a family.

Sarah's vision in her right eye was getting worse by the day, so on Friday, 13 February 2009, I took her to the hospital for her MRI brain scan. The MRI scanner is a large cylinder and requires the patient to lie very still on a couch that moves backwards and forwards into a tunnel. Sarah was very nervous about this. She knew it was painless but had reservations because of its associations with claustrophobia. The scan was to take around thirty minutes. I waited anxiously for over an hour. A nurse told me it was taking longer as Sarah was very agitated and finding it difficult to lie still. Again I was helpless, frustrated and concerned – feelings that I was becoming familiar with.

When the scan was completed, a nurse took me in to see Sarah. She told me that Sarah had had a bad reaction to the scan. She was lying on a hospital bed having some kind of seizure. Her whole body was shaking violently and she was shivering. I was very frightened and held her tight in my arms, pulling her close to my chest. I was trying to warm her up and relax her. I thought that this was the moment I would be saying goodbye. I was shocked, scared and depressed. Sarah eventually stopped shaking and the colour returned to her face. Her first words were, 'I am such a wimp.' I told her how concerned I was and how I thought she was dying. She smiled and simply asked, 'Were you relieved, baby? I would completely understand if you were.' I didn't experience feelings of relief but I was finding it increasingly disturbing watching Sarah suffer these ordeals. Her reaction to the scan was not a panic attack. The severe convulsions I had just witnessed and the recent fall in the shower were caused by something far more serious and sinister than what I was willing to let my mind think about.

On Sunday we took the children to London again. This time Claire, Sarah's sister, came with us to be part of the memories that we were creating. Samuel and Olivia were the only ones amongst us who didn't know that their mum was going to die. I wondered if they would have enjoyed or appreciated the day more if they had known she wouldn't be with us for much longer. In fact they were having a great day, oblivious to the heartache surrounding them. Sarah found the day very tiring, though, and her impaired vision made it more difficult as a result of walking into people on the escalators and pavements. We travelled by taxi as much as we could, seeing as many sights as possible, which ended with the London Eye. Somewhere near the top I took a photograph of Sarah standing with our children. She was wearing large sunglasses and her favourite wig from Hong Kong. The sunglasses were to make her feel less conscious of being blind in one eye and the wig was to cover up cancer's most obvious give-away. All of my senses recognised her except for my sight, as the cancer and the treatments were changing the way she looked. Her face was becoming puffy as a result of the steroids and her spirit was in conflict with her body, wrestling with wondering if it was time to give up the fight.

The following Thursday was a chemo one. We were in the hospital all day and as it was scheduled quite late, I had to leave Sarah to collect the children from nursery and then I brought them back to the hospital to collect Sarah. She was still in the middle of treatment and the children climbed up onto her lap. They were fascinated by the drug-filled tube that was connected to their mum's chest. They both had magazines which came with a cheap toy to keep them occupied and they were soon engrossed in these, oblivious to what was going on around them.

Recovery from chemotherapy was taking longer each time and Sarah needed to spend the best part of the week that followed in bed. She was suffering from regular headaches and the nausea was worsening. After about six days in bed Sarah came downstairs dressed and ready to go out to do some food shopping. Her friend Jenny was due back in the morning from a holiday to America and Sarah wanted to buy her some groceries to leave outside her front door. She didn't want her friend coming home and not having all the items necessary for breakfast, lunch and drinks. Sarah was very poorly but still thinking of others. I was so moved, but not surprised, by her kindness and selfless nature that I started sobbing. She stared at me wondering what had caused this sudden outburst.

Sarah had barely recovered from her last treatment when the next one was due. We were also getting the results of the MRI scan on this visit. Sarah had been taking the herbal tablets regularly and I remained hopeful, praying to God for some good news even though He had refused to answer my prayers on previous occasions.

At the hospital we were informed that the constant headaches and the loss of sight in her right eye were because of cancer cells colonising the meninges. Sarah sat there and cried, which she rarely did in hospital.

'When am I going to get a break?' she replied.

I told the doctor that we had a family holiday booked for June and he recommended that we bring it forward. I suggested May and again was told to make it sooner.

Her treatment would continue and other ones were offered. Radiotherapy was an option – as was more chemotherapy injected directly into the affected area. Sarah refused the latter at once. I hoped that the herbal tablets alongside her regular chemo and sessions of radiotherapy would be sufficient to rid the cancer cells from her brain. We were only asking for a couple of years' grace. Our last wish was for Sarah to live long enough to take Olivia to school.

Into March and Heaven

Sarah had a "bucket list", albeit small. This was a list of all the things she wanted to do before she "kicked the bucket". She aptly called it this after watching a film of the same name. We had our holiday in Cornwall booked for May and tea at the Ritz in London to look forward to in April. May was only two months away and I was confident that we would enjoy it as a family. Sarah wanted to see a comedian who was performing at a local theatre, but I had left it too late to buy tickets and felt guilty as it was sold out. I called them and explained about Sarah's "bucket list" and was told that seats would be found for us. I really wish it didn't take the onset of death to make things possible.

I was responsible for all the driving now as it was illegal for Sarah to drive in her condition. We were out driving in her car one day, when I said how scared I was about the future and how my list of fears was endless. My main fear, which was unavoidable, was coping without my wife and the mother of our children. I couldn't for the life of me see how I would manage this mammoth task.

Sarah told me that she had only two fears: me being lonely every night was her first. Her second was that she was really afraid of losing her dignity as the cancer spread further. She told me that she wasn't afraid of dying or leaving her children, because she knew that I would do a great job of bringing them up. She had a lot more faith in me than I did in myself. She believed in me totally. She was extremely upset that she would never see Olivia in a wedding dress or Sam getting married, though. I was in awe of her strength. She knew she was going to say goodbye to her children quite soon, yet somehow she found a way to cope and accepted it.

She spoke to me about my future without her and suggested that I grieve for eighteen months before moving on. During that time she told me to go out and get as much sympathy sex as possible. She said it wouldn't prove to be a problem as ladies would come out of the woodwork offering themselves. She warned me not to get involved with anyone on my own doorstep, pointing out that this included family and friends. I continued driving as she joked about me getting a Thai bride because I would be well looked after. Sarah told me that she wanted me to be happy and find love again. She smiled as she jokingly told me not to love anyone quite as much as I did her. I said that I didn't want anyone else and that the only person I wanted, I was losing.

Remarkably, Sarah was strong enough to prepare me for my future without her at the same time as she was preparing for her death. Together we made a list of potential qualities for future relationship material. I said anyone I got involved with would have to be selfless, thoughtful and loving. I didn't want a fussy eater, someone with tattoos or a dog owner. I wanted someone with a similar sense of humour and taste in music. She had to be at least five years younger than me, intelligent and definitely a non-smoker. Sarah joked that I would be on my own for a very long time. I couldn't imagine being alone at the time as Sarah was still very much alive and still making me smile from the passenger seat of her car. I believed that that somehow a miracle would occur, enabling us to stay together.

Sarah found it very difficult to leave her bed two days after chemotherapy and a day after another Friday the thirteenth, her headaches were so bad that she had to be kept topped up with painkillers every few hours. Chewing and swallowing had become a problem, which made eating increasingly difficult. I still believed that radiotherapy would improve her condition, but Sarah told me that she wanted it all to be over. She wanted to hurry up and die so that everybody could move on and get on with their lives. She asked me to stop the children from seeing her if she ended up in a hospice suffering. The oncologist told us that in some cases cancer of the meninges can lead to a horrific death. She could lose the sight in both eyes and her hearing. It was also possible that her bodily functions would fail.

On Saturday, 14 March, Sarah was very agitated. Her headaches were less responsive to the painkillers and the muscles that controlled her chewing were not functioning properly. She said that she needed to get out of the house and suggested a walk. We took a short stroll along the river near our home. I was finally accepting that we might not make our last holiday together and wanted to share my thoughts. I eventually stopped and hugged her before sharing them. She told me that she wouldn't make it and insisted that I still go with the children. She then told me that she loved me and that I had been a brilliant husband. I had received birthday cards from her over the years, telling me the very same thing. Cards that were eventually put in a drawer and forgotten about. Written words that were taken for granted. Hearing Sarah tell me this filled me with a joy I had rarely experienced. Time stood still as she thanked me for being in her life and told me how lovely and kind I had been. Certainly the biggest compliment I had ever received, especially considering it came from someone I believed to be as brave as Jesus. I still needed to accept that she was going to die, however, and that it would be soon.

I had to call Jacqueline the following morning. I had been awake for most of the night because Sarah had spent the majority of it being sick. I had read that this was one of the symptoms from having cancer of the meninges, but I told myself it was more to do with her having had chemotherapy a few days earlier. Surely her condition would improve.

I took Sarah to hospital that afternoon. She was admitted straight away and given her own room. I was relieved when I went to bed that night that Sarah was in hospital being looked after and under observation.

After an assessment on Monday morning it was decided that radiotherapy would start on Wednesday. I was only working mornings and would go to the hospital at lunchtime. I would take a box of melon along with me because Sarah couldn't eat much else. Her mum was at the hospital most of the time and was reluctant to leave her bedside.

Throughout the week the children kept asking me when their mummy was coming home. I could only tell them that I didn't know as their mummy was very poorly. I said that the doctors were doing everything they could to make her better.

When I picked Samuel up from school on Wednesday, he told me that he really wanted to go to the hospital to see his mum. I thought it would do them both good, so I took him in with me. When we arrived her bed was empty, but a nurse soon directed us to the radiotherapy ward where we would find her. She was sitting in a wheelchair waiting to be measured up for radiotherapy. She didn't look like my Sarah.

Cancer had made her look very ill. She was without her wig, which was very unusual for her. She also had a very dark purple bruise on her arm as a result of an injection.

As soon as she saw Samuel she came to life. 'Hey! Hello, you,' she said with the utmost excitement.

If she could have powered a bulb at that moment from her sudden burst of energy, it would have been blinding. Samuel was staring at the chair and the bruise on her arm. He didn't ask any questions about what he saw; he just wanted to know when she was coming home. We had shared so many traumatic moments as a family and here was another. I was very moved to see Sarah and Sam holding each other but at the same time I was desperately sad that he would only ever experience it as a child. We stayed for about an hour before collecting Olivia. Sam was very happy after his visit to the hospital.

I headed back to the hospital once the children were asleep. Sarah was sitting up in bed when I arrived and she told me that my parents had been to see her. She joked about my dad being as work-shy as me and using her illness as an excuse to slack off work. She asked me if I was working in the morning and how she hoped that I was. She also told me that our parish priest had visited her during the day. I didn't really pay much attention to this. I didn't see that it had any significance and assumed it was merely a formality with patients who were unwell.

While I was there Sarah got out of bed to use the bathroom. Her legs could barely carry her and she looked relieved once she was back in bed. She asked me to chase up the nurse for some painkillers. She was having high doses of pain relief now to relieve the discomfort in her neck. She wanted me to stay with her until the nurse had given them to her, telling how tight and forgetful they were with the medication. Within five minutes Sarah had taken it and a short while later I said goodbye. But then she told me that I couldn't leave until her medication had arrived and was bemused when I said that she had been given it already. This was the first time I had noticed any signs of confusion. Sarah was always very sharp and had the memory of an elephant. She always won arguments with her ability to remember everything I had ever said that could be used as evidence against me at a later, relevant date. I left her to rest and headed home, guessing that her confusion was a result of all the drugs she was taking. I kissed her goodbye and went home.

Radiotherapy was to begin on Thursday morning and was our last hope of prolonging Sarah's life as far as I was concerned. I was frustrated because there didn't seem to be any urgency with the staff at the hospital. She had been there since Saturday and should have had radiotherapy sooner. Did they even care? I had stopped praying for my wife to be saved, as God didn't appear to be hearing my prayers at all. I still prayed, but this time my prayers were for her to die without suffering, for I was constantly concerned about her final days. All I asked was that she die in her sleep with her dignity intact and without suffering. Maybe God would at least answer these prayers. I had desperate thoughts about Jesus, as God didn't intervene to stop His only son from dying, so why would He help my Sarah? Jesus was destined to die and there was a purpose to His death. Maybe there was a purpose to Sarah's death, too. Her work and her life here with me had come to an end and she was now needed elsewhere. An image presented itself to me of an angel in Heaven with bright green eyes and a smile of pure happiness.

After work on Thursday I went straight to the hospital, hoping that radiotherapy had taken place. I discovered that Sarah had refused treatment. The doctors had lifted her onto a wheelchair and taken her to the radiotherapy ward but once there, Sarah had sat rigid in the chair refusing to go ahead with treatment. She wanted to accept her fate. Sarah was now in bed and unconscious. Her mum left the room so I could be alone with my wife. I climbed onto the bed and put my arms around her from behind. Then I held her hand and cried. She moved her little finger against mine. This was the only sign that she was aware of my presence. All the years of love and closeness between us could not compete with the intimacy I felt at that very moment.

It was soon mid afternoon and I had to kiss her goodbye because the school day was coming to an end. Her mum stayed and would do so until she needed sleep.

I spoke to her mum later that evening and she told me how agitated and restless Sarah had become after I left. She told me how Sarah had called out Samuel's name at around ten past three. Instinctively, she must have still been very much aware in her unconscious condition that it was school pick-up time. Her mum was heartbroken but I didn't have the strength to connect or to feel her pain as my own filled me to maximum capacity.

Friday morning at work was extremely difficult. I didn't want to be there. I couldn't concentrate or stay focused on any task. I just wanted to go to the hospital to see if Sarah had woken up from her deep sleep. Claire had flown down from Leeds with her husband, Stuart, to be with her mum and to help provide extra care for her sister.

I received the biggest shock when I arrived at the hospital later that day to see Sarah. Her breathing was laboured and there was a loud rattling sound coming from her chest as she breathed. I had brought along my iPod and speakers to play our favourite music to her. Her mum told me that Sarah would not survive the weekend. I checked Sarah's mobile as I had sent her a message midweek from the children telling her how much we all loved her and missed her and was pleased to see that she had read it. I then climbed up onto her bed and through sobs of anguish, told her that she didn't have to worry about anything. I said that I would take care of the children always and then I told her I would tell Samuel that evening about her imminent death. I told her I loved her so much and proceeded to thank her for making such a difference to my life. I think that is what the real definition of a celebrity should be: somebody who really makes a difference in another's life and improves it, not just anybody who stands in front of a camera for TV or magazines, famous for just looking good.

I was in a state of shock when I left the hospital. Sarah had maintained her dignity when she had given birth to two children, when I had walked away at the final hour, only to return and feast my eyes upon a new life in her arms. I felt that this was also now the final hour, where I would walk away to protect myself from years of trauma. Sarah once told me that nobody should ever die alone. Her mum and her sister were not about to leave her side and let that happen, so what she had said had been fulfilled.

Walking back to my car I realised for the first time that Sarah was going to die. I had refused to accept it until that moment when it had become definite. I needed to see my dad, so I drove the 5 km to my parents' house. I was numb and I blocked out every thought that tried to enter my mind. Years of driving enabled my arms and legs to function automatically, without guidance. I wanted to travel at lightning speed because I knew I couldn't hold myself together for long. I walked through the front door of my parents' house and passed by my mother, asking her where Dad was. I usually confided in my mum and turned to her in my hour of need, yet this time it was Dad I needed. Olivia was staying there for a couple of days and was having a nap upstairs at the time. Dad was at the bottom of the garden, working in his garage.

I couldn't speak but I flung my arms around him and wept solidly for ten minutes. After releasing all of my hurt and sadness, I told him that Sarah wasn't going to survive the weekend. My dad did exactly what I wanted from him. All he said was, 'Oh dear,' over and over. He didn't cry, which would have made me feel bad for him. He soaked up my pain with all of his love for me. This was the closest I had ever been to my dad emotionally and I was so aware at that moment how dearly I loved him. Why did I only ever seem to have such feelings of deep love during a tragedy? My dad had been in my life for forty years and I had taken so many of those years for granted. I had enjoyed so many moments, but had never actually stood still and been overwhelmed by them before they passed. My life with Sarah had been like that, too. We'd had fifteen wonderful years together and so many unappreciated days.

I pondered this as I left my parents' house to collect Sam from school. I tried not to think about how I was going to tell him that his mummy wouldn't be coming home. I was shaking as I parked outside his school. I called my friend Dominic, who worked close by, and told him that Sarah wouldn't be with us much longer and how scared I was. Within five minutes he had left work and was sitting in the car with me. He hugged me with the understanding that words were superfluous. I told him how I was dreading having to tell Samuel and cause unavoidable hurt. I wasn't thinking about Olivia at this stage. At 3 years old, I didn't think she would understand or that it would even have the same impact. Dominic went back to work and I was alone once more.

I managed to stay strong as I collected Sam from school and take him home. My breathing was deep and my chest tightened as his bedtime approached. My heart was pounding when I chose my moment to tell him. We were in my bedroom when he asked me when his mummy was coming home. I answered clearly, telling him how poorly she was and although the doctors had tried really hard to make her better, they were unable to do so. I wept as I told him how sorry I was, because his mummy was going to Heaven soon and not coming home. I expected him to cry immediately, but instead he laughed and said, 'You are joking. Let's go downstairs and play a game.' I certainly wasn't expecting that reaction.

I followed his lead and we played a couple of games. A while later he asked me when his mummy was coming home and how many days it would be. I told him again that she wouldn't be coming home. I felt I was being tortured and it was getting worse. I had been given a book by a friend aptly titled *Mama's Going to Heaven Soon* by Kathe Copeland. It's a book to help a child with the anticipated death of their mother. It is illustrated very well by Elissa Hudson and gives a very hopeful message about life after her death. I asked Sam if he wanted me to read it to him. He sat in silence as I read to him and relayed how much his mummy would always love him. No parent should ever have to read such a book and I found it to be, without doubt, the hardest moment of my life. I read clearly and without tears. My hands were shaking and it worsened as I neared the end. As soon as I had finished, Sam cried. I held him in my arms and we cried together. I kissed him goodnight and left him to sleep. I felt as if I had just run a marathon. I had a feeling that there would be many more exhausting days ahead of me.

Jacqueline and Claire were still at the hospital – and would stay there until Sarah passed away – while I sat in my front room with my brother-in-law, Stuart, convincing myself that I didn't need to go back to the hospital. Sarah wouldn't want me to. Maybe I would go in the morning. I was lying on my usual sofa and Stuart was sitting on Sarah's. We were watching a comedy and laughing, when his mobile phone rang at 10.00 p.m. He put it to his ear and I immediately saw the look of sheer shock on his face. 'She's gone,' were his first words, directed at me.

My Sarah had gone. She had been taken from me far too soon. I wasn't with her for her final breath. I hoped she would forgive me. My prayer that she wouldn't suffer had been answered. I believe she consciously gave up her fight after I told her it was okay to die and that I would take care of everything for her. I called my mum immediately and told her that Sarah would suffer no more. It was 20 March 2009 and from this day forward, Sarah would only be alive in my memories. Stuart asked me if there was anything I needed and I told him to put the comedy back on.

We were laughing when Jacqueline and Claire returned from the hospital. Maybe they thought this was as odd, as I did when I heard Sam laughing earlier that evening. Jacqui told me that she was certain that Sarah's spirit couldn't wait to leave her body behind – a body of no hair, one original breast and lots of scars all brought about by cancer. A cancer that grew so fast, leaving her blind in one eye and very quickly shutting down the rest of her senses. Even the strongest of spirits could not remain in such a damaged body. I just hoped that her hearing was still responsive on my final visit when I had told her how much I loved her one more time.

On Saturday morning Sam pulled out a card from his school bag. It was a Mother's Day card that he had made. He asked me what he was supposed to do with it. I told him that it was beautiful and that he should put it on top of the fireplace. He waited until bedtime to ask me when mummy would be coming home. I gave him the same answer as the night before. There was a pause before he asked if she would be home by Christmas. I stroked his head as I told him that Mummy had died and was in Heaven like the lady in the book. He asked me to read it again. Reading it a second time was just as hard as the first. When I had finished, Sam was quiet. A single tear ran from his left eye. One tear was all it took to drown me with sorrow and make my heart cry a lifetime of tears.

I had booked Olivia into nursery for Monday. It wasn't one of her usual days to attend, but I needed time to arrange the funeral. I didn't realise that it was the day of the Mother's Day tea, where all of the children's mums were invited in to join their children. I was glad that they still went ahead with it, though. Samuel went into school as I wanted to keep to the same routine. At school collection time his teacher told me that he had walked into class in the morning and announced to them that his mum had died over the weekend. We both agreed that this was quite astounding considering Sam was only 6 years old. I was really pleased that he wasn't uncomfortable mentioning his mum's death. He was too young to understand how uncomfortable some people feel when confronted by a mourner, though.

A small number of people I passed every day would try to avoid me because they didn't know what to say. This was also true with phone calls, which you would think were easier because you are not in the same room as the person you are saying sorry to. If I did manage to corner one of the avoiders, they would apologise for not calling because they didn't know what to say. I never took offence at this and would tell them that I understood, as I had been guilty of the same thing in the past. Unless you are selfless, it usually takes a close family bereavement to understand another person's grief and to know what to say to them.

I also didn't take offence at the handful of friends who, on being told of our loss, replied, 'You're joking.' I was aware that adults behave in strange ways in these situations and would try to do my best to alleviate their discomfort.

When I walked into the school playground I would approach the groups of mums and dads who had just struck up an impromptu conversation on seeing me and I would join in. I would tell them not to feel awkward and that I didn't expect any words of wisdom from them. I told them all when the funeral was taking place and that they shouldn't feel obliged to wear black if they wished to attend. Surprisingly, one lady approached me and said that she might not be able to make it to church as her 2-year-old had a swimming lesson. A few days later she spoke to me again to tell me that she could now come along. How very privileged I felt to know that I had her support!

My sister, Tracy, had just arrived from America to offer her support and within a day of arriving we noticed to our horror that Olivia had head lice. In all the time that Sarah was alive her children had never had head lice. What I do know is that it would have grossed her out and made her scratch for weeks – obviously if it had occurred while she'd had hair! Spending thirty minutes combing through Olivia's hair, searching for nits, made it harder for me to get her and Samuel to bed at their usual time. I thought if I kept to the same routines that we had spent years creating then I just might keep my sanity. I would take the children out shopping with me and feel proud when they told strangers that their mum had died. I would cringe and be extremely embarrassed when Olivia would tell them that she had nits, though. I am quite sure that I had more stunned reactions from ladies with long, curly hair on hearing about nits than some of the reactions I got from others hearing about the loss of my wife.

Sarah had told me that she wanted everybody to weep at her funeral. She then wanted us all to put our grief to one side and enjoy celebrating her life. Planning a funeral is a little bit like planning for a wedding, except that one is celebrating a future and the other a past. We'd had about a year and a half to plan for our wedding and I only had a week to arrange the funeral. Sarah had chosen a venue, which would have been fine if only a dozen people showed up. There was only enough parking for about eight cars and so I needed somewhere more spacious.

It came to me immediately and it was obvious. I booked the same hotel and meeting room that we had chosen for our wedding reception. In 2001 we had celebrated with our friends and family the start of a new life together. We had exchanged rings while swearing our love for each other through sickness and health and until death did us part. We had danced for the first time as husband and wife in front of an audience following weeks of dance lessons to avoid shuffling around in a circle to a cheesy love song. It seemed very fitting to celebrate Sarah's life in the same venue.

I was thinking about songs to play at the funeral and at the hotel afterwards. Sarah had chosen two songs for the church service. The entrance song was to be by Kate Bush called "This Woman's Work" with "Movin' On Up" by Primal Scream for the exit song. Instead, I ended up choosing "Sarah" by Thin Lizzy for the exit song as I thought it would touch more people. I saved the Primal Scream one for the crematorium, as thought it was more appropriate. Sarah couldn't have chosen a more perfect song for her farewell. The words, "Well, I was blind. Now I can see," followed by, "I'm movin' on up now. I'm gettin' out of the darkness. My light shines on," captured the sentiment perfectly.

Weeks before Sarah died I had introduced myself to a local charity called Simon Says which specialises in helping children deal with bereavement. At the time I was taking Olivia to her gymnastics class, when I saw their advert about an annual meeting at a local hotel. What I didn't realise until I arrived was that it was their annual finance meeting. The conference room was filled with all of their staff. A middle-aged lady approached me and asked me who I was and I told her I would need their help very soon. I was introduced to each and every staff member and I told all of them my story. When I arrived back home Sarah was in bed and she asked me if it had been upsetting. I'd answered without a single word by proceeding to weep. Once I had calmed down I told her that I felt very hopeful about any future help and input they could give me. I was certainly needing their help now and finding it to be invaluable. One of the ladies I had met a few weeks prior to Sarah's death was a counsellor for the charity and she now called me every day, guiding me with helpful advice. She told me to share my grief with the children by crying with them. She also advised me to be as honest as I could when answering any questions that they might have. A growing concern of mine was about the coffin, as I was worried that Sam would ask me what it was and what happens to it, though I was told by the charity that he probably wouldn't mention it.

I went to see the priest the day before the funeral and told him I wanted to get up and speak about Sarah in church. He advised against it, arguing that the day would be too traumatic for me to be able to. I had always been a terrible public speaker – this was one of the reasons it took me seven years to propose to Sarah. I'd also had a serious phobia concerning the groom's speech, during which I knew that I would shake, stutter and sweat while holding an unsteady piece of paper – and I was right. I assured Father John that I would keep it short and have a few friends standing by in case I couldn't manage it.

He then told me about his visit to the hospital to see Sarah. They had never met before and he told me how much he was moved by the moment. He had written a few things down himself about Sarah to relay in church. He told me about the time when he was sitting by her bedside and told her how angry she must have felt at God for not helping her. He said that she must have been asking herself, 'Why me?' Sarah had listened quietly up until this point and then she turned to him and said, 'Why not me?' Father John told me how these three words broke him. I wasn't surprised by Sarah's response, but I was very moved that during his short visit Father John had been so touched by her spirit and her wonderment. I was glad that he told me this before the service and not just before I had to stand up and speak.

Walking through the church doors holding Samuel's hand and carrying Olivia was a calm experience. The church was full, vanquishing Sarah's fears that not many people would attend. The line from the entrance song was clear and beautiful as it filled the church. "All the things I should've said that I never said, all the things we should've done that we never did." I cried during this song many times. Today it was everybody else's turn. Sarah wanted a celebration and I had to stay strong for her to ensure that she got one. The only dry eyes in the church belonged to the three of us, as our tears were already spent. It seemed that this time all of my pain and sadness was being shared by the friends and family around me and my own tears were having a much-needed rest for a time.

The children and I moved forward through the sea of grief on either side as the tears fell from the watching onlookers along every pew who had been touched by Sarah's life. I felt that we were the only bright light as we sat at the front holding hands. Everywhere else there was darkness as sorrow descended and extinguished the lights of loved ones as they thought about Sarah.

I stood facing everyone as I read out the words I had written the night before, thinking about Sarah as I read. Her face filled my mind, blinding me from seeing the faces before me and her coffin that lay alongside me. I finished reading and noticed my children's faces smiling up at me. The counsellor from the child-bereavement charity turned out to be right. Neither Samuel nor Olivia had asked about the large basket covered in flowers. Flowers that they see every day in Sarah's hand in our wedding photograph. The only conversation that we'd had about the coffin was when we had painted our handprints on a large piece of paper to place in the large basket with Sarah. I told the children that they would go to Heaven with her, so that she would forever be able to hold our hands. I think it is a fair assumption that angels have little need for wigs. Understanding Sarah's wishes for dignity, I thought it necessary for her to wear the bargain wig that her friend Jenny had bought her for one last time, so that went with her as well.

We left the church in the same way we had entered, but hearing a different line from a different song: "When you came in my life you changed my world. My Sarah."

Close friends and family headed to the crematorium to say final goodbyes. I watched the priest smile as Sarah's chosen song was played and she moved out of the darkness, into the light.

Her light will shine on.

The children were with my parents outside the church. They each had a balloon that they had drawn a picture on and written a message for their mummy. They wanted to let the balloons drift higher and higher, eventually finding their way to Heaven. A crowd had gathered to watch and as the balloons sailed up into a clear, sunny blue sky, two planes formed a cross, marking a path for them before they disappeared from sight.

Everyone then made their way to the hotel to share stories and to celebrate Sarah's life. I had chosen our favourite music to play on a loop all afternoon and songs filled the very same room that we'd had our wedding celebration in, eight years previously. Photographs of Sarah sat on a table at the edge of the dance floor, where we'd had our first dance as husband and wife. I had also left some plain cards on the table with pens for people to share their thoughts about Sarah and post them in a box, the idea being that the children might like to read them when they were adults and had a greater understanding of events. I proudly watched the children from the dance floor, running around laughing, drinking lemonade and telling everyone what a great party it was. But this time I stood alone, as there would be no last dance. My marriage had ended – death parting us.

I was now a single parent and a widower. Although I was now without Sarah, I had gained far more than I had lost. I told myself how lucky I was. How could I not be thankful for having her in my life for fifteen years? I admit that the love that we had showed each other since cancer had come into our lives was very different from the love without it. Obviously the love was still there, but there didn't seem to be any urgency to show it. Like most people we went from day to day, taking each other for granted. I showed Sarah more love during the years that she was ill than I probably would have in a lifetime together if she hadn't developed cancer and that's quite shameful. I counted my blessings that she had given me two beautiful children, for whether I realised it or not, they were going to get me through the hard days that lay ahead. Without them, I wouldn't have had a reason to get up in the morning. I would continue as a lone parent in the same manner as I always had.

Sarah's strong will continually encouraging me to cook would prove very worthwhile. Her equally strong feelings about education had also rubbed off on me. A shelf in our dining room is full of pictures of Sarah and her family wearing graduation gowns and holding certificates. I used to joke that the only way my picture would get up there would be if I hired the gown for a day and borrowed a certificate. My photograph is still absent from there. I had left school with grades that are best forgotten about. The children's education was now my responsibility and I really didn't want to fail. It was now my job to ensure that they achieved the same level as they would have done if Sarah was still in charge.

Sarah had mostly taught me how to be thoughtful. She would always write thank-you cards for gifts and she always considered other people's needs. She might have had a foul temper and a stroppy side, but the overwhelming warmth of her personality outweighed this temporary occurrence.

Women's Work is a Tough Act to Follow

The funeral had kept me busy for ten days and cards dropped through the letterbox on a daily basis. I read them all, but was unable to store a single word in my memory. The only thing missing from the post was an invoice from the funeral directors which had been hand-delivered two days prior to Sarah's cremation. I wondered if payments of this nature had always been a matter of urgency. Someone would certainly have to pay me a lot of money to turn up at the family home of the deceased with an invoice. After about a week, most of the cards had been received. Friends and family had returned to their own lives and I somehow had to adjust to my new life.

'I want Mummy,' should be such a simple request to fulfil. But hearing these words as I put the children to bed each night was exhausting. The one and only thing that they wanted, I couldn't give them. I could take them anywhere in the world and buy them anything they liked, but I would never be able to grant this wish from the top of their list. My own grief was bubbling away beneath the numbness, trying to force its way through, using anger to make its way to the surface.

Everything felt different and alien to me. Part of me had died and the remaining part was trying to make sense of it and adjust somehow. I tried not to think about the future. I didn't want to think about having to feed, wash and clothe the children for 365 days a year for at least the next ten years. Sarah had reinforced the importance of education and I didn't want to let her down by ignoring it. Samuel had homework every night and I had very little enthusiasm for it. I wondered if my enthusiasm would return though, as it appeared lost throughout the day. Neither did I see the point in joining in the children's games any more, as Sarah wasn't there to witness it.

I spoke to my mum about this and compared it to cooking a fine three-course dinner for myself. Some things are meant to be shared to be enjoyed. When the children had gone to bed I would look through our photo albums that were filled with pictures of Sarah and would have to resort to a glass of whisky to take the edge off my grief. I would sit and watch camcorder footage of past holidays and was dismayed by how little Sarah featured in our films. I thought it was important to have the children on film to show them later in their life when they became adults. I also knew that I would enjoy looking at them myself in years to come, to remind me of the happiness we shared jointly. For now, though, I just wanted to see Sarah on my television screen and although there wasn't much footage of her, every brief smile and wave could be enjoyed forever. At times it made for frustrating viewing, as largely she could only be seen from the neck down as I had focused on the children. I would be craning my neck, getting closer to the screen in the vain hope of seeing more of her. Holding the remote control in one hand and an empty glass in the other, I would sit alone on my sofa, surrounded by photographs. My throat and head would ache from the pressure of emotion.

The philosopher Kahlil Gibran states that when you are sorrowful, if you look into your heart you will realise that you are weeping for the joy and delight that you have experienced. The more joy you have experienced the deeper the sorrow will be. He wrote about joy and sorrow being inseparable. While one sleeps the other is awake. I understood this and agreed with every word as my sorrow was now fully awake while I looked at Sarah in our photographs and on the television screen. I welcomed the intense grief as it made me feel closer to her. The more my eyes blurred from the tears, the clearer my memory and my feelings for Sarah became. My happy and sad emotions had switched places and appeared to be all mixed up, for I had a strange feeling of happiness during and immediately after grieving. My grief was all that felt natural and real. Everything else seemed to be forced or a distraction, enhancing my depression. I forced myself to get up in the morning and get the children to school. I forced myself to cook and clean and somehow entertain the children, even though they knew that my heart wasn't in it. Once the necessary jobs were completed, I would find as many ways to distract myself as possible before I felt the need once again to shake hands with my sorrow.

I climbed into an empty bed at night but I didn't feel alone. I could still feel her presence and see her smile. I just wished that I could feel her hand and hold her tight or have a conversation. Cancer may have taken my Sarah but it could never destroy our love. That will never die.

All of our shared experiences were so important, the good and the bad, because all of those precious moments have created a lifetime of precious memories. This is why death can never completely take away the person that you love.

When I turned the light out I felt as if Sarah was lying next to me. Sometimes I would move my leg across to her side, feeling for her cold feet. She always had cold feet at night and I was her human radiator. She relied on me to warm them up. A heat battle ensued as she drained my heat with her abnormally cold feet. We used to joke about her having thin blood and that she only married me because I was so hot!

I would fall into a deep sleep very quickly when clutching her nightshirt, which would enhance her smell in the dark. I would only awake during the night if the children disturbed me. Olivia would often come in during the middle of the night looking for her mummy, hoping that she had returned from wherever she had gone. Another time I woke to hear Olivia screaming in distress because she had been sick. It was 2.00 a.m. and the most unsocial time to be sick. I went to her room and she was completely covered in vomit, as was her bedding. She was very upset and even more so when I stripped off her soggy clothes and lifted her under the shower. The heating had long been turned off and the house was cold. I washed her hair and body while she shivered and she stayed under the shower while I put clean linen on her bed.

I was feeling so alone and didn't think I could feel any more miserable until I wrapped Olivia up in a towel. Her bottom lip was sticking out and she just managed to say, 'I want Mummy,' before throwing her arms around me and weeping. From the very first moment I had walked into Olivia's room, she could sense my stress and upset because of my inability to hide my frustration and tears. I told her how much I was missing her mummy, too. But when someone or something is missing, there is usually a chance of finding them or it. Sarah, my wife and the mother of my children, wasn't missing. She was gone and she would never be coming back.

I dressed Olivia in clean pyjamas and put her back to bed with a kiss and a hug. Then I got back in bed and was just drifting off when I heard her being sick again. There was so much sick the first time that I didn't think it was possible that there could be any more. I only had one more spare set of bedding. My stress levels were really high and I could feel my temple pulsing as the panic started to grow. Thankfully she was only sick on her pillow and there was a little bit on her cheek. I hummed nervously as I cleaned it up. Nervous humming is good if you want to cause a child more distress. I settled for silence and tried to turn my scared, miserable appearance into a regular, tired look. I needed Sarah so much to keep me calm and help me to be less dramatic about a bed full of sick. I was worried that Olivia would continue to be sick throughout the night and I would soon end up having to put her in bed with me next and then possibly the couch. Maybe the car would be the only clean option left once all the bedding had been soiled.

I was worried that my food might have poisoned her. I didn't think a jacket potato with cheese could cause food poisoning but it crossed my mind. At three in the morning I couldn't really call anyone. I had lots of offers from friends and family to help me and some said call us any time, day or night. Eventually I picked up the phone and called Tracy. She was on American time and I was so relieved to think of calling her. It must have taken me a whole minute to say hello as a result of being overwhelmed by grief. Tracy told me that Olivia would be fine and she doubted there would be any more vomiting. I put the washing machine on as we chatted and I guessed I was lucky to live in a world with modern technology. I had a telephone which I could use to chat any time of the day and use to call for help. I also had a washing machine which, I admit, I had only learned how to use when Sarah became ill. When I was a child my mother used to do all of the washing by hand and she would point this out to me frequently. I am sure that if it wasn't for these important inventions I would not have been able to manage alone. I thanked Tracy for listening and felt so much better for sharing my worries. I fell asleep immediately, aware that what most people saw as "morning" was only three hours away.

Chatting on the phone was something I was spending a lot of time doing. Most nights I would chat for hours to anyone who would answer. Before she died Sarah had been spending a lot of time chatting too, and she had complained to me about the battery life in our phones. She told me that she only had about an hour of battery life each time and asked me to replace them. I would constantly forget as my mind would be full of thoughts about Sarah and her illness. I didn't have any room in my brain for remembering things that I considered unimportant. Both phones were fully charged now, as I needed to keep chatting to avoid the silence in our house during the evening. I could visualise Sarah shaking her head as I placed the brand new rechargeable batteries into the handsets now that I wanted to have lengthy conversations.

I didn't feel the emptiness that I had expected to, though. But if the children weren't sleeping upstairs then I would most definitely have felt it. I still felt Sarah's presence in every room. It was as if she left a room just as I entered. I would be cooking in the kitchen, sensing her sitting on her sofa in the living room. Sometimes I had to suppress the urge to call out to her. I couldn't accept that she was dead and completely refused to face it. I told myself that all of my responsibilities as a single parent were only temporary until Sarah returned. I wondered if I felt this way as a result of not witnessing her take her final breath. Having not visited the funeral directors to see her body had also helped with my denial. I had decided against seeing her body because I wanted to remember her full of life and smiling, not as a damaged body without her soul.

Getting the children ready for school was something I was used to being part of. Breakfast was easy as Sam could serve himself cereal and he could also pour his own apple juice. I was getting through a lot of milk and juice but for now, it was a big help while I stared into Olivia's wardrobe, hoping to be handed an outfit by a magic fairy of some kind. Sam would be fed, washed, dressed and waiting downstairs each day for me to finish my daily battle of wills with Olivia regarding her clothes. I would dream about the day when she started school and how much easier a uniform would be.

I couldn't wait to get them into the car and dropped off so I could be alone for the day and have less to stress about. Some mornings it took ages to get them into the car. On one such morning, Olivia asked me if I could tie her hair up into bunches. As we had about ten minutes to spare I thought I had plenty of time to perfect it. I had been shown how to do it by Claire when she had last visited. She had made it all look very easy and was finished inside of a minute. Olivia has very fluffy, curly blonde hair; if it was pink it would resemble candy floss. Claire had found a parting and separated the hair within seconds. I was using the same comb that she had used but it took me ten minutes to get a neat line down the middle of her hair. I was sweating and Olivia was starting to get very restless. My nervous hum had returned, just to make her even more anxious. I managed to tie up a bunch on my first attempt. It would have been perfect if my finger and thumb hadn't been attached. If I went to nursery with her and sat behind her all day it would have been okay. After at least ten attempts I was angry and tearful. I had thrown the comb and had upset Olivia by shouting at her for not sitting still. In all fairness she was crying before I had shouted as a result of having her hair pulled too tight on so many occasions, but she was crying nonetheless.

We were running very late and I have never been late for anything in my life. I get very stressed if there are unnecessary hold-ups so I admitted defeat and decided I would ask one of the staff members at her nursery to tie it up and maybe show me again how it's done. I was incredibly tense as I climbed into the car, wondering how I was going to raise two children if I couldn't even complete a simple task involving hair. I was a precision engineer and could make anything out of metal, wood or plastic. I could wallpaper and hang doors. But I was beginning to think that only women had the natural skills to raise a girl.

I was about to drive away when I realised the children didn't have their coats. I closed my eyes, took a deep breath and slammed the car door behind me as I went back indoors to get them. While inside I tilted my head skywards and roared like a threatened lion. I cursed a number of times too, before returning to the car with the coats.

I was pulling away a second time when Samuel told me he didn't have his book bag. I slammed the brakes on and shouted at him. I asked him why he had left everything to me. I pointed out that he'd had loads of time while I was upstairs pulling Olivia's hair until she screamed. I told him that there were only three of us now and that he had to help me out sometimes. He was only 6 years old and I was being completely irrational owing to my grief.

Anger hadn't just arrived when the cancer had, though. I had been a short-tempered teenager, which had continued into my twenties. I was a lot like a volcano. I regularly felt my temperature rising and my blood would appear to boil moments before I exploded into a rage. Sarah had calmed me down over the years and my volcanic eruptions were infrequent as my anger slept. It was now wide awake and I was very unstable as my loss and my situation became apparent.

After I had dropped children off I would wander aimlessly around the shops in the town centre. I would sit in coffee shops and stare out of the window in a daze. I was constantly looking for someone who reminded me of Sarah. I wanted to see somebody who had similar hair to her or perhaps had the same style in clothing. There were no similarities to be found. Sarah was unique and I would have to face up to the fact that I would never see her again. As I looked around I saw some ladies who reminded me of Sarah wearing head scarves with no eyebrows. It was then that realised I needed to distract myself because I didn't want to dive head first into grief. I was worried that if I did then I might never come out of it. If I remained in denial, I thought I could manage better.

Nearly everything in the present reminded me of the past, though. I had frequented most of the coffee shops and bars with Sarah and had been shopping with her numerous times. I once passed a card shop and was drawn to a card that was for a loving husband and I would briefly be shaken from my denial. Sarah would never buy me one of those cards again and she would never tell me that she loved me. I keenly felt a huge void in the absence of her love. I would wipe the tears on my sleeve and continue to window shop until it was time to collect the children, when I would climb into Sarah's car and drive to school.

My car was parked at home unused, so I decided to distract myself by buying a new car. I would part-exchange both cars and get myself something practical. I had bought a car magazine and I would study it cover to cover, learning about every car in my price range. Reading hundreds of reviews and dreaming about a new car distracted me from grieving for days.

When I wasn't in town I would be at home cleaning. I struggled to keep the house clean and I struggled to keep my temper in an untidy house. I really did want a tidy house but could not be bothered. The more I cleaned the angrier I became about losing Sarah. I had no idea how hard it actually was to maintain and run a home. I thought about all the single mums who were raising children as a result of a failed marriage and understood why some were so bitter as a result of getting very little help and attention from their husbands. Unless you have family and friends to help, it is impossible to have a life of your own and escape the daily chores. Dusting was the biggest chore and it was my worst enemy that kept coming back. I was always told to ignore my enemies and eventually they would leave you alone. Would the dust stay away if I ignored it?

I don't know why people feel the need to say that they have a million and one things to do. Surely a million would suffice, but even that is a tad over exaggerated. Adding one more to the huge number of chores is a little unnecessary and pointless. I had about a hundred and six things to do.

There was something to do in every room. Sweeping, hoovering, scrubbing, washing and clearing up all the clutter that the kids had scattered about. If I stepped on one more piece of Lego or skidded on another Hot Wheels car I would gather them all up and fetch my sledgehammer. Sentenced criminals should be made to walk barefoot through a room filled with Lego as a punishment. They might think twice about reoffending once the pain had stopped. I would pile up the Lego, pens and cars on a stair for the children to tidy away. Days would pass as they stepped over them hundreds of times. Were they ignoring them to annoy me? I could hear Sarah's voice asking me if I understood this inconsideration. I could also picture her face with a smug grin. If it was possible to spend two minutes with a loved one after they had died, I would sincerely apologise to Sarah for ignoring her hard work.

Then my mum offered to come round on Tuesday mornings to hoover up and wash the floors for me. Each time I couldn't believe how much she had achieved in a little over an hour. But by the time the weekend had arrived the three of us had managed to mess the house up again. My anger would increase as I moved from room to room. Dirt, dust, spilt food and clutter was like the tide. It would keep returning forever more.

My increasing waves of anger could be heard from every room and from every neighbouring house. I now understood why sharing the cleaning duties had been so important to Sarah and why they had been at the forefront of most of our arguments. I had developed some kind of controlled Tourette's. I would walk away from the children as I started to swear under my breath, but by the time I walked in to my bedroom the obscenities of fuck, bugger, shit bags, bum, cock face and bastard bollocks were replaced with tears. I would then grab my memory foam pillow and punch it with both hands until all of my strength had drained away. Finally, I would smile when I thought about my memory pillow that shared similarities to a bag of cement. Did it really have a memory?

My memory had been severely affected by Sarah's death. I struggled to remember events that took place before she was first diagnosed. I almost laughed out loud when I remembered that Sarah had made a joke about my pillow. Whilst Sarah was terminally ill we had invited our friends Dave and Sian over for dinner and Sarah had asked us to smother her with the pillow if she got to a stage where she didn't know her own mind. Dave had joined in with her dark humour and pointed out that it would be impossible to get away with it because our handprints would remain indelible in the pillow. I put the pillow back in its place and went to join the children. I hugged them both and knew that eventually we would be okay and that we would get through this mist of confusion that followed a death. They knew how much I loved them and felt quite secure as a result. Through all my heartache and pain, the love I held for my children was by far the strongest emotion and would eventually conquer the sadness and the void that surrounded us.

Cooking dinner for the three of us after school was the hardest part of the day for me. I was aware that a new routine would have to be established but for now it proved impossible. The children were used to having my attention at this time of day while Sarah had prepared the dinner. Now, they would constantly demand my attention as I tried to keep up the tradition of cooking a meal with raw ingredients. I would be in the kitchen for an hour making a shepherd's pie or a cheese sauce to accompany the pasta and my stress levels would reach new heights because Sarah wasn't there to help.

I had spoken to a lady whose husband had died a year earlier, leaving her to bring up two young children, and she told me that she could only muster up enough enthusiasm to make scrambled eggs on toast, which they lived on at dinner time for three months or so. I should have kept it simple, too. I wanted to give the children my attention but I couldn't be in two places at once. Cursing under my breath, I would bang pots and plates down hard. I wanted to throw every plate and glass against the wall, but was sensible enough to realise it would cause more stress in having to be tidied up and it would have been expensive. Also, the children might have ended up cutting their feet if I didn't do a thorough job of cleaning up, making me feel terrible.

I would call them to the table when it was ready and would sit in silence as they prodded it around the plate while feeling the tension in the air. Within minutes I would be screaming at them, telling them how ungrateful they were after I had slaved away in the kitchen for an hour. The whole neighbourhood must have heard me. The children would cry first and I would follow suit. Samuel would be out of his chair first to give me a hug, closely followed by Olivia. The three of us would then hold each other as I apologised for being so mean. I explained to them that I couldn't help my moods and I was mostly angry because Sarah had died. I told them how much I loved them and said that I would take care of them always. Telling Sam and Olivia that their mummy didn't want to die was upsetting, but I needed to keep reassuring them of this fact and also that she would always love them. These conversations mainly took place at the dinner table and at bedtime. No wonder they had little interest in eating their food.

Once the tears had stopped I then told them to sit down and finish their food or I would have to put them to bed immediately. While they ate I would send a desperate text to a random friend concerning my helpless situation. Today's text went to a female friend I had known for years. I became totally depressed and angry when all I got back was a text saying "hug". I thought this was about as much use as sending a text sandwich to a starving person or a text kidney to someone on a waiting list. I was well aware that the text could have been filled with words of comfort and wisdom and still it wouldn't have been able to improve my state of mind, but it was how I felt at the time.

After about an hour of watching my two children chase food around the plate until it either dropped onto the tablecloth or the floor, I could stand it no more. I would yell at them and tell them to go to their rooms while I cleared up. My legs would be aching from standing too long in the kitchen and my hands were sore from all the washing-up that followed mealtimes. Time seemed to run in slow motion while I cleaned the kitchen. I desperately wanted it tidy so I could sit down for the evening. I didn't seem to be able to get the portions right and was still cooking for four people. Even when I intentionally cooked less, there was always plenty left over.

I don't quite know how I managed to dirty nearly every cooking utensil that we owned. Every saucepan would have stubborn food glued to it that required all of my strength to scrub it away. This was my reality

– as was putting the children to bed. Every time I cooked for the children and every night that I got them into bed was a constant reminder of my widowed status. These constant reminders were a trigger for my grief and impossible to avoid. We ate out in a restaurant every Friday after school to give me a break from cooking and to allow me to spend some quality time with them.

Friends came round in the evenings to keep me company and offer me a shoulder to cry on. My friend Dominic helped me with all the necessary paperwork that follows a bereavement. Sarah used to fill out all the forms during our time together because she knew that I had some kind of form phobia. The correct name for this phobia was laziness. I now had a large pile of them and they were building daily. When I say I had a large pile of them, what I really meant was that Dominic had a large pile of them. Tax credits, family allowance, widow's pension, bank accounts and a will were amongst the pile that I would at some point have to start filling out myself.

While Dominic was at our house one night, Samuel cried out my name, which he did most nights. I frequently hoped that sleep would come quickly for him so that both of us could avoid the bedtime anguish. I was apprehensive because I knew it would be traumatic when I went up to see him and I didn't know what to say to console him. He told me he really wanted to give mummy a cuddle and I told him that I did, too. I told him again how wonderful his mummy was and how much she loved him and how proud she was of him. My grief joined his as we wept and I told him that his mum had been in my life for fifteen years. I repeated the same words each night and he absorbed everything that I had to say. He knew that his mum loved him and that her death was unavoidable and that she didn't want to die. Nobody was to blame. I would tell him it was late and he needed sleep as there was school in the morning. Then I kissed him goodnight and left him to cry alone until he slept.

This particular night I went back downstairs where Dominic was waiting and started punching the wall next to him out of sheer frustration and helplessness. I was grunting like a wild animal and hyperventilating. Then I walked into the kitchen and grabbed an empty Coke tin, which I crushed in the palm of my hand like a crisp packet then proceeded to beat it against the worktop.

Moments later I was running my hand under cold water to reduce the swelling. I admitted that it was a stupid thing to do and Dominic said that he wouldn't disagree with me. I shouted at him, telling him that he had no idea what it was like for me and that my behaviour could not be helped. The frustration from not being able to make my children feel better whenever they cried for their absent mum always sent me spiralling out of control and into grief. There was no medicine or plaster that I could give them to relieve the pain that they regularly experienced.

The difficulty I had was trying to determine whether or not their behaviour was the result of grieving or just being children. I decided to tell them off for every misdemeanour I witnessed. At least if I did that, I would have well-behaved children. If they cried and said it was because of their mum then I would hug and comfort them. Tears usually occurred at bedtime and mostly came from Samuel.

During the day, school would distract him from thinking too much about his loss. In bed, where it was quiet and when he was tired, there was no escaping the thoughts and memories from entering his mind. Many evenings after kissing them both goodnight and telling them not to call out I would wait anxiously downstairs, hoping they would fall asleep quickly. Even if all was quiet, I would be too nervous to go upstairs in case I woke one or both of them up. I would even take extreme measures to avoid doing so. The toilet in our house is upstairs and it is the only one we have, so I would go outside and relieve myself into the drain rather than risk disturbing the children or waking them and renewing their sorrow.

Quick-fix Distractions

I was still working part time but finding it increasingly hard. Challenging children at the school were not the best therapy for my raging grief. I would stand in class and stare out of the window across the playing field. I imagined Sarah walking towards me dressed in her brown-and-yellow blouse with a brown skirt and boots. My eyes were looking at the grass and my mind was trying hard to project her there. She was smiling at me and giving me one of her signature waves.

An argument taking place behind me broke my reverie and Sarah disappeared. I shouted at them to stop. I noticed I was shouting a lot more in school, too. Even my hands and body were starting to shake as I tried to contain my anger.

A boy at school and of a similar age to Sam had been told that his dad had developed cancer and was terminally ill. He became more unruly and disruptive as the days passed and as the news sank in. I could see that he was a lovely boy through all of the confusion, though most of the staff were wary of him because he often became violent and he was regularly excluded for this. When he was in school his poor behaviour was largely ignored and he often left the classroom without asking, having had special dispensation to do so. Quite soon he learned that he could get away with most cases of bad behaviour because his dad was ill and it was assumed that he couldn't help it. I remained strict with him though, and he usually listened to me because he sensed my sincerity and appreciated my positive attention. Witnessing an 8-year-old boy become reckless and scared, finally resulting in expulsion, was heartbreaking. It did, however, reiterate to me that we had made the right decision in not telling our children until we had no choice.

Even though I was only working part time and I had reduced my working hours considerably, I was still struggling to remain focused owing to extreme fatigue brought on by grief. One midweek morning as lunchtime approached, one of the teachers asked me to look after the class because she had to attend a meeting. I should have told her that it wasn't a good idea. There was about twenty minutes until the bell rang for lunch, so I took a deep breath and wiped my sweaty palms down my flanks. I was in charge of around thirty children and had been in this position many times. This was the first time since losing Sarah, though. The children were meant to be reading quietly, but as soon as the door closed behind the teacher, many of them started chatting and fooling around. An argument broke out and a chair was kicked over. I had asked them to settle down a few times but to no avail. Aged between 9 and 10, I thought that they should listen to me as they all knew I had recently lost my wife. My trembling, nervous voice went unheard. I gritted my teeth hard, feeling the anger course through my veins. My lungs emptied fully with my first shout. I had been ignored, but I was unable to control or ignore the grief monster that wanted to surface and change places with my rational, sane self.

'I have asked you to be quiet, why are you still talking?' I bellowed, creating silence in the room as I imagined the windows shattering from the force of my anger. 'How dare you be so rude!' I roared even louder.

I ranted for over a minute until my anger had subsided. Every adjoining classroom heard every word. I had calmed down by the time the bell rang for lunch, but I immediately made my way to the head teacher's office and requested a leave of absence. I only had about four weeks of my contract left to work and I was unsure if it would be renewed. My request was accepted and understood. The staff had been very supportive throughout Sarah's illness and her death. The head teacher had been at her funeral and told me afterwards that it was the most moving ceremony that she had ever attended and how it had affected her.

The children stayed at my parents' house most Saturday nights. They were very happy there and with good reason, too. Everything at my parents' house had remained constant for them. They were used to sleeping there as they always stayed there when Sarah and I had a night out or went away to a hotel for a couple of nights. There was more fun to be had at their house now than there was when I was a child. They had a swimming pool, a trampoline, a pool table and nearly every room had a television that was connected to a games console. I imagine it was a relief to get away from a shouting dad and a home that was temporarily broken. Most importantly, they were given lots of love and attention.

My mother's fridge is always filled with chocolate and Samuel, like his mum, shared the same unhealthy addiction for it, so he never had any reservations about staying there. Olivia was reluctant to leave my side, however. Her separation anxiety was increasing by the day and she would cling to me and cry whenever I said goodbye. I understood that this was because her mum had never returned from hospital and she was worried I might disappear, too. I would always get a phone call shortly after I left, telling me that she was happy and laughing, moments after I had driven away. She was exactly the same when I dropped her off at nursery during the week. On occasions at home she would be asleep and hear the front door opening and closing as I went to empty the bins. She would cry out in panic, thinking that I was going out. I kept reassuring her that I would always be there for her and that nothing bad was going to happen to me.

Knowing that the children were happy and safe at my parents' house, I headed into town, which was becoming a habit. Shopping was a very good distraction. In one shop I tried on about ten polo shirts and ended up buying seven of them. I tried on lots of shoes after realising that buying a pair made me feel happy, if only superficially. I had discovered this when I walked into the best shoe shop in town to buy some black boots for Sarah's funeral. I liked them so much I bought a brown pair, too. I was pointing them out to friends and family at the funeral. I even asked a couple of people if they wanted to try them on.

Having just purchased my latest pair of shoes I decided to get some trousers to complement them. Weighed down with shopping bags I rode home in a taxi. I opened the front door and stepped into an empty house. I carried the bags into the front room and stood there holding them in the centre of the room, while staring at the photographs of Sarah on the fireplace. I threw the bags down and cried because she wasn't there for me to show them to. Buying them was completely pointless and as I stood there feeling lonely and depressed I said, 'I am so pathetic,' to an empty room.

Although I couldn't see Sarah or know for sure whether or not she could still see me, I hoped that she had heard my words and could understand why I needed to distract myself by shopping. I tried not to think about the existence of Heaven, just in case I convinced myself that it didn't. The children asked me about it quite often. I would be driving to school and Olivia would point to random buildings en route and ask if they were Heaven. Samuel would tell her that Heaven was in the sky and that Mummy was watching us.

Walking to school one morning Olivia was too close to the road. I told her to walk on the other side of me as I was worried a car might hit her. She wanted to know if one hit her would it 'make her dead'. I said that it might and she smiled and told me that she would be able to see her mum. This worried me and I told her she could never choose to go there. I said that her mum didn't choose to and would have remained here with us if she could have. Olivia would tell her friends and her carers that her mum was now an angel and she gave her mum wings in all of her drawings of her. Occasionally the staff would give Sam and Olivia a balloon each. They would draw pictures and ask me to write "I love you, Mummy" on them. Once outside they would send them up to Heaven. These moments seemed to bring them great comfort. I didn't want to think about Heaven or question its existence. I opted for temporary, quick-fix comforts instead.

The comfort I had felt whilst on the spending spree soon passed and left me feeling very depressed. My shopping bags remained untouched on the floor, having been my temporary drug for the day. It was my escape from reality, where superficially I enjoyed myself. Standing alone in an empty house was all that was required to feel the reality of my loss. I felt even more lost without my children to take care of. Taking care of them was proving to be difficult, but at least it kept me busy and gave me a purpose. I wanted to hug and kiss them and I promised myself that I would give them loads of love and attention when I collected them in the morning.

I had arranged to go out for the evening with some friends and was looking forward to getting out of the house. For years I had taken for granted the fact that I could go out for a walk on my own during the evening. Occasionally I just wanted to clear my head for twenty minutes or so. Now that it couldn't happen unless I called a babysitter I wanted a walk even more. I was very privileged to have such wonderful parents to look after the children at weekends. They love my children like their own and without their help, I would surely have lost the plot.

I put on some music as I got ready, which took longer than usual because I had so many clothes to choose from now. I ended up getting very drunk and spent most of the evening telling everyone how lucky I was to have been married to Sarah. I thought my grief was visible for all to see, as it appeared that I was in colour and they were all in black-and-white. I was important and they were not because I didn't care about anyone but myself. As I spoke about Sarah, which was for most of the night, I felt very proud of myself. I was proud to have been her husband until the very end and I was proud for giving her the funeral she had hoped for. My friends intended to get me up dancing before the night ended and they achieved it. Shortly after I danced, the night ended and I walked home.

I turned the last corner into my road and saw the lights on in our house. Many times I had come home to a house that was lit up. Usually I would open the door with my key and head straight for the bedroom to see Sarah. Most of the time she had waited up for me, because she would worry about my safety in a town where fighting was a regular occurrence. After saying hello and telling her about my night whilst trying to stop myself from falling over, I would go back downstairs for drunken snacks. There would always be a complete mess in the kitchen to clear up the next morning. I would then return to the bedroom and tell Sarah about my night again, giving away my drunkenness through repetition. Climbing into bed, the last thing I would remember was Sarah telling me to face the wall and not to breathe beer all over her.

I put my key in the door and tried pretending that nothing had changed. I shouted out, 'Darling, I'm home.' After spreading crumbs and butter all over the kitchen worktop I needed my bed. I really hoped that Sarah was in bed waiting while I brushed my teeth. Maybe I had just woken from a nightmare and I could hold her and feel relieved that her death was only a dream. I turned out the hall light and walked into a dark bedroom. I climbed into bed and reached out, pulling her pillow close to me before falling asleep. I always welcomed sleep because as I did so, Sarah was neither dead nor alive. I was neither happy nor sad. Sleep was the only true escape from constant reminders unless I had a dream – but they appeared to have left me, too.

As well as dealing with my household chores, the homework and my grief, I had to do thirty minutes of physiotherapy with Samuel every evening as he had short tendons as a result of rapid growth spurts. Sarah had noticed him walking on his tiptoes from around 3 years old and decided to take him to the doctors. I didn't take it seriously as I thought he would grow out of it. My argument to back this up was simple: I had walked on tiptoe until I reached my twenties and a girlfriend had laughed at me, forcing me to stop. I always told people it was a habit that started owing to wearing trousers that were too long and I didn't like stepping on the back of them. The result of the appointment was that the doctor referred us to the hospital and said that Samuel might at some point need surgery to lengthen his tendons. Sarah smugly told me this and also mentioned that we needed to be strict with daily foot exercises to try to stretch his tendons and avoid surgery.

The day after we had been informed that Sarah was going to die of metastatic cancer, Samuel had woken up and found that he couldn't put any weight on his right foot. It was a school day and he sat on his bed and clutched his teddy really tight and cried. Excessive physio on his foot had caused it to spasm. In normal circumstances, it would have been on a par with teething. Sarah turned and walked away from the impact of such a defining moment. I felt the blow too and instantly realised that it symbolised his whole childhood. Sarah realised that one day soon she would not be there to offer motherly comfort and see him through it.

It wasn't long before I handed over the responsibility of physio to Sam and trusted him to complete his daily routine. An appointment to decide whether or not to operate was only a month away, but I put it to the back of my mind because Sarah had died at the same hospital and I wanted to stay well away. I had spent so much time in hospitals since Sarah had found a lump in her breast that I hoped Sam would miraculously start to put his heels down.

Even though my mum cleaned on a Tuesday, I felt as if I had a huge mountain to climb concerning the house, so I decided to get a cleaner in on a Saturday for a couple of hours. Maybe then my mountain might only feel like a small hill. My cleaner was due at lunchtime and I spent my morning running around stressed, trying to clear all the floors for her to be able to clean. I wouldn't let the children get any messy toys out and had to enure they were washed and dressed so we could go out and let the cleaner do her job. I usually took them to the park for a run around and a play on the slide and swings, though I had never really liked these places where there is usually graffiti informing me that Jodie is a slut or that Tia Maria loves Romeo.

To my relief it was fairly quiet. Mainly it was young children who played, which usually meant that the bad language would be minimal. I sat on a bench and watched my children play and entertain themselves, or at least try to. They were so used to having me chase them around and entertain them that they couldn't get used to me not doing so. I sat and stared at them and thought about the joy it had once brought to me. Would I ever be able to enjoy them again and feel true happiness? I didn't know why I was unable even to pretend to have fun. I was merely there as an observer. Other children playing nearby called to their mothers, filling me with envy and more sadness. The twenty minutes felt like two hours, but they didn't argue with me when I said it was time to go to the sanctuary that was my parents' house.

My sanctuary was the town centre, where I could shop and drink coffee, and I was there within the hour. I would have liked to be able to sit in coffee shops and read a book. Like Sarah, I had been an avid reader and had no trouble working my way through a sea of books before she had died. Now, I couldn't read a single page or even begin to lose myself in a story. I couldn't bring myself to look at newspapers, either. As already mentioned, Jade Goody, the celebrity, made famous from appearing on *Big Brother*, had died of cancer on Mother's Day and two days after Sarah. A number of papers ran daily stories about her life and her death. There were no stories about Sarah's death, but it was equally important. No strangers were talking about her courage or the importance of her life, like they were with Jade.

Before Sarah had been diagnosed with breast cancer and had had her breast removed, I used to read all the trashy papers. Pages filled with celebrity gossip, naked girls and readers' relationship problems. Now I thought that girls who bared their breasts in papers were vulgar and I stopped buying them or looking at them. It angered me that they were flaunting their breasts at the world when my wife had just had hers removed. Some celebrities should be referred to as celeb-titties, because a large number are only famous as a result of flashing for cash. I have heard that some even tip off the paparazzi themselves in desperation for front-page coverage. I often wonder if, when spending their hard-earned cash, they resist the urge to say, 'Suckers,' because that would be quite fitting for boob-lovers.

Towards the back of the papers and past all the breasts, the problem pages filled with readers' trivial and usually self-inflicted woes annoyed me, too. Vanity problems were the worst kind. Fat people and thin people, bald and hairy men, all awaiting a miracle cure from an agony aunt. I would have asked them if they had a terminal illness and if not, then they should count their blessings and enjoy life. I thought that girls who were awaiting or who had already had breast enlargements should be ashamed. Thousands of ladies are having their breasts removed every year while shallow, narcissistic girls are either furthering their career or pleasing their partners by paying for extra cup sizes. I am sure it would be a much better idea to develop their personalities or to get an education and be loved for that – probably cheaper, too.

I guess it must be nice to be so self-absorbed and have little else to be concerned about in life other than how you look. Men are ultimately to blame for this with our transparent need for titillation and a breast fix of some kind. A work colleague of mine had paid for his second wife's new breasts as a birthday present. She ended up having an affair and leaving him soon after her op. I don't think he ever asked her to give his presents back. He is on his third wife now and has hopefully learned from his mistake. He was, however, a bit insensitive towards me quite soon after Sarah's mastectomy. Albeit very aware of my situation, I was quite surprised when I walked into his office and he had a fake silicon breast on his desk. He laughed as he picked it up and threw it to me, telling me how real it felt. Maybe it was one of his ex-wives' presents that had been returned. I put it down and left the room. I was uncomfortable for him, because I knew that he would realise soon enough why I had walked out.

After Sarah's mastectomy, breasts had seemed to be everywhere, in a similar way that I noticed every pregnant lady at the same time that Sarah was. Breasts would try to catch my eye from newsagent windows and calendars at work were filled with them, but I wouldn't allow myself to look. Girls walking along the road revealing a large percentage of cleavage would make me avert my gaze towards the floor. Arc eye is caused by looking directly at the sparks produced by a welder or looking at an eclipse. I looked away in a similar way to avoid the pain from the image burning itself into my eyes. Breast cancer had changed the way I viewed my environment. Sarah used to wear low-cut tops and I had encouraged her to do so. After her mastectomy I had missed her breast and felt ashamed and selfish because Sarah was the only person who had the right to miss it. Her scar and her reconstructed breast would always be a constant reminder that cancer might return.

Sipping my coffee in between shopping, I was now able to glance at ladies who passed by who were revealing their cleavage. I still had a problem with tabloid breasts, but less so now. I thought about the conversation I had with Sarah concerning sympathy sex and wondered if it actually existed and was possible. Would ladies be approaching me and offering themselves to make me feel better? I thought about the many times the two of us had stayed and relaxed in luxurious hotels. Would I ever stay in one again with another girl? Sarah had joked that I was now the result of a lifetime's work and how she had turned me into a good catch for the ladies. She had certainly refined me and helped me to become the person that I had always wanted to be. Having children had played a big part in this too, as they made me feel complete.

A day spent shopping and drinking coffee was more draining than had I thought possible. Every now and again I would pull out the photograph of Sarah from my wallet and sit and stare at it. I would look into her eyes and concentrate, hoping and wishing I could bring the picture to life, if only for a brief moment. I wanted her death to feel real, but it did not. I was certain that if it did, I wouldn't have been able to cope as well as I had. Numbness and shock follow death for a reason – a defence mechanism as a result of the loss being too great for a human mind and spirit to deal with straight away. The waves of grief that hit are hard enough to deal with, but if the waves kept coming in a relentless onslaught, then grief would have drowned me and made it very difficult for me to resurface. The strain from the grief was debilitating and was the main reason why I was left so drained after a day of sipping and shopping.

I arrived home with another new pair of shoes and proceeded to get ready for my second Saturday night out in a row. This time I had a night planned with my friend James, who had been very supportive since Sarah's death. At short notice he would turn up at my home so that I wouldn't be crying alone. He often telephoned, too. I was very honoured to have such wonderful, supportive friends in my life.

Looking out of the window of the hotel bar that evening, I saw an attractive older lady smoking a cigarette. It had been a while since I had smoked one and I suddenly felt an almighty urge to have one. Sarah had died from cancer and although her cancer wasn't connected to smoking, here I was craving one. I opened up an imaginary box in my mind and forced the shame inside, shutting the lid. I had quit smoking on a few occasions since I took it up at the age of 19. I found the quitting part easy. It was staying away from them that was the problem. Just one cigarette was enough and all it took to reignite the habit. I ignored this sensible thought, too, as I stood up. I walked outside and approached the lady. First impressions are important, which I also ignored as I proceeded to tell her that my wife had recently died of breast cancer and I could really use a cigarette. Her mouth immediately fell open in shock at the same time as she handed me one.

Smoking does kill and the packaging states this fact quite clearly as required by law, so I was more than aware of the dangers from smoking. And whilst I felt very ashamed, my loss was significantly greater than any shame that I felt or concerns I might have about my health. I was self-harming with nicotine and thought I could be in control of the amount in which I indulged. I felt the dizziness after just one puff. I had no respect for myself, my lungs or my children as I puffed away until it extinguished itself and left behind the usual foul taste in my mouth. I felt bad for the lady who had given me the cigarette. She obviously felt very uneasy and uncomfortable. Literally seconds after lighting it for me, she offered her apologies for my loss and jumped into the nearest taxi.

Grief had completely removed any shyness or embarrassment that remained. I used to be quite shy and nervous before we had our children. But the shyness was dissolving with age and couldn't remain alongside the seriousness of cancer. Hours spent on the chemotherapy ward, chatting openly to ladies about breasts, hair loss and death, made it impossible for shyness to exist. My shyness might have made me tremble during my wedding speech but at Sarah's funeral I was a different person. The only time I feel a little shy or self-conscious now is when I am bending over in the shower at the gym, but maybe that's just a self-dignified courtesy.

The children and I were invited to one of Sarah's friend's for dinner one day. She had a new man in her life and I was meeting him for the first time. The children were really well behaved during our visit until I was driving away, when Olivia asked me to open her window so that she could say goodbye. The second that the window was down she shouted, 'Bye, fat man,' as loud as she could, presumably as a result of his slightly overweight condition. I put my foot down hard on the accelerator, but the words had already reached him.

Public tantrums are always embarrassing. As a result of either good parenting or sheer luck, our children rarely had tantrums in public. They have never been witnessed lying on their backs kicking their legs in the air on a supermarket floor. Olivia's first full-on tantrum happened in the school car park as I was collecting Samuel from after-school club. We were having a disagreement over her apparent need for a pushchair to take her from the car to the building that Sam was in. I thought she could manage the thirty-second walk and so I refused to get it from the boot and Olivia came at me with both fists clenched and held level with my face. She was screaming in tandem and I was horrified. It was not a regular tantrum. She had not seen Sarah for over six weeks and now never would and she was scared and confused. Realising very quickly that it was down to her grief, I told her to let it all out. Teachers and parents were staring at us but I remained unusually calm. When I was new to parenting I used to run from shops with a crying baby, filled with embarrassment, but this was different.

I waited until she had calmed down, which only took about a minute but felt like ten. Then I put my arms around her and held her tight while she sobbed against my shoulder. I didn't know if anyone was still staring at us because my eyes were closed and all I could feel was our hearts beating close together and my hands on her tiny back, pulling her close. Her one minute of screaming didn't even scratch the surface in understanding or representing the enormity of her loss. I was finding it difficult to understand this as an adult, so it must be very confusing for a child and would no doubt take years for her to grasp the concept.

I was determined not to fail my children. The trust Sarah had put in me and the love I felt for them would supersede any mistake I might make owing to my early grief. We had a very bumpy ride ahead before we could reach smoother ground, but for the first time, as I held Olivia, I was confident that I would make Sarah proud.

Mostly at bedtime and usually after getting upset, Samuel would ask to see the memory box that I had put together. It contained pictures that he and Olivia had drawn and cards that they had made for their mum. I had kept cinema tickets and Sarah's Race for Life medals which she had been awarded after raising money for breast cancer. There was a bag of her hair too, which looked and felt as if it had been shaved off that morning as opposed to nearly five months ago. There was also a memory book that Sarah had bought, which she'd wanted to fill in but never got round to. Most of the questions I could answer, such as her favourite colour, song or book.

I flicked through it but was unable to write in it myself because of the rawness of my grief. There were questions such as: do you have any regrets? This was one question that I couldn't answer. I relayed this question to Sarah's friend Cathy the following day during a telephone call. Cathy had been a friend to Sarah since their university days and had been with Sarah the night we first met. I had spent a lot of time during the first few weeks after Sarah died chatting to Cathy. Sarah told me that Cathy should always be my first port of call for advice. Cathy had last seen Sarah on the Wednesday the week before she had gone into hospital. They had been sitting together on the sofa, when Sarah took hold of Cathy's hand and told her how much she loved her. Time stood still for Cathy as she looked at Sarah's hand.

In our telephone conversation Cathy told me how Sarah's hands were now always prominent in her dreams as she knew the back of Sarah's hand as well as her own. I had been completely oblivious about the significance of Sarah's hands. They had carried her wedding ring, emphasising our commitment to one another, and every hand writes a different signature, making it unique. Sarah's hand, though, had caressed and soothed. It had held her children's heads to her breast and in her own childhood it had been held by her own mother as a means to love and for guidance. It was also the last part of her that I had touched before she died.

Cathy knew the answer to my question because she had looked through the book with Sarah and discussed it with her. I waited with anticipation for her to tell me what Sarah had claimed to be her one and only regret. I was thinking it was going to be something like not having a third child, or marrying me, or having caravan holidays. But it turned out that her only regret was that she never got around to knocking down our kitchen wall to make one big kitchen-diner. Her only regret after fifteen years with me! I was so overwhelmed at how content she must have been with her life that I laughed real laughter for the first time in a long while. Cathy's memories, as well as my own, would always keep Sarah's memory alive and in the children's thoughts. I was privileged to have inherited Sarah's friends. Cathy would prove to be as invaluable as my parents in guiding me through my grief and helping me to find the correct path forward.

The last Sunday of April was our first visit as a bereaved family to the Simon Says charity organisation. They hold one meeting every month, where the children get to meet others in a similar situation. Sarah had wanted me to take the children regardless of whether or not I wanted to go. Having already introduced myself at their annual meeting, it made it a lot easier for me as I walked in and introduced my children. I was surprised by how many children there were. Being amongst single mums and dads in the same situation as me was comforting. It was our own bereaved club where we had a good understanding of each other's feelings. The children were entertained by the helpers and counsellors before taking part in an activity relating to a topic connected with bereavement. I was joined by the other adults in a separate room, where we would discuss the same topic.

We were put into small groups of five and asked to share our experiences. I wasted no time by speaking first and telling my group all about my loss. I had told my story many times but always added to it with every mention. The lady who followed me shocked me with her story. She was raising her four grandchildren after her daughter had been murdered. All of us had lost loved ones prematurely in different tragic circumstances. All of us had to raise children by ourselves. But we all realised that the children were the key factor in our cycle of grief that would help us reach acceptance.

I thought that a bereavement group would have been depressing because on paper it doesn't look like the best choice for an afternoon out. But the afternoon turned out to be very fulfilling and gave me more hope for my future. I drove away feeling less alone, waiting for the sugar rush to send the children into a frenzy after they had helped themselves to sweets all afternoon. It was difficult to know if their current happy state was the result of two hours spent with other bereaved children and counsellors or the handfuls of sweets.

When someone dies you have to get through a lot of firsts during the first year. Birthdays, Christmas and finally the anniversary of the departed are all huge milestones to get through. My first of these firsts was our eighth wedding anniversary on 28 April 2009. I always bought Sarah a traditional present for each of our anniversaries. The first was supposed to be something made of paper. I had joked that a card would suffice for that one or possibly divorce papers. I looked on the Internet to see what gift was recommended for the eighth year together and it was pottery or bronze, so I spent an hour wondering what I would have bought her. I was satisfied when I decided that her gift would have been a pair of earrings.

When I collected my new car I looked upon it as an anniversary gift from Sarah, making myself a promise to clean it and hoover it regularly, as my cars usually only get an annual wash. It wasn't a flash, midlife crisis kind of car but merely a practical purchase focusing on our needs as a family.

Our family holiday was a couple of weeks away and although it was meant to include Sarah, I really wanted us to have a good time as I knew that was what Sarah had wanted. When the children were in bed I paid tribute to our special day. As it was our wedding anniversary, I thought it would be fitting to watch our honeymoon video, when we'd had the pleasure of swimming with dolphins in Mexico. I was so glad that I had purchased the video. It was quite expensive and fellow honeymooners were reluctant to buy them. I told Sarah that if we bought it we wouldn't spend our life regretting doing so and saying I really wish we had that £40 now. If, however, we had not purchased it I would certainly be kicking myself right now.

Sarah can be seen smiling throughout the whole experience. I thought about our honeymoon as I watched. Almost instantaneously after walking down the aisle and tripping over a stool at the front of the church I had become accident prone, much to Sarah's amusement. She had always been a "laugh at someone slipping on a banana skin" type of girl. The night of our wedding as I ran into the honeymoon suite and jumped onto the bed had proved no exception as I bounced straight off again and hit the wall. I lay on the floor groaning with a pain in my back as she laughed.

On our first day in Mexico we were eager to use the Jacuzzi in our room and wasted no time in doing so. I tried not to think about all the couples who had used it before us and all of the dead skin and bodily fluids that may be circulating around the jets. We relaxed for about an hour drinking champagne before I pulled the plug. I didn't realise that the jets of water would still be active as the water level fell, so powerful jets of water hit the ceiling, followed by the bed and then the walls. I was naked and trying to stop the water with my hands and feet. But my feet and hands could only cover four jets as the other two drenched the room. There were some instructions of some kind on the door at the other side of the room, so I made a run for it and slipped. Sarah's infectious laugh could be heard on every balcony as my naked posterior proceeded to skid the length of the room until my body hit the door like a fly hitting a windscreen. Meanwhile, Sarah had calmly pressed the only button on the Jacuzzi which we had used to turn it on. The jets of water ceased but the laughter continued for some time.

We enjoyed our honeymoon immensely but it was also tinged with sadness as Mike, Sarah's stepfather, had been admitted into hospital while we were away. He had been in her life since she was five and had done an excellent job raising her as his own. We were both silently aware that he might not be alive on our return owing to his incurable lung cancer. Thankfully he was, but tragically he died in July, two months later. Although he had many wishes for the future, he was very proud that he had walked Sarah down the aisle and had seen her start her new life with me.

I finished watching the dolphin video and could neither use shopping nor smoking as a distraction. All I could do was cry and then sleep, spending my eighth wedding anniversary alone.

A Surprising Distraction

Just two days after my wedding anniversary a lady I barely knew approached me and asked me how I was coping. I had only spoken to her on a few occasions, even though our paths crossed most days. I knew her name, which wasn't Alison but I will call her that for anonymity purposes. She was a single mother of one, in her thirties. Beyond that I knew little else.

I told her how difficult everything was and how much I was missing Sarah. She made a facial expression that pleased me, which was somewhere between sympathy and admiration. Her hand reached out and clasped mine. Since Sarah's death I had been lost in a fog of grief. There was no obvious direction in which to turn because my emotions had been consumed by it. The fog was at its thickest when my mind focused on the past or the future. I thought of Sarah constantly, but all that my memory could concentrate on were her final few months. I would often think about my future without her and whether or not I would remain alone. I even wondered if I would ever hold another girl in my arms, or indeed have any sexual encounters. Briefly, my fog would clear during moments of shocking reality, bringing me firmly into the present. It always cleared during intense sorrow, when it became awfully apparent that I was a widower.

The shock I suddenly felt from Alison's touch jolted me into a clearing amongst the fog. Still holding my hand, she suggested that I call her if I ever needed to talk. She said that she would be more than happy to come to my house for a glass or two of wine one evening. The fog that enveloped me appeared to be significantly thinner, brought on by the increase of warmth through my veins. I was disappointed when she removed her hand and I realised that it was the source of my warmth. I told Alison that I would take her up on her offer.

While I was cooking the children's dinner that evening, I wondered if Alison was genuinely concerned for my well-being. I sent her a text message informing her that I had lots of free evenings, including the one that was almost upon us. She sent a message straight back telling me that she would be with me by eight o'clock. Maybe she was, as Sarah had pre-empted, the first of many girls offering me sympathy sex. It was a nice feeling, knowing that I was going to have some company on a Friday night. It would make a change to have a conversation with someone who wasn't at the end of a telephone.

The children were asleep by 7.00 p.m., giving me time to shower and dress in some of my recently purchased clothing. I had a feeling we were going to be sitting close to each other, so I wanted to smell and look good. At eight o'clock I was looking through a gap in my curtains wondering if Alison was going to show up. She arrived fifteen minutes later and I was glad of the rest from pacing up and down for that amount of time. She was holding some cigarettes, so I suggested we go outside for a smoke.

Not unlike excessive shopping, smoking had become a big distraction for me and I regularly stepped outside the back door with various babysitters if they were smokers. My guilt over my views towards smoking would not let me go into a shop and purchase some, though. We were soon on our third cigarette and I was on my third glass of wine, feeling quite relaxed. Chatting to a girl used to make me feel very nervous and I used to get embarrassed easily. Here, I suddenly felt like I was on the easiest date in the world. I talked about Sarah and the children, opening up my heart to Alison, and she took in every word, which appeared to fill her with admiration. She kept smiling at me and stroking my arm.

I had noticed recently as I opened up to lots of strangers about my loss that they would in turn share their woes with me. Alison told me that she was divorced but her ex-husband, Edward, wanted her back and she was considering giving the relationship another go for the sake of their child. She neither loved him nor wanted him, but she did want to be a family again. I had found out about a lot of broken relationships since Sarah's death. Divorce and separation seemed commonplace. People I mixed with were telling me how they had fallen out of love with their partners or in some cases, were filled with hatred. Adultery seemed to be the most popular reason. I would feel even more cheated when I heard these stories about wrong relationships, ruining families and creating single parents. Mine had not been perfect, because that would have been boring. I was, however, in the right relationship as a result of either good luck or hard work and yet it was taken away from me without being given a choice.

I told Alison about the afternoon that I came home from shopping with lots of clothes and cried because Sarah wasn't there to show them off to. She asked me if I wanted to try them on for her now and model them. One after the other I tried them on and paraded in front of her. She complimented me on my choices and told me which ones were her favourites. I was enjoying all the attention that I was getting. I settled back down on the same sofa as Alison to watch a film, having just opened the second bottle of wine and feeling very relaxed.

As the film played out we ended up getting more comfortable, lying side by side and stretching out. I didn't feel uncomfortable In any way and it didn't feel unusual when Alison started stroking my bare arm again. After she had been doing it for a few moments she apologised and said she didn't realise that she was doing it. I told her it was okay and she put her arm around my shoulder and cuddled up closer. She was lying on her back now and I was on my side. To get comfortable I had to lower my head onto her chest. I held it up for a while until my neck muscles were burning and then rested my head against her bosom in defeat. She continued to stroke my arm while her heart beat faster.

Sarah had lost a breast to cancer, followed by her life, and here I was feeling excited by the feeling of having my cheek pressed against another girl's chest. Again I thought about the sympathy sex from willing girls that Sarah had told me to take advantage of. I wasn't sure if I was in the fog or out of it as we both took full advantage of the situation. My pain was being soothed away. The truth is Alison could have been anyone. I had loved Sarah completely. Her body had died but her spirit never can. The spirit has to be loved for a relationship to work. So many people make the mistake of just loving the body of their partner. I was now connected to the body before me and enjoying it, but I had no connection with its spirit. The longer our bodies remained as one, the less pain I felt as I momentarily forgot about my loss.

I realise now that I must have been in the densest part of the fog, because I can only recall snippets of our evening as my mind was not engaged. I didn't feel uncomfortable in any way and when it was time for Alison to go home, I said goodbye as if she had simply dropped in to cut my hair. I was relieved that the children hadn't woken up during the evening. I wanted to keep both of my shameful distractions from them. I would have been mortified if they had seen me with another woman or smoking a cigarette.

As I climbed into my bed that night, which I considered sacred and had consciously avoided, I was in a state of bewilderment. I couldn't quite believe what had just occurred. I should have felt guilty. But I had been given Sarah's permission, which absolved any guilt that I might have. I wondered if I should have felt ashamed or was in denial of the possibility. Surely Alison had more cause for shame by getting involved with a recently bereaved man. I had lost my wife less than six weeks ago. Did Alison think for one minute that there might be a chance of a future between us or was she using me, too?

In the days that followed I distracted myself by exchanging text messages with Alison. She was telling me how great I was and how much she liked me and I was enjoying the compliments. The huge void in the form of Sarah's love for me was impossible to replace. Compliments and attention from someone of the opposite sex, however, was better than being alone, so I focused, welcomed and pre-empted them.

In between texting and evenings spent with Alison, I had to pack for our rapidly approaching holiday. A holiday is about spending quality time with your family, relaxing with them and having fun. A week away in Cornwall was meant to be a final holiday as a family, which should have included Sarah. She had insisted that I still take the children and try to enjoy it without her. Sarah had always packed our cases for holidays. She used to tell me that I had it easy and how much she disliked doing it. I used to tease her about her endless lists categorising all the necessary paraphernalia required. The chore of packing was now solely mine and I found it to be rather depressing.

I had no intention of backing out of the holiday, but I knew how difficult it was going to be. I had so many apprehensions about going away without my wife and the mother of our children. I thought about what Sarah had said to me as I worked my way through my mental list of things to pack. She had a better idea than I did as to how tough it was going to be for me. I completely understood why she had told me that she would rather be the one to die than to be the one left behind. I had to make all the decisions regarding the children's future. I had to cook, clean, grieve and deal with Sam and Olivia's grief, too. Packing suitcases always looked easy and they always looked neat and tidy once finished. Mine looked like I was in a rush to escape a fire. I practically threw everything in. I wanted to climb in myself and close the lid. While I was aware that I didn't need a pair of shoes for every day of the week, in they went anyway.

Packing, alongside other chores and thoughts about an uncertain future, was tearing me apart. The one solitary thought at the centre of my soul that was connected to Sarah's remaining spirit was that she had faith in me. Sarah believed in me completely. She had chosen me in marriage and as a father to her children. Her telling me in the weeks leading up to her death that she had no doubts about my abilities to do a great job inspired me and motivated me even on the darkest of days.

With most of the packing done we still had a week before departure and at times I had to dress the children from the suitcase. Samuel was only interested in the suitcase that Sarah had had with her during her final days. He told me that was his mummy's suitcase and that I shouldn't be using it. I told him that his mum would be okay about it and then he asked me if he could pack his things into it. Personal items belonging to Sarah were precious to him and he regularly slept with her scarf or her dressing gown.

On Friday night Alison was coming over to my house again. She was providing me with both of my addictions, which were the necessary distractions for me in my time of grief. Smoking and female companionship soothed me and were my own form of antidepressants. I was aware that at some point I would have to give up both the smoking and the Alison drug, but I put the thought at the bottom of my priority list. I kept both addictions a secret from my children. I did, however, tell my friends and family about my involvement with Alison. I did not mention my smoking though, as I was still deeply ashamed about it.

I am not sure exactly why I felt the need to call Sarah's mother to tell her about my liaisons. Maybe I was subconsciously hoping that she would give me a hard time about it. Many men have been known to confess to their wives about an affair to unburden them of their guilt and seek forgiveness. I was confessing to my mother-in-law in a similar way. She did not appear to judge me or scorn me in any way. She had experienced losing her husband and so understood how the senses were as lost in the fog as the mind was. She told me how lonely she had felt, especially after the first six weeks when the phone doesn't ring as often. However, I now wish that I had considered her feelings and kept it from her.

Moments after Alison arrived I started to relax, giving me a break from my grief and stressful thoughts about the approaching holiday. After an evening of using each other and an overindulgence of cigarettes and alcohol, I would climb into bed and say the words, 'I'm so sorry, baby.' Sleep would once again take me to the place where no changes had ever taken place and to where the past, present and future were as one.

The Return to Cornwall

My boot should have only contained two suitcases but I ended up with an additional twenty bags, filled with last-minute items that I had forgotten to pack. I was feeling very tense as we set off on our four-hour journey. To make my life a little simpler I had purchased a satnav and simply typed in Mawgan Porth.

Sarah used to have the unfortunate task of being my navigator. She was quite a good map reader but couldn't stare at a map for too long or she would suffer from car sickness. This would always prove a problem as we neared our destination, especially if it was in Devon or Cornwall, where narrow country roads are commonplace. Sarah also had a problem determining her left from her right, which at times was comical and other times quite dangerous. Knowing how stressed I got if I took a wrong turn made her a tense passenger. She would often shout at me to slow down to give her time to get her left and right directions correct. I would hear, 'Left, no right, I mean left, yes left.' I would always ask her if she was sure, at which point I wouldn't have time to indicate as I did a sharp manoeuvre into the wrong side of the road. We would always end up arguing as we neared our holiday destination, sometimes while driving around for an hour.

We used to joke that a Cockle holiday would not be complete without an argument at the start. I wondered why I hadn't bought a satellite navigation system a long time ago to avoid such arguments. I guess we would have found something else to argue about, though. My obsession towards timekeeping also meant that we used to set off early in the morning. The children would be sitting in the car in their pyjamas and eating their breakfast on the motorway by seven o'clock. Most journeys were about three hours, which would always end up being four after going left instead of right a few times or vice versa. We would always arrive at our destination before midday and would have to wait for over three hours to collect a key or for our room to be ready.

It was now around mid morning and the children were dressed in the back seat. I had dehydrated them to try to avoid toilet stops as I wanted to get to the hotel as soon as possible and without complications. I remembered how excited I used to get as we headed away from home. I would reach out and squeeze Sarah's hand and tell her how I felt.

I was feeling depressed as I daydreamed about the last visit to Cornwall in 2007 with Sarah. When cancer was behind us and a future together lay ahead, or so we thought. I recalled how I'd cried when our week away came to an end. Now I felt like crying at the start of our holiday. I reached out and stroked Sarah's empty seat. Part of me wanted to walk the same pathway to the beach as I had done with Sarah. I wanted to sit at the same table in the restaurant in the vain hope that it would bring me closer to her. I knew it was going to be difficult.

Olivia disturbed my thoughts by asking me if Chloe the clown was going to be at the hotel. The hotel provided entertainment for the children every evening before bedtime and Olivia had obviously remembered how scared Chloe had made her two years previously. All of the other children seemed to like her and her considerate approach of applying her clown make-up during her act. Olivia was crying in the back seat, pleading with me not to make her see the clown. The idea of holding a tarantula and a snake on a different night didn't bother her at all. At least I was guaranteed to get Olivia into bed early on one night.

It took me an age to unpack the car on my own. Conveniently, every item in the boot was either too big or heavy for the children to be able to help. If I had a piece of chocolate that weighed as much as a horse, I am sure they would have found a way to manage it. I emptied all the cases and bags into the relevant drawers and wardrobes while the children ran around jumping on the beds. The view of the beach from the patio door could possibly cease wars for a moment or bring love back to couples on the brink of divorce, but it could not penetrate my open eyes. I felt as if I was at the base of a volcano that had erupted some time ago, covering everything in a sheet of black dust.

The children needed to burn off some energy, so I took them to the play area. I had very little enthusiasm for playing or for being a spectator.

Claire and her family were joining me on the holiday to keep me company. They had arrived before me and it was their first time visiting this place. I failed to realise that Claire was also grieving for the loss of her sister and thought that my loss took precedence over everything else. I don't know whether or not she was able to appreciate all of the beauty surrounding her, including her husband and her three daughters, but I certainly couldn't.

While the children played together I stared out to sea. The seaside has always been the most idyllic place for me. This area with its sea views had brought me so much happiness in the space of a week and provided me with so many happy memories, some of which I had captured forever in the form of a photograph. I thought about the permanence of my loss. For the past couple of months I had managed to convince myself that it wasn't real. One distraction after another made it possible to do so and allowed me to obtain complete denial. Millions of Elvis Presley fans convinced themselves that he was still alive as a result of not being present at his death or witnessing his lifeless body. I had only ever seen Sarah alive and so she remained that way for now.

Distant but familiar laughter brought me back from my dreams as the children played on the climbing frame together. Their resilience and natural ability to have fun should have been an inspiration and while I felt relieved to see them play, at the same time it made me wish I was a child, so that I didn't have to take on the burdens and responsibilities of an adult and a parent.

I hadn't taken my eyes off the sea but only saw it occasionally. It was calm and very blue. Surfers waited patiently for the next wave and my own catastrophic wave hit as a vivid memory of Sarah's infectious laugh suddenly struck me like a bolt of lightning. It penetrated my senses and shook me back into reality, forcing me to hold my face in both hands to catch the tears.

Bedtime for the children arrived soon enough and I welcomed it as I did at home. They were excited to be sleeping in bunk beds and I was pleased that they had their own room. Olivia fell asleep very quickly owing to extreme tiredness and her love of beds. Samuel, however, started sobbing as a result of his mummy's absence and I was at a loss as to what to say or do. I was tired from the long drive and very upset myself at being alone. I screamed at him, telling him it was bedtime and he should sleep. I asked him why he'd waited until now to get upset and want my attention when he'd had all day to do so. Ashamedly, I told him it was now my time as I hugged him and kissed him goodnight, leaving him to cry into his pillow.

Claire, who was staying in the room next door, entered the room through the patio door to see what all the commotion was about. Olivia had woken up and was crying and Sam was still crying as I threw myself into an armchair and shouted out, 'I can't do this on my own,' before breaking down for the second time that day, giving into my sorrow once more. Claire was as helpless as I was because there is no quick fix when dealing with death.

Dinner on the first night was extremely difficult. The children had eventually fallen asleep though, allowing me to switch on the listening device on their wall and have a peaceful dinner. I was very aware that the chair opposite me was empty. I was also aware that I was surrounded by loving couples, including Claire and Stuart on my own table. During my last visit with Sarah I hadn't paid that much attention to other diners. Sarah had my full attention, even when enjoying the sunset as other couples were doing now. I looked around the room, watching them with envy as they laughed together and shared a bottle of wine. I assumed that they were all very happy and were making the most of their lives.

During dinner I told Claire and Stuart about Alison. Claire just stared at me and told me that she was shocked. Previously Claire had told me that it was quite common for widowers from strong relationships to move on in a short period of time owing to having faith in relationships. I certainly wasn't moving on. I just needed the regular buzz that intimacy brought me.

I wanted everybody I met to ask me why I had come away with the children on my own. I wanted to tell them about my tragic loss, partly because I wanted their sympathy, to emphasise the importance of Sarah's life. The other reason was so that they didn't assume that my wife had left me through choice.

After dinner I sent Alison a text telling her how much I had enjoyed our evening together the night before. She sent me one back telling me how much she liked me and how good I made her feel. I smiled as I enjoyed this fantasy that had been created.

Later that evening Alison sent me another text regarding the situation with Edward. They were planning on getting back together as soon as an apartment was available to move in to. They had found one and Alison had insisted that it be decorated before she would move in. She told me that she was staying there with Edward the following night after trying really hard to get out of it and failing. I was overcome with jealousy, which was very surprising, as I had already decided that our encounters would have to end if she gave her relationship with her child's father another go. I sent her a message telling her that I didn't like the idea of her spending the night with another man. She explained that it wasn't another man but a familiar one and that she had no feelings for him whatsoever. She said she intended to avoid intimacy if possible. I asked her if I would see her on the Saturday night when I returned and she told me I could only if she wasn't in her apartment.

My reply didn't go down very well when I asked if she found it exciting, not knowing which one of us she would be spending the evening with come Saturday. Knowing that she was annoyed and that rekindling their relationship was imminent, I felt the pain of sadness rapidly returning. Alison had become my drug for escapism and I needed her in similar way I imagined a heroin-user needed a fix. The thought of her not being there panicked me.

The children were fast asleep as I entered the room before getting ready for bed myself. I kissed them both goodnight as they slept and told them that I loved them – a ritual I had performed every night since birth. I had been shouting at them a lot lately but nothing could stop me from loving them. I watched them for a short while as they slept and was suddenly aware that I was smiling. But that brief moment of pure happiness transformed itself immediately into sadness. I wanted to share my feelings of love towards my children with Sarah. I wanted to tell her that no matter how tough and traumatic some days might be, I would never let her down. As far as the children were concerned I wanted to continue to make her proud.

Once in bed I opened up the bedside drawer and took out the photographs I had put there earlier. I spread about ten photos of Sarah across the bed and looked at each one in turn as I tried to remember how I had felt as I pressed the shutter down to capture each moment.

Sunday was a reasonably stress-free day. At bedtime Samuel cried again for his mummy and his longing for her hugs. I didn't always shout at him during these moments. I did get really angry with him one night, though, when it was obvious that he was using his loss as an excuse to stay up late. I told him that he should never pretend to be upset and reminded him of the story of *The Boy Who Cried Wolf*, at which point he was genuinely upset and I wrapped him in my arms, feeling bad for all of the times I had shouted at him. I told him how sorry I was that his mummy had died. I also apologised for my shouting and asked him if he felt loved. He told me that he knew how much I loved him. I reminded him about his mum's heavenly dream of bed and chocolate.

I was childlike in my grief. I wanted to be held in somebody's arms and to bury my head in their shoulder. This was mainly why I sought out female company. I had tried doing this throughout my spare moments alone during the day. I had initiated conversations with female members of staff and told them what had happened to Sarah, hoping that they would take pity on me. I wanted someone to hold me as I drifted off to sleep, though I could not replace Sarah and there could be no substitute. I felt that if I had female company then my situation would feel less abnormal. Surprisingly, there weren't any offers of sympathy-hugging or bed-sharing.

On Sunday night Alison was staying in her apartment with Edward. She asked me not to text her until Monday, which made me feel miserable. I wanted her to be available to make me feel better on a whim. Claire and Stuart were good company and kept me from complete depression but that was not enough. Their eldest daughter, Evie, kept Samuel amused for most of the holiday, which was good for him and a big help to me.

On Monday I texted Alison. She had spent the night with Edward and claimed that they had just slept. I knew that our time together was coming to an end.

When the week came to an end Claire and Stuart went home and I booked to stay for an extra day. I took the children to the beach for the first time on my own. It was cold and windy and they complained constantly. I felt as if we were trapped on a desert island after falling overboard and had lost Sarah to the sea, leaving just the three of us waiting to be rescued. We managed to get through the day without a fight, though.

I went to dinner alone and sat at a lovely table in the window that I had once shared with Sarah. I ordered champagne and held my glass up to the sky above the sea. I imagined Sarah holding one too and said, 'To you, my darling.' My food arrived at the same time as my tears. My blurred vision made the sunset look like a firework display. I didn't wipe the tears away but ate my dinner while they dried naturally on my cheeks.

After breakfast the following morning and the near-impossible task of fitting everything back in the car, we set off for home. I had managed to get through our first holiday without Sarah. I wondered if she would have enjoyed it if she could have been spared a few more months. Blind in one eye and very weak from a quick-spreading cancer, I doubted that she would. It would have been selfish of me to want to prolong her life for one last upsetting holiday. I was lost without her but I believed that she was guiding me somehow. Her soul was entwined with my own and she was like a star watching over us as each day passed.

The journey home took a long time as a result of an accident and a road closure. My satnav directed me along narrow country lanes, which we followed for miles in solid traffic. We were at a standstill when Olivia said that she needed to go to the toilet and not the liquid kind. I couldn't open either door as I had a bush on one side and cars on the other. I started to feel extremely stressed as I told her she would have to wait. We hadn't moved more than a car's length for over twenty minutes and I wanted to cry. She said that she couldn't wait and I told her she would just have to soil herself. She then told me that she was just joking with me and didn't need the toilet at all. The pressure from all the stress was desperate for release. Unfortunately, I didn't have a lid like a bottle of pop, so the air came out of my mouth in a series of shouts. My shouting made the children nervous and they started to laugh, which made me shout even louder. I had rarely been as angry and then they started crying. I wanted to get out of the car and run as far as my legs would carry me, but for now we were trapped inside, miles from home.

It was a relief arrive back home. The children were at my mum's and I had Sunday evening and Monday to relax.

From One Distraction to Another

Alison was coming over at eight o'clock. It was a lovely sunny afternoon so I took a stroll to the nearest supermarket for a couple of bottles of wine.

But she didn't show up, telephone or text. I had a miserable evening as I waited for her either to show up or contact me. I heard from her on Monday. She sent me a text saying how sorry she was that she didn't get in touch but couldn't because she was with Edward all evening. I drove straight to the shopping centre for a coffee and some shoes.

Alison came over to my house on Friday night for the last time. She was moving in with Edward indefinitely. She wanted to continue our farcical arrangement, but I knew full well as we lay together that it would be her last visit to my house. We still exchanged texts but it was different. Companionship was our only connection. We were two very different people. This became obviously apparent after an exchange of texts about grieving. I told her how upset I was one evening after putting Olivia to bed. Olivia was asking me to play her the recordings of Sarah that I had kept on my phone. We then looked at photographs together and cried. Olivia hugged me and patted my back as she did so. Alison told me to get a grip and not to show the children that I was upset. I explained that it would be far worse to pretend that everything was okay. Surely the children would think it rather odd if they only ever saw me smiling and not weeping for their mummy. Alison disagreed and said it would scare them seeing me cry. I explained further that I had taken advice from experts at the local bereavement charity regarding the matter. Alison disagreed with them, too. I gave her some advice which was never to tell a recently widowed man to get a grip.

I now had an opportunity to face my grief completely but still I didn't want to. I was not ready for the intense pain that it would bring. Sarah was always on my mind even in the midst of a distraction. Frequently and without warning, she would take over my mind completely and then the reality of her death was impossible to avoid. Once the tears had run dry I would always feel happier and more prepared for my next distraction.

Grief is like a huge debt that someone has built up. You want to forget it and avoid dealing with it. You can never escape it fully because it can always be felt in the pit of your stomach. But grief, like debt, will eventually catch up with you and will need settling to be able to move forwards in your life. The longer it is ignored, the more damage it may cause in the future. It is very hard if not impossible to get over the loss of a spouse. If the grieving process is dealt with in the correct manner then it's entirely possible to learn to live without your husband or wife. The grieving cycle does not have to be dealt with in the correct order. Everybody's way of facing their loss is different. I knew I was stuck in denial and jumping in and out of anger.

Now that Alison had returned to her old life, I returned to my recent one. I was once again working my way through the phone book, spending my evenings chatting to friends and family.

I called Cathy regularly for advice and worried her with my obsessive talk about Alison. She advised me to focus on the children and not complicate things by getting involved with women so soon after Sarah's death. She was astonished that any girl would get themselves involved with a man who was still raw with grief. I reminded her about my being given permission by Sarah to do so. I said that Sarah knew me better than anyone and must have realised that it was what I needed to get me through.

Cathy suggested that I search the Internet and find sites where I could chat to other widowers. She also suggested signing up to Facebook, where I could catch up with old school friends and make lots of new friends. I had been asked months earlier if I was on Facebook and had replied that I had a life and a wife, so why would I want to spend my evening in front of a computer. I found Facebook to be a lot like the programme *Big Brother*. I could sit at home and spy on other friends' lives. Occasionally whilst married I wondered if the grass was greener on the other side. I could only assume that other couples were laughing more, kissing more and being more intimate than us. Facebook would have answered these curiosities for me. I discovered that there were a lot of lonely and unhappy people in my growing list of Internet friends. Indeed, I was intrigued and regularly shocked to read so many personal updates. On a daily basis I would learn far more than I thought possible. Live relationship arguments for all to read were the most entertaining. I wondered if this was as a result of not having any credit left on their mobiles.

Facebook was my new distraction and I was adding people daily to my friends list as the weeks passed by. I was innocently talking to a girl one day while out and about. I didn't know her very well, but her name was Rita and I remembered that Sarah had once referred to her as "the pretty one" at a party. She was a mother of two in her mid twenties. I casually mentioned Facebook during our conversation when she said that she would look me up and send me a friend request.

I was now purchasing my own cigarettes and keeping it a secret from nearly everyone. Mostly I smoked after I had put the children to bed. I had even got into a bad habit of smoking while cooking their dinner. I would close the kitchen door and tell them not to open it or the smoke alarm would be triggered. I would then go outside and smoke as fast as I could. I would always imagine Sarah standing at a safe distance from the smoke pollution. She would be shaking her head and wagging her finger at me. I would direct my words towards her imaginary position, telling her how sorry I was and that my smoking was only temporary.

The children had thoroughly enjoyed our last holiday so I thought we should get away on another. I proceeded to book for July, but I was neither ready to go on my own with the children nor wanted to. Jenny and her family had agreed to accompany us this time, so we had booked two caravans on a family-owned caravan park. Although we had booked late, after explaining my situation to the owners they agreed to find two caravans which were next door to each other. At the time I was thinking about the caravan holidays from my childhood that provided me with happiness but I was too raw from grief to think rationally about a self-catering holiday.

My job at the school had come to an end and I was told that my contract could not be renewed owing to poor funding. The head teacher was very upset as she delivered the news to me because she didn't have a choice in the matter. I told them that I would return after the summer break on a voluntary basis. It wouldn't make much difference, as teaching assistants were paid a pittance anyhow.

I soon received a friend request from Rita and accepted it immediately. I could be found in cyberspace most evenings, where the lonely would feel less so. I saw Rita a couple of days later and thanked her for looking me up and welcoming me into her friends list. Whilst talking I sensed that she had her own sadness. From the little I knew, I guessed this was wholly the result of a lack of money and love in her life. She hadn't completely missed out on her youth as she regularly partied and socialised and yet she took her parental responsibilities seriously.

On Friday evening of the same week I was sitting at my dining-room table with my laptop, alone and sipping wine from a bottle that wouldn't be shared, yet feeling as if I had company. Suddenly Rita's name appeared at the side of my screen. I don't know if I was consciously aware that I was trying to find a replacement for Alison, but I had a feeling that Rita and I would soon be involved. Based on a look she had given me and the way she had laughed at my jokes earlier in the week, flirting was natural and immediate as we engaged in an online chat. Within a week she had given me her phone number, which led to me inviting her over the following Friday night.

Grief was impossible to escape. Distractions helped with avoidance temporarily, but constant reminders were everywhere. Driving to school one day I heard a familiar and favourite song of Sarah's on the radio. The song was finishing as I parked the car and I was doing my best to stifle my sobs and hide my face from the children. I didn't want to upset them moments before school and nursery. Samuel was fully aware of my tears and was out of his seat as soon as the car came to a halt. He squeezed between the front seats and hugged me. I still shouted on a daily basis but I was consistently proud of him. He told me that although Mummy was in Heaven he was still able to have fun. 'At least we have still got you, Daddy,' he said as I held him tight to me, drying my tears on his shoulder.

More than three months had passed since Sarah had died, when I drove to the funeral directors to collect her ashes. I had not consciously avoided picking them up, but decided in an instant that the time was now right to do so. I had imagined that they would be in a highly polished gold container about the same size as Aladdin's lamp. I certainly wasn't expecting an army green plastic container that resembled a large sweet container found in confectionery shops. It weighed a lot more than I had anticipated, too. It was difficult to comprehend that these ashes were Sarah's remains. A mixture of grey-and-white powder with small chalk-like stones, they could have come from any fire. I stared at them for some time, hoping for some kind of spiritual enlightenment. Then I reached in and felt the smooth powder-like ashes between my thumb and finger. I had touched her hands, neck and arms many times as she slept with the thumb and finger I was now using and I wondered which part of her I was touching. I guessed that the ashes were a mixture of Sarah and her casket. I made a mental note to check if a body is lifted out of the casket before cremation. Maybe after the cremation is completed the casket is sold back to the funeral directors at a discount price.

Without realising I had instinctively brought my thumb to my nose and inhaled. The burnt aroma remained in my nostrils for a few seconds, etching itself into my memory for an eternity. I was suddenly struck by irrational thoughts about cancer. Could I catch it by inhaling the remains of a body destroyed by it? I smiled and heard Sarah's laugh once more from within. I screwed the lid back on and placed it on the shelf in our dining room between the graduation photographs. It towered over everything and I hoped that the shelf was sturdy enough and that the children wouldn't ask me about them. I was worried what I was going to tell them if they asked about them. I didn't want to tell them that their mummy's body had been cremated because I thought it would upset and scare them. I needed to think about what I could tell them that would satisfy their curiosity. Hopefully, they would just ignore the huge green pot and its large white label with their mum's name on it.

The questions and upset from the children continued at bedtime but mostly from Samuel. They had both missed the industrial-sized ash pot, though. One night I heard Samuel crying from the kitchen and reluctantly went to his room. I repeated to him my usual words and finally told him that I had a lot of jobs to do downstairs. I had been telling him this a lot lately, pointing out all of the chores that that I had to endure now.

'My mummy is far more important than any jobs,' he shouted while sitting up to face me.

I was momentarily shocked by his reaction and extremely proud of him. I completely agreed with him and promptly apologised.

'How did Mummy die?' he asked in a much calmer voice.

When you inform an adult that someone has died of cancer, they generally give their condolences and understand its devastating effects. But with a child it is different, usually accompanied by lots of whys and wherefores.

'Mummy died of cancer,' I said, hoping that my short answer would suffice.

'What is cancer?' he replied, unaware of the difficulty in answering such a question.

I reminded him that his mum had her breast removed when cancer was first detected. I told him that lumps had been found in her breast. I started talking about how healthy cells work in our bodies and what happens when they mutate and grow. He stared at me blankly, in a similar way that I probably would have if someone tried to explain quantum physics to me. I continued telling him about how his mummy's cancer had spread to her brain and that the doctors had done all they could to save her. I didn't really understand it myself, but I wanted to be as honest as I possibly could be. Most importantly, I told him that not everyone dies from cancer and that for many a long, healthy life awaits. The only consistency in my answers was telling him that his mummy didn't suffer and that she was now in Heaven. He asked me to read him the book I had read to him the night his mummy had died about going to Heaven, which I did. He remained quiet throughout my confusing answer and the difficult story about a mum preparing to die. Then I kissed him goodnight and he was asleep within minutes of saying, 'I love you, too.' Exhausted, I could only sit in silence on my couch and wonder why this was happening to us.

Text messages increased between Rita and myself as Friday approached. My suitcases were once again filled with clothes that looked like they had been thrown in from the other side of the room. I should have been planning an early night for Friday, as we were going on holiday number two without Sarah on Saturday. Instead, Rita was due to arrive at 8.00 p.m. and I had a feeling it was going to be a late night.

On Friday afternoon I was meeting Jenny at the supermarket to buy all of our holiday food. I had been away on holiday twice before with Jenny but Sarah had been part of it both times. Jenny and Sarah used to do the shopping whilst I entertained the children at home. They would plan the meals between them and know how much food and drink was required. I had not given the holiday meals any thought and I arrived without a list. I assumed that Jenny would have everything organised and I was merely there to push the trolley, pay for my half and then load the car.

As soon as Jenny asked me what I would like to eat during the week, I knew there were going to be problems. I had been to this very same supermarket hundreds of times but it felt like the first time. Filling the trolley with enough food for our holiday was an impossible task for me. An alien or a child would have fared better. Jenny was finding it equally difficult, because she should have been shopping with Sarah. Her grief for her friend was different to mine and I had no understanding of it. After a number of grunts and nods of my head in agreement, we somehow managed to reach the checkout without either of us breaking down. As we left the shop Jenny reminded me that Andy was finishing work on Saturday afternoon and that they wouldn't arrive at the caravan until 7.00 p.m. She also pointed out that their car was smaller than mine and asked if I could take all of the shopping.

I drove away with very little space in my boot for our three cases. I was angry and depressed at the thought of having to go home and unload it. The idea of going on holiday with friends was to make it easy for me. My hallway was soon cluttered with bags that I rifled through looking for the cold items. After an hour of persistence, my fridge was full. I was not looking forward to putting everything back into the bags and into my boot, along with our luggage, in the morning. I certainly didn't want to think about unloading everything once at the caravan with two children in tow.

I put the children to bed early, telling them that we were going on holiday in the morning and that they needed a good night's sleep. I got showered and dressed and then poured myself a drink. I was feeling nervous about Rita's arrival and couldn't sit still. After an hour of impatient waiting I was about to admit to myself that she wasn't going to show, when I received a text from her. She told me that she had every intention of showing up but was currently having a drink with friends. She told me how nervous she felt and that she wanted a couple of drinks before arriving at my house. I should have taken this opportunity to pack the car but instead I spent my time looking out of the window towards the bus stop.

It was gone 10.00 p.m. when she finally arrived and the first thing we did was go outside for a drink and a cigarette. I already knew that she was in an unhappy relationship with a man of a similar age and I asked her what she had told him about tonight. I was shocked and a little worried when she told me that she had ended the relationship that day. She continued to tell me that the relationship was coming to an end regardless of my recent involvement. She sensed my concern and told me not to worry about it.

I was a 40-year-old man about to get involved with an attractive girl in her mid twenties. Was this about my grief, a midlife crisis or a mixture of both? Sarah had once said to me that she thought I would have a midlife crisis. She predicted that I would get involved with a blonde in her twenties. Rita wasn't blonde, but I was entering into a crisis that I thought I could be in control of. We didn't have a lot in common and we were worlds apart, but I was really enjoying her company. Surprisingly, I talked very little about Sarah to her.

It was getting cold outside and as the cigarettes were our only form of light we moved to my living room. Rita joined me on the sofa and our conversation ceased very quickly. I used to be very uncomfortable with silence but this time I was positively calm. Rita was breathing very heavily and I could tell she was feeling very nervous

'Don't you just hate these uncomfortable silences,' she said in between the quickening of her breath.

'I had better do this then,' I said as I leaned across and kissed her.

What was happening to me? I didn't want to be involved with Rita and there could never be a future for us. I had been honest about this fact and explained that I could never have a relationship with her. I told her that all I wanted was some fun. She assured me that that was all she wanted, too. But while I knew what I was doing was wrong, I didn't care. My wife had died and I selfishly ignored everybody else's feelings as I proceeded to cure my heartache temporarily once more. I lost myself by directing all of my focus towards Rita. Pleasure would vanquish the pain.

As her taxi arrived and we said goodbye, she told me that I had made her feel more attractive in one night than she had felt in years. I was too tired as I climbed into bed to be shaken back into reality. I had escaped into a world of fantasy because it was more appealing than grieving.

Caravan Holiday from Hell

I awoke at 7.00 a.m. unsure if the night before had happened or if it was just a dream. My suitcases remained on the floor, answering my question. I wasn't feeling particularly excited about a week in a caravan. Instead, I was thinking about the following Saturday night when I would see Rita next. I had to pack the car before I could give the children their breakfast as my fridge was so full, so I set about the task and finally managed to pack the car. My thoughts then turned to Sarah. I had feelings of guilt from the previous night but my sadness from losing Sarah was too strong to be overpowered by it. If Sarah was with me now, I would have been singing as we set off to the caravan. Samuel and Olivia wouldn't need to feel nervous in their seats, brought on by the constant cursing under my breath and my anxious silence. I don't know how she would have fitted into the car though, as her seat and the surrounding area was filled with shopping bags. I had a bad feeling as I set off, but it was difficult to know whether it was about the week ahead or the previous few months.

It was lovely to see the children's happy faces as I opened up the caravan door and watched them run around and claim their beds for jumping on. This brief happy moment brought back my own memories of being a child and doing the same thing. I remembered how I had laughed innocently with Tracy, filled with the same excitement I was witnessing now. As our parents unpacked the shopping, we would play together, as mine were doing now. I was a happy boy surrounded by feelings of security and love. I started to cry for Sam and Olivia and their loss, wishing and longing for Sarah to stand next to me at the caravan door and be proud of our own innocent and beautiful creations. I wanted to scream at the sky and at God. I could also really have used Sarah's help in unpacking the car and putting all the shopping into the world's smallest fridge.

Once everything was inside I took the children to the reception area so that I could enquire about Wi-Fi. I had brought my laptop along and intended to distract myself in the evenings by chatting to Rita and other Facebook friends.

Jenny, Andy and their two children arrived early evening. It couldn't have been an easy decision for them to come on an expensive caravan holiday with the three of us so soon after Sarah's death, but I was unappreciative of this fact as I expected too much of everyone. As soon as the children were in bed I should have gone and socialised with Jenny and Andy in their caravan. But I did not want to spend my evening with another couple and be reminded that I was no longer part of one. Instead, I spent a frustrating evening trying to get my computer to connect to the Internet so I could escape into my fantasy world. In fact, I had been immersed in my fantasy world throughout the day by exchanging text messages with Rita and we were both looking forward to the following Saturday night. I should have been focused on the holiday and my children, but I just wasn't able to engage in the present for very long or in anything outside my own needs.

A couple of days into the holiday my anger surfaced and was a cause for concern amongst my friends. Struggling to cope with being a single parent in a caravan, I started shouting. Andy appeared at the door and told me to take it easy, which fuelled my already unstable condition.

'I have just lost my wife; don't tell me to take it easy!' I shouted as I proceeded to kick the seating in front of me.

Jenny had rounded the children up to take them to the swimming pool and I thought they had left. But they were all standing behind the door, to witness me fall to my knees and punch the dusty caravan seat. I was punching, screaming and crying all at the same time. My excitement about getting together with Rita on Saturday night was completely forgotten – as was she. Sarah was untouchable in any comparison list. She scored top marks in my mental perfection list. I had canonised her to angelic proportions. But she was gone and every cell in my body was missing her. I continued to kick and punch the furniture because my anger could do it no harm.

'Darren, you are scaring me,' Andy said from a safe distance on the outside of our caravan door.

My hands and feet had rid me of my anger and instead of beating it up I used the seat to sit upon and rest. I was now calm as I thought about Sarah and our last caravan holiday together. Indeed, I thought about all of our caravan holidays together. I thought about our whole life together. There was nobody who looked like Sarah and nobody could ever replace her. There could never be a substitute as she was unique. My head hurt from the madness coming from inside. I wanted to wake up and see Sarah standing before me. I would tell her how beautiful she looked as I was feeling guilty for the lack of times that I did so.

I waited for the tears to stop before composing myself and then went to find my children to reassure them that I was very much in control as a single dad again. I didn't know how, but I knew that I would find my way out of the smog that enveloped me. I wanted to be the best dad I could and live up to Sarah's expectations of me.

The children were happily splashing around in the pool when I arrived there after my breakdown. They appeared to have forgotten my latest outburst, but I decided that I would seek out a counsellor when I returned home. There was an increasingly bad atmosphere between our two caravans that I simply ignored. I had expected to go away on holiday and put my feet up whenever I felt the need to. I tried to remember if Sarah had done all of the hard work during our holidays. I guess I was expecting Jenny and Andy jointly to fill in for Sarah while I mended my broken heart and mind.

Andy told me that Jenny was unhappy with my behaviour as she felt like she was doing all she could to support me. She was upset about not being appreciated and fed up with my attitude towards everyone. If I had broken both of my legs or arms I would have been guaranteed a lot of help from family and friends. They would have seen my physical disability and provided me with the necessary help. I was paralysed in a similar way but it was not obvious by sight alone. I was able to move my arms and legs but my mind didn't feel like assisting them. My mind didn't even want to get my body out of bed in the mornings. I was numb from shock and crippled by grief. Years of routine and consistency had all been undone. I didn't know what to expect from day to day. Children need routine for a calm, happy childhood. My new routine was to expect the unexpected.

My second involvement with a girl in as many months probably hindered my grieving process. I thought that my false involvement with them helped me in some way, but keeping the children from finding out was my top priority. It was difficult to predict an angry outburst or a wave of tears, but I certainly didn't expect to get involved with girls who were too young for me and on a completely different wavelength. I guess close friends and family of Sarah's didn't expect it, either. My ongoing texts and Internet chats with members of the opposite sex probably confused most of them. They must have thought that I cared very little for Sarah because of my recent involvements. They probably had grave concerns that I would lose my house to an ill-chosen girlfriend and mess up my children's future.

Having sole responsibility for the children was the sole reason for my staying in control. I had managed to get them to school every day and on time since Sarah's death on 20 March 2009. They were always clean and well dressed. I was on my second holiday and was in the process of booking a third to visit my sister in America for two weeks in August. But the children required all of my attention, which I wasn't giving as a result of my many distractions, including my mobile phone. 'Dad, Dad, Dad, Daddy, Dad, Daddy, listen to me,' Olivia would repeat until I answered her. Instead of listening to her, I was giving my time to a girl I barely knew via a text message. Olivia would be in my life until my death, not just until I decided to allow myself to grieve for Sarah.

We only had a couple of days left of our holiday and tensions were running high. The seven of us travelled a short distance to the local beach. Compacted into a small area next to the beach were some shops, a funfair and an amusement arcade. We grabbed our buckets and spades and walked for about ten minutes before choosing a suitable place to stop. It was sunny but also quite windy. All of the children except Olivia proceeded to fill their buckets with sand. Olivia was complaining about the cold wind and she was crying. I decided to leave Sam with the others and take Olivia to the amusement arcade. I checked with Jenny to see if she had a phone with a camera to get a picture of the finished sandcastle. She told me that Andy had his and so I left them to it.

I quickly forgot about Samuel and the others while pushing Olivia around in her buggy. She jumped out occasionally and demanded some money for a funfair ride or some sweets, but generally I was feeling relaxed. Wandering aimlessly, I had very little regard for the time. An hour or possibly two may have passed. Most of which was spent in a daze, watching and listening intently to the families around us. Every child was with their mother and every mother spoke lovingly to her children. Most of them undoubtedly took their children's and their own lives for granted. I was terrified of my single-dad status and panicked by it, but at least I wasn't losing sleep over it. I appreciated how lucky I was to have two wonderful children and always remained proud of them, even on the darkest of days. Apart from my own, theirs was the only grief I understood. Their loss saddened me more than my own. Children will always need a mother more than a man needs a wife. As a small boy I always ran straight to my mum whether it was comfort I was after, or a biscuit. I was now completely in charge of the love and the biscuits and soon found out that one is closely linked to the other. A biscuit before bedtime brought about a much bigger smile than my hugs and kisses managed. I needed to evolve into a mum and a dad for them which wasn't going to be easy, but by now I was getting used to difficult situations.

I decided to rejoin the others at the beach. I had just started walking in the direction of the beach, when Olivia noticed Jenny walking towards her car. I approached her and asked her if everyone was still on the beach.

'Andy has been looking for you everywhere. Where have you been?' she said in an agitated tone.

I asked why they hadn't called me as I had been checking my phone regularly. Jenny then told me that Andy had left his phone in the caravan. At that moment I saw Andy and the children approaching. I started to say something to him and he immediately interrupted.

'I don't want to speak to you; I'm not happy! You clear off for two hours, leaving us with the kids on the beach without sun cream. It's lunchtime and they are hungry and grumpy,' he said angrily as he continued to walk to the car.

My own anger didn't need much of an excuse or an invitation to show itself.

'You have no right to get angry. You have each other and I am on my own,' I shouted.

The children were oblivious to the angry scene taking place in the middle of a public car park. An image from a favourite western of mine popped into my head, where a final showdown between three unhappy individuals about to settle their differences was taking place. Usually the good guy with the fastest trigger remains standing, pleasing his audience. I knew that the two friends standing in front of me were good people. Jenny was missing her best friend and Andy was affected by his wife's grief. He was obviously very saddened by Sarah's death and missing her too, adding to his frustration. Andy was now quiet as Jenny confronted me.

'That's not fair using your widowed status as an excuse,' she remarked or words similar to that effect as I can't recall them exactly.

As my anger built and poured out of my body, I could feel the tension being released with it, calming me slightly.

'I'm sorry that I asked you to come on holiday with me. I really wish I had come on my own now as it would have been a lot easier,' I revealed selfishly. I didn't care if I came across as ungrateful or rude.

'Why don't you clear off home, then,' Jenny screamed as her own anger reached a crescendo and hopefully cleared the thick air surrounding her own grief.

She had actually used a far ruder word that suited the moment, but I will leave that to the imagination of the reader.

I didn't respond this time as realised that we both needed some distance between us. I opened my car door and asked the children to get out. Then we walked back to the promenade as Jenny and Andy drove off. I wasn't angry any more. I felt extremely relaxed and focused. The children were hungry and I went straight to a pub that I had noticed earlier and bought them lunch. They were very happy and well behaved.

They had got used to eating out as we still enjoyed our Friday afternoons, where we would choose a different restaurant each week and try to spend some quality time together. Arguments at the dinner table born out of frustration in getting the food to it did not apply to Fridays. I would ask about the children's day and they would ask how big a dessert I would let them have and we would always talk about their mummy. I constantly told them how proud of them she would have been if she was there and that she would have made them have fruit for dessert.

As I ate my lunch I wondered if Jenny would be packing up to go home and how she felt now after our argument. I wasn't surprised by the argument because it had been brewing for days. I was as surprised by Jenny's reaction as she was by my behaviour. We had both lost someone important and we were both hurting in different ways. My pain and how I dealt with it was all that mattered to me at this stage. I was very aware of the frustration and discomfort that my grief caused for anyone trying to help me. My anger and tears had regularly shown themselves to family and friends. I didn't want anyone trying to fix me by telling me that all would eventually be okay. I didn't want to be told that things would only get better. I just wanted a hug. Hugging a male mourner seems a very difficult thing to do. Men rarely do it because it might be considered a bit gay or because they are worried by how it may be received. Women who knew me well did hug me, but most appeared uncomfortable by the possible sexual connotations involved and the unknown boundary rules. I made no secret about the sympathy-sex permission that Sarah had given to me, so that could have added to the lack of hugs. I thought about the long hug that I would be receiving at the weekend from Rita and it filled me with excitement.

I drove back to the caravan park with nervous anticipation. Andy's car was parked alongside their caravan but there was no sign of them. We had talked earlier about going swimming, so I guessed that they were by the outdoor pool. The children must have read my mind, because they asked if we could go swimming. I dressed them in their swimwear, grabbed some towels and walked the short distance in the hot afternoon sun to the pool. I saw Jenny and Andy straight away sitting on a grass bank close to the pool. I slowed my pace to give myself some more time to decide whether or not to join them or to sit elsewhere. The children made the decision for me, as they ran towards them. I placed my towel on the grass next to Andy.

'I'm sorry about earlier,' he said so earnestly that I nearly cried.

I didn't reply with an apology of my own. I didn't say much at all. I lay back on my towel and hid behind my sunglasses. I hardly spoke all afternoon. The children managed to persuade me to join them in the pool and I appeared to be having fun as I swam, splashed, jumped and laughed for the whole ten minutes that I was in there. I then resumed my solemn position back on the grass. I don't know why, but I wanted Jenny and Andy to feel as bad as I did. I wanted someone to understand and recognise how lost and hopeless it felt to be a widower.

Andy asked me if I wanted to join them for dinner as I got the children ready for bed, but I told him that I wanted to be alone. Once the children were asleep, I turned on my computer and sent Rita a message. I looked towards my friends' caravan and saw their shadowed outlines through the curtains, sitting at their table. They could probably see my outline too, and a light from my computer screen as I shared my evening with a keyboard. A knock at the door a while later gave my eyes a well-earned rest from staring at the screen. I opened the door and Jenny stepped into my caravan. I could tell that she had been crying as she sat on a stool in the middle of the floor.

'You don't seem to realise that I have lost someone, too,' she said.

She was right. I was unable to understand or care about her grief. All I cared about was myself and the brutal fact that Sarah was dead. My wife and the mother of our two wonderful children had gone forever and I was at the top of the grieving list alongside Sarah's mother.

'I feel like I have let Sarah down,' Jenny cried.

We both stood up and hugged each other. Jenny had not let Sarah down. She had been there throughout her illness. She had spent hours talking to Sarah on the telephone until our batteries had lost their life. Sometimes they would talk for over an hour on the phone before meeting up for lunch. Jenny had bought Sarah her first wig, using her initiative and understanding her friend. She would organise the children's parties with Sarah, as we generally had joint ones to keep the cost and workload down. Jenny had been a very good friend to Sarah since they had met at a baby group just after Samuel was born. I didn't think that Jenny had let me down either, but it was a mistake to go on holiday in the depths of grief. My expectations of her were unreasonable and would have been impossible for anyone to meet, but I was a desperate man.

Our friendship had become damaged by our few awkward days in caravan hell, but I felt it could be glued back together when the time was right and our grief was less raw.

The following morning I drew back the curtains, to see Andy putting the last of their belongings into the family car. We still had a day of the holiday left, but they had decided that it was best to leave early before any more upset. I decided to stay for the rest of the day before heading home. I bade them farewell without even a thanks for coming away with me.

I took the children to a castle, which turned out to be a ninety-minute guided tour. The door was locked behind us and the loud echo of it slamming was still bouncing off the walls as the children's boredom set in. There were about twenty adults on the tour and two children.

Olivia was intrigued by the sound of her own voice as we moved slowly forward. I shut my eyes, hoping that when I opened them again I was no longer in the present.

Olivia told everyone that she needed a wee after forty painful minutes. I had been drinking quite a bit of water myself but had sweated most of mine out through anxiety. I interrupted the guide mid sentence to ask discreetly for toilet directions. She told me that they were at the entrance and I would have to be escorted there by a member of staff. I asked Olivia if she could wait, even though I already knew the answer.

We were escorted to the main entrance and to the other side of the locked door. We would not be able to rejoin the tour but would have to wait an hour for the next one. I should have demanded my twenty-five quid back and caused a scene, but I left quietly, saving my anger for another triviality.

I took Olivia to the Ladies at her request, which was becoming a habit and made me feel very uncomfortable. I would get strange looks from some of the ladies I encountered due to unfortunate timing. Men's toilets, especially public ones, are not the cleanest or nicest-smelling places. The floors are often wet with a mixture of overflowed water and urine, and toilets remain unflushed, revealing the last visitor's deposit. I didn't feel overly comfortable taking her to the Ladies, but I was more uncomfortable with her seeing men pee into urinals and listening to them break wind. I wanted to lift her onto a clean toilet seat and help her pull up a dry skirt that hadn't soaked up the contents of the floor from a poor aim. Some ladies reacted as if I had caught them naked in the shower and proceeded to inform me that I was in the wrong toilet. One lady made me laugh when she apologised before walking out again after thinking she had gone through the wrong door. I always felt uneasy, as Olivia insisted on talking to me whilst on the toilet. I would answer in whispers to avoid drawing attention to my being there. I wondered if there was such a crime similar to a peeping Tom called a hearing John. I didn't cover my ears or whistle as the ladies on either side went about their business, but tried to time it right so I wouldn't meet them at the sinks. I already had a speech planned for anyone who might tell me off. I was sure that once I told them that Olivia's mum had died and was unable to take her to the toilet, I would be forgiven for intruding.

The chickens and other small creatures in the castle grounds provided much more entertainment for the children than its costly tour, teaching me a valuable lesson for the future. Another day was nearly ticked off. We found another pub close to our caravan to enjoy one more meal before I drove home. Olivia must have had sausages and mash on five of our seven days and hungrily cleared her plate once more. I would need to become more organised and plan our meals a lot better than I had been. At least we weren't eating at fast-food restaurants every day. Not yet, anyway.

On the way home the children told me how much they had enjoyed the holiday. I envied their innocence and their needs. I am fully aware that Hell was a far worse place than a caravan park in Dorset. Hell was a place that I was trying to escape from. Sarah was in Heaven which meant that I was in the worst place, regardless of my location. I must have been doing something right though, for the children to have had such a lovely holiday. Would I ever be able to enjoy a holiday again? I only had two weeks until I found out the answer to that as Tracy was already preparing for our arrival in Pennsylvania.

Time for Counselling

Clothes were unpacked and washed, the house was clean and the children were at my parents' house. It was Saturday and Rita was due round soon. We had been texting and chatting on Facebook for most of the week. Apart from drinking and smoking and the obvious, we had very little else in common. Most of our texts were about the obvious that had passed and the obvious that approached. But I was feeling excited about another encounter and an evening with some female company. I wanted to feel close to a member of the opposite sex, regardless of whether or not a future with her could exist. I had been honest with Rita about this and I had no shame about our involvement. I imagined I was feeling the same way as a man who is involved in a secret affair does. I was excited by my liaison with Rita and told lots of male friends about her and her age. I liked the fact that a lot of them were envious. It was a relief to cause envy instead of pity for a change. Unlike a marital affair, I could not be found out. I would not feel the strong guilt that should be felt with such relationships. My wife had given her blessing and could not be hurt by my selfish needs.

Sarah had said that her biggest fear was that I would be lonely. She didn't like the thought of me sitting on our sofa every night with a meal for one resting on my lap in a silent room. I didn't like sitting on a sofa all alone, either. My involvement with Alison and my recent one with Rita seemed far more normal than loneliness. There was a huge void left behind by Sarah's death as I had been used to her company for fifteen years. Sharing my sofa with a girl I liked the look of was a much better prospect than feeling the silence and confusion that surrounded me. Being with someone, anyone, was less confusing for my mind to adjust to. I had so much to adjust to and I needed to mend all of my damaged feelings. I felt that sharing someone's company would help me mend quicker by giving me occasional boosts and an escape from the regular turmoil of grief.

Later, I opened the door and stood aside to allow a smiling Rita to step into my house. I returned her smile and offered her a drink. I did not greet her with a kiss and I did not hug her. She was young, she was pretty and she could burp the alphabet. I had not heard Sarah burp once during our time together. I was a bit shocked by the random burps, but pleased that it would stop me getting too attached. I would just have to be careful that I got the timing right as I moved in closer for a kiss. I had never had a purely sexual relationship until becoming a widower. Many men tell their wives that the affair they were having didn't mean anything as it was just sex. My grief was my excuse. My only worry was that the children would find out and I still wanted to keep my temporary affairs a secret from them as much as the men having affairs wanted to from their wives.

After sharing the evening and my sofa with me, I phoned for a taxi for Rita. Although it remained unspoken, she knew that it was not possible for her to stay. I always hoped that the taxi would arrive quickly and when it did, I closed the door behind me without offering a hug or a kiss.

'I'm so sorry, baby,' were my last words, once more directed at Sarah's pillow as I escaped from my conscious mind and slept.

I was starting to establish some kind of routine in my upside-down world. School uniform and nursery clothes were waiting to be put on in the morning. Breakfast was easy, as was driving the children to school. Samuel was becoming more independent as he was putting on his own tie and packing his school bag. His pyjamas remained on the bedroom floor in a heap, but I wasn't expecting miracles. We continued to eat out every Friday night and the children slept at my parents' house on a Saturday. My home-made cheese sauce with pasta was their favourite meal and on our weekly menu rota. I was taking Olivia to gymnastics every Friday morning and Samuel swimming every Tuesday after school. On one occasion I was at the swimming pool with Sam waiting for one of his friends from school to arrive who could already swim.

'I don't need my armbands,' said Sam with confidence.

I was surprised as he had always insisted on them before. Anyway, he got into the pool and both attempted to and succeeded in swimming without his swimming aids. Peer pressure had got him swimming. He swam around the pool for twenty minutes enjoying his sense of achievement. He was so excited and I was in awe. I was fourteen when I had learned to swim and I still remembered the thrill of being able to do so. The thrill I was feeling now soon turned to tears though, because I wanted Sarah to share this moment with us so badly. I was telling Sam how proud I was and I was smiling while at the same time the tears fell from my eyes. The swimming pool is a good place to cry discreetly because splashes of water from the pool take on the same form.

His friend soon arrived and already Samuel was the stronger swimmer. I couldn't take my eyes off him and his smiling face. The sun was shining through the large roof windows, reflecting off the water's surface and into my moist eyes, almost blinding me. I could still see the smile on my son's face and hear his joy though and I hoped that through the rays of light coming down from the sky above, Sarah could see it and hear it, too.

I was aware that my female distractions were probably causing more harm than good. I saw them as a temporary fix until I gained some strength and confidence as a single dad so I could be in a better place to confront my grief. But at some point I would need to confront my demons. My first session with a counsellor was arranged by Sarah's employer. There were six free sessions available with an option to continue if necessary.

I knocked on the front door of a big house in a very affluent area. I both expected and had imagined a female counsellor, but a man past the age of retirement opened the door and welcomed me. His trousers were too short for him, which I thought odd as only children should outgrow their clothes. My initial impression was not very good.

'Hi, you must be Darren,' he said with confidence as he held his hand out to me. 'I'm Victor. Pleased to meet you. Please come up,' he said with a smile.

I followed him up his winding stairs and into a room opposite that overlooked a well-tended back garden. The room was colourless and small. A dark leather sofa faced a leather chair that stood next to a small coffee table, on which was a box of tissues and some relevant books about grief. I positioned myself in the centre of the sofa. I wanted to leave but couldn't think of a decent excuse. I wanted to say that I wasn't expecting an elderly gentleman and that I would give it a miss. But Victor had already made himself comfortable in the chair opposite.

Before we could begin I had to answer some questions that he had on a sheet in his hand. He wanted to know things like whether or not I had harmed myself or others since Sarah's death or had wanted to. After answering his questions and signing the form to indicate that I wasn't a risk to myself or others, Victor told me a little bit about himself and his relevant background. He smiled as he told me that he makes people cry for a living.

I proceeded to open up and tell Victor my story. I had told it over a hundred times and could never begin to tire of doing so. I started with Sarah's birthday and the cancer diagnosis and spoke solidly for twenty minutes before getting to her death. I informed him that she was my life's gift and how lucky I was. I told him how I had loved her more in two years than most people do in a lifetime. I also acknowledged the importance of my wonderful children and my disappointment towards some friends. I continued for a further ten minutes, talking about my recent caravan holiday and my involvement with Rita and the "fun" agreement between us. Finally, I told him how frustrated I was that my memories of Sarah were mostly about her being ill. When I had finished, the tissues that I had been staring at remained untouched.

There are many styles of counselling and I expected Victor to recap what I had told him and repeat it back to me. To some, this kind of counselling might appear to be a little lazy or annoying. This was not Victor's style. First, he told me that the two years I had spent with Sarah during her illness wasn't real. By this he meant that it was unusual and based around traumatic circumstances and therefore not a true reflection of a relationship. He told me that I would have to face my grief and could not avoid it for long. He explained the grieving cycle to me and how important it was for me to go through the necessary stages. Then he recounted a story to me about a lady who had lost her husband and how she had appeared happy at her husband's funeral and in the months that followed. She still hadn't started grieving properly after ten months had passed. Finally, she had a breakdown and ended up in a psychiatric hospital. I was starting to feel worse than I had before I had walked in to his spare converted bedroom.

Victor told me that it is very common for widowed people to focus on the death and the illness leading up to it. He assured me that my memories would return once the numbness had faded. He seemed very confident that I would reach acceptance and smile when I thought about Sarah owing to what was called tipping the balance. By this, he meant that my happy memories of her would eventually outweigh those of her terminal illness and her death. He warned me not to canonise Sarah, based on my flattering tribute where I said she was perfect. If there are no flaws in the person or relationship, then it would be harder to move on.

I interrupted him when he said it could take me five years to come to terms with my loss. I argued that I was already two years into his prediction owing to grieving early on when Sarah was alive. I knew this was nonsense because I was ill prepared. I thought that it would help me in some way, knowing what lay ahead, but nothing could have prepared me for her complete absence. The only solace that I had was that Sarah had not suffered and we had been given the chance to say our goodbyes.

We talked some more about my recent holiday and the upset surrounding it. I expected him to agree with me and to understand my disappointment about the lack of help.

'If you have expectations of people which they do not fulfil then it is your fault, not theirs,' he said firmly. 'You can't tell people that they have no right to feel the way that they do,' he said, referring to my car-park argument with Jenny. 'Furthermore, she has every right to grieve for her friend and be angry, too.'

He continued to speak as I sat there staring at the tissues. Then he lost himself in another story about himself. His brother had died some years earlier, leaving behind a wife and two children. His brother's wife couldn't see past her own grief and had expected everyone to see that her grief was far worse than theirs. Victor told her that his brother was only in her life for fifteen years but had been in his for over fifty. I was staring at him now, intrigued by the fact that grief becomes a competition. I understood that he had lost his brother and how tragic his loss was. But I also felt that his brother's wife had lost her loving husband from her daily life and her children's father from theirs. Their whole future as a family had ceased abruptly. A family life that so many of us take for granted until a tragedy occurs. In my mind there was no contest, but I guess I am biased. Maybe I didn't understand Victor's argument because I don't have a brother. I also believed that Victor could only pass judgement and understand the enormity of our loss if he had lost his wife. Every person's loss is different and their grief is individual. Victor's love for his brother is always going to be greater than any love he may have for his sister-in-law, making it difficult for him to sympathise with her more than himself. My parents had the most sympathy for me because they are the closest people in my life who love me unconditionally and the grandchildren wholeheartedly. While Victor was talking I was thinking about Claire and her individual loss. I hadn't really given it a thought until now. I was feeling guilty for not considering her feelings concerning her sister's death.

I looked at the clock. I only had about seven minutes left of the session. I wanted to hear Victor's views concerning my recent involvement with unsuitable girls. He told me that my involvement with Rita would end in disaster and be very painful for me. His advice was to stay well away from women.

'No sane woman would touch you with a bargepole. The only women who would get involved with you are broken ones. Broken people attract broken people,' he said, highlighting the word broken in a louder tone. He took a deep breath and continued. 'You should not get involved with anyone you have no future with. There is no such thing as no strings attached.'

I thought about this for a few seconds and although I knew that he was right, I didn't want to admit it. I tried to convince him that it was okay because Sarah had given her consent and had insisted that I take advantage of any sympathy sex on offer.

'Your children are far more important than you getting your leg over and you should be concentrating on them because they need you,' he said rather loudly, creating silence in the room.

He had a look on his face that he probably has during checkmate in a game of chess. "The game is over and you can now hang your head in shame and defeat" kind of look. The time was up as my first hour of counselling came to a close and we shook hands at the door.

'It was lovely to meet you, Darren. Take care and I will see you next week,' said Victor with a warm, caring smile.

We had covered so much in one hour and I had plenty to be thinking about.

'I'll look forward to it,' I said, smiling back at him as I climbed into my car.

I switched my phone back on and sent Claire a text telling her how sorry I was about her sister's death. I sent another to Rita telling her that I was looking forward to Friday night. I thought about Victor's comments. I was confused by some of them. My love for Sarah and our appreciation for each other had felt very real to me during the two years of her illness. 'You can't tell people that they have no right to feel the way that they do.' These words were having such an impact on me because I was guilty of this on many occasions. My head hurt from processing too many thoughts whilst trying to concentrate on driving. I wished I had taken some of the tissues from the table as I wiped the tears into my sleeve. I was glad of the tears, because they always managed to wash away some of the pain. I enjoyed telling different people about Sarah and her courage. I would always grow prouder of her with every telling of my story and miss her more, too.

I continued with my involvement with Rita, who was endearing in many ways. The age gap was obvious but our involvement wasn't. Apart from the friends and family that I chose to tell, our relationship remained a secret. We never went out in public together. We were in our own soap opera that took place in my front room twice weekly. Sometimes the scenery and location changed to Rita's flat, but the reality was that I had created a fantasy bubble and I wanted us to stay inside it. My grief and the real world wanted to get in, but I fought to keep them out. I could manage the necessary functions like keeping a tidy house and cooking meals. And I could take care of the children, but I was still unable to give them my undivided attention.

I started packing for our holiday to America to visit Tracy. They would get my attention for two weeks then.

An American Birthday

I was nervous about the long-distance flight to America and the length of time involved. The children were very excited at the airport but behaving themselves. Including the time difference, it would be twenty-four hours from door to door. Surely I would be at the end of my tether by then. During the flight I wondered how I would feel if the plane was about to crash. At least we would all be together as a family and wouldn't have to suffer any more grief. I pushed the thought from my mind. My parents were travelling with us, which stopped me from panicking too much. I hadn't been on holiday with them since I was a teenager and it enhanced Sarah's loss and my need for them. I was a needy child once more and I didn't like the feeling at all.

The children were incredibly well behaved but extremely tired when we arrived at Tracy's. It was late and so they went straight to bed. We were staying in the guest house, which was next to and very close to the main house. It stood on about an acre of land next to a wood and a river. I felt very isolated and lonely being away from my family home and on holiday without Sarah once more.

The sun was shining brightly in the morning and the children ran around the huge garden, demanding attention. They wanted me to chase them and play hide and seek, and they wanted to go swimming in their auntie's pool. Each request was met with the same vacant look and disinterest. I didn't see the point of pretending to enjoy myself, so I relied on my parents and sister to do the entertaining. I sent Rita a text about the weather and my need for sun cream and a pair of administrating and accommodating hands. I knew how pathetic my fantasy world was, but my reality appeared to be far worse in comparison and a lot harder to live in.

I had turned forty-one and it was the first birthday in sixteen years that I hadn't received a card or gift from Sarah. I was feeling relatively depressed. I thought the absence of her pinches and punches on the first day of every month were hard to live without, but my birthday seemed utterly pointless. My thoughts turned to my twenty-fifth birthday, which was the first one that she had shared with me. We had travelled down to London for the day on the train and were sitting opposite each other at a table, when Sarah asked me to close my eyes. I did as I was told and kept them shut until she instructed me to open them. When I opened them there was a cup cake in the middle of the table with a candle with a dancing flame. Sarah started singing happy birthday to me in her own unique singing voice, ignoring the other passengers on the crowded train and focusing completely on me. At the time I was feeling a little uncomfortable and embarrassed to be fully appreciative of her personal birthday wish. Thinking about my birthdays from the past was the best way to celebrate my current one.

To take my mind off the day, Tracy had booked nine holes for me and my dad at her local golf course. I had only been playing for a couple of years and was still very much an amateur. Dad had never played on a golf course before, so it was bound to take my mind off things and prove interesting.

On the tee at the first hole I watched Dad trying to hit the ball. There were a few people waiting and more approaching. His first attempt struck air, sending him spinning around in a full circle. Sarah's singing felt less embarrassing as my dad's second attempt sent the ball trickling off the tee. He was fretting and I was sweating about our inexperience on an experienced golf course. His cursing saved us from hearing any noises of disappointment from the other players and the phone calls to their wives, informing them that they would be home late. We finally got moving and into the swing of things as the sun burnt our skin. It was three hours later before we were able to enjoy a beer while we waited for Tracy to collect us. I hadn't thought much about my past or my future all morning. I had thoroughly enjoyed my dad's company and the first half of my birthday. I had cried, laughed and suffered embarrassment as I forgot my woes while driving around in a golf buggy, and all in just a few hours.

Tracy had baked me a cake and it was waiting to be eaten by two very excited children on our return. My family sang happy birthday and hoped that it would give me a lift, but I was feeling too depressed even to pretend. My parents were doing all they could to help lift my spirits and help with the children. It must have been incredibly difficult for them to see how unhappy and lost their son was.

My first angry outburst of the day came in the middle of the afternoon. Olivia had wet herself and my mum was talking to her about it. I was telling everyone to ignore it and not to make a fuss. I was feeling very grumpy and got quite aggressive about it. My mum walked away because she was angry and upset and I was left feeling guilty amidst the uncomfortable silence that I had caused. I walked back to the guest house and wasn't disturbed for a couple of hours, when Dad appeared at the door and picked up a cue. I'm surprised that he didn't whack me over the head with it for being difficult. We started playing pool and after a short while he asked me why I felt the need to be mean to my mother. My anger spoke before I did and informed him that I was feeling far worse than my mum.

'You obviously have no idea how hard it is for me. I have lost my wife and you are getting upset about a few grumpy comments.' In my head I could hear Victor telling me that I had no right to tell people how they should feel. I ignored all of his advice as my anger grew. 'I just want to throw myself off a bridge into a river,' I screamed as my whole body shook. 'It's my birthday and Sarah isn't here to share it with me,' I ranted, before storming out of the front door.

My feet were hurting before I had even reached the road at the front of the house. I looked down and I was still wearing my sandals. They were fine for sitting around the pool but very uncomfortable to walk in. I couldn't possibly go back inside and change them, so I walked for a mile until I came to a bridge that crossed a river, where I stopped and peered down into the water. The sun was going down but the entire river still reflected a strong glow. I stared at it, hoping to see Sarah's reflection. She had taken over all of my thoughts and my love for her was far stronger than I was. I started talking to her and looked up at the sky.

'I miss you, darling. It's my birthday and all I want is for you to be here with me.'

I leaned over the bridge and watched my tears splash into the river. I must have stayed there for about two hours before limping back in the dark. My feet were incredibly painful by the time I arrived back at the guest house. Dad was still there playing pool. He put his arms around me and held me.

'I'm so sorry,' he said with such emotional sadness.

Mum was sitting at the table in the corner and I apologised to them both. In the depths of my grief, I could not yet see how difficult and impossible I was to deal with.

The following morning I went shooting. Only five months had passed since my loss so it probably wasn't the best idea to hand me a loaded gun. In fact, I was handed several guns. I was at a friend's house which happened to be a couple of kilometres from neighbouring houses. I was told to shoot low and towards the sloping hillside. I was surrounded by trees on either side. The only sound I could hear was the barking of a distant dog. The silence allowed my ears to hear the sound of grass flattening beneath my foot as I moved around. I was nervous because I had never fired a real gun before.

I was given a hand gun to begin with. I think it was a 9mm but I might be getting it confused with an action movie that I had watched recently. The power was frightening and I wondered if I would have fired a gun, had I not been grieving. My ears were ringing after just two shots even with good-quality ear plugs inserted fully.

I fired from a few rifles before being handed an AK-47 in the same manner that someone might hand me a sandwich. It had an eighty-bullet drum attached which I guessed was for saving time. I was holding one of the most powerful semi-automatic assault rifles in the world. I asked why it wasn't fully automatic and was told that being found in possession of one of those could mean a spell of twenty years in the state penitentiary. I thought this was the craziest thing I had ever heard. I was allowed to shoot continuously and as fast as my finger could repeatedly pull the trigger, yet if I fired continuously with my finger holding the trigger tight I was committing a crime.

I aimed at a milk carton. The noise was deafening and it drowned out my grief. One shot sent the carton spiralling into the air, then I lifted the nose of the gun skyward and continued to fire. I heard shouting amongst the gunfire. I stopped shooting and was told to keep my shots low because there was a store just over a kilometre away and I could hit somebody. Nothing felt real any more. My wife had died, I was involved with a girl who had been born when I was sixteen and I was pretending to be Rambo. I pulled my ear and tried to wake myself from a possible coma. Maybe this whole situation was a dream from an unconscious mind.

My phone beeped and it was Rita telling me that I had a nice smile. Maybe a dream was the best place for me at this time.

The final gun I tried was a shotgun and the recoil really hurt my shoulder. I had been warned, but was not prepared for the intensity of the shock. It nearly knocked me off my feet and it frightened me. The recoil was a lot like my grief, but it would never come close to causing as much pain. That pain was far too real for a dream. My shooting day was over and I headed back to put the children to bed.

I frantically continued to text Rita with an unhealthy intensity. I wondered if she knew how much her texts cost to send or if she even worried about it. Her worries about money were considerably less than the amount that was coming in. This was certainly the case regarding unpaid mobile phone contracts. I didn't worry too much about it because she was doing a great job of keeping me distracted and making me smile somehow. I would help her out with her phone bill on my return if it was too much.

I continued to text Rita for the remainder of the holiday, each time getting disapproving looks from my mum, especially if I was texting while the children were talking to me. I sent her a text message asking her if she wanted to go away with me to a hotel for a night. I had received a favourable response from her even before I had put my phone back in my pocket. I connected to the Internet and within an hour had booked a five-star hotel that overlooked a beach which wasn't too far from home. Two weeks had passed quickly – most of which I had spent on the Internet.

The children had a fantastic time in America because my parents gave them all the attention that they needed, especially my dad. He had an endless amount of energy and enthusiasm for them as he swam with them and chased them, running from the bombardment of water bombs on a daily basis. I was proud of my dad and aspired to reach the same level of enthusiastic involvement with the children that would make me equally as happy.

The hotel was booked for the first Saturday after returning home. Only five months had passed since Sarah had died and here I was about to stay in a hotel with another girl. Although I knew that there could never be a future between us, I was really looking forward to it.

A Five-star Distraction

Dressed in my new clothes and shoes and wearing a cool pair of shades, I arrived at Rita's flat at around four on Saturday afternoon. She had been looking forward to this day from the moment she had agreed to it. I was feeling a bit like James Bond in my pretend fantasy world, where I made up the rules as I went along. I didn't have a licence to kill or a car with gadgets, but any girl I charmed could only be temporary.

Rita was waiting out front with her bag because she didn't want her children to see me as I pulled up. She was smiling for most of the forty-minute journey, unable to hide her excitement. She told me that she had never been taken out for dinner before and had never stayed in a hotel. Her jaw dropped when she saw the hotel and the beach that was directly in front of it.

We checked in and within twenty minutes were sitting outside, enjoying a beer in the sun. The beer garden overlooked the beach and I was feeling as calm as the sea in front of me. I looked at Rita and thought how good she looked. She was like a chocolate sundae. Very sweet and inviting but not something I could have every day for the rest of my life. She was merely a pleasurable treat that would leave me feeling guilty for a day or two when the sweetness turned sour. I was using her and taking advantage of her, but justified it to myself by pampering her with charm and materialism. I also believed that she was both using and taking advantage of me, which helped me to deny my mistreatment of her.

We stayed outside until the sun disappeared into the sea and the cigarettes disappeared into the ash tray. Rita wanted to go for a walk along the sand before we dressed for dinner. I was wearing an expensive pair of shoes, so I kept to the tarmac that ran parallel to the sand. It was a very mild evening and if I had been with Sarah it would have been a very romantic moment. We would have walked along hand in hand, relishing the togetherness and peace. I sensed that Rita wanted to hold my hand, which was within easy reach of hers, so I put my hands in my pocket to avoid any uncomfortable disappointment.

The restaurant was nearly full and mainly with married couples. The waitress seated us at a table and I noticed the split-second glance at our hands and at the one wedding ring between the two of us. It could have just been my paranoia, but I was aware that it might stand out to people. Women are very good at noticing and forming an opinion about possible affairs. I wondered if everyone in the restaurant was looking at us and deciding whether Rita was my secretary or my daughter. Sarah had been without her wedding ring during the final year of her life as a result of excess fluid and I had never considered such thoughts. She was my wife and it was obvious, with or without a wedding ring.

Rita stared at the menu with a look of confusion on her face that she might have if she was holding a French map. She started to fire questions at me about some of the words.

'What is a parfait, a noisette and foie gras?' she asked without embarrassment.

I told her it was part of a joke where a parfait, a noisette and some foie gras walks into a bar and the barman says, 'For starters we don't serve snobs.' I admit that this was a crap joke and would be rejected by any stand-up, but Rita suddenly got the giggles and told me that I was really funny. She was still smiling about an incident in the room before dinner, where she'd tried to kiss me while she was chewing gum. I'd stopped her and asked if she would kiss me if I was chewing on a piece of broccoli. Her laughter at my jokes and silliness fuelled my fun side, which was enjoying the limelight for once. My depressed and traumatised side was taking a holiday for the day but I could feel it beneath my pretence. Whilst I knew I could not avoid it for long, I wanted to for as long as possible.

Rita chose the fish soup. No chewing gum was going to be strong enough to hide that for the evening. I could tell that she was struggling with it and that it was a burp trigger. I ordered a bottle of wine after refusing to get Rita a cider. She had only ever tried cheap sweet wine and so I encouraged her to try some dry wine that mirrored my humour. I could tell that she was enjoying the wine as she downed it in one. I had enjoyed just a few sips but reached out for the bottle to top up Rita's empty glass nevertheless. Her hand beat me to it as she grabbed the bottle and after filling her own, she proceeded to fill my glass to the top.

'Stop, stop, whoa, whoa, whoa,' I said as if I was trying to stop a stampeding horse.

She stopped before the wine could run out of the glass and onto the tablecloth, but that was more to do with the bottle being empty. The glass could not be moved or lifted. I had to lower my head to shield my embarrassment and to drink from the glass as it rested on the table. I slurped the wine in the same way that a dog would until it was at a safe level to be picked up. I was convinced that everyone in the restaurant was looking at me. I was more paranoid about the uncouth pouring of the wine than I was about the age gap between us or my obvious wedding ring that shouted out, *"Affair!"* I could hear Sarah's laughter in my head and her words telling me that I sure knew how to pick them.

In the midst of my embarrassment, I felt like a complete snob. Rita couldn't care less. She lived her life in her own way, not caring about what strangers thought. Her public burping and her ignorance towards many topics and problems gave her what I considered to be an endearing quality. She reminded me of what I was like aged 17. She was honest and pleasant in her own way, but she had a lot of growing up to do and a lot to learn about the world. She would probably remain a lot happier if she didn't, though. I was feeling more like Richard Gere than James Bond now as I thought about the film *Pretty Woman*. In no way was I comparing Rita to a prostitute or myself to a rich businessman. The age difference and our social differences were wholly responsible for this comparison.

Rita didn't know me at all. She was getting a little part of me. Sorry, I should have rephrased that. She was getting the fun, charming and relaxed part of me. I hadn't introduced the grief-stricken, angry, confused, scared and lost soul that was at the very centre of my being. I didn't talk about my loss with her. I kept it separate from the fantasy world that I was living in. She would go home and smile about a wonderful weekend away in a glorious hotel. She would probably tell her friends about the wonderful time that she'd had. Instead of telling my family and friends about my weekend, I would sob until my head could no longer cope with the hurt it caused.

I had enjoyed her company immensely and I'd had a good time, yet I was confused about being able to enjoy myself with Rita and about our night away. I had only been home for a couple of days and was feeling sad and guilty. Though I continued to text her after the tears had stopped and we made arrangements for the coming weekend.

A couple of weeks later, having spent a few evenings together, I went to stay with family for the weekend and Rita had made arrangements to go out with her friends. Just as I was getting into bed she sent me a message informing me that she had something to tell me. In her next message she confessed her strong feelings for me and said that she wanted a proper relationship. My heart sank and I panicked. I should have expected this natural progression that occurs when two people spend a lot of time together and become intimate. I sent her a message back telling her that I was unable to offer her any more. Rita was very upset and disappointed by my response and I cried myself to sleep.

Rita came to see me during the week. She told me that although she was disappointed about my commitment issues, she wanted to continue with our unusual involvement. 'If I stop seeing you then I would only be sitting alone at home feeling bored, so I may as well continue,' she said rather confidently.

For the first time since this fantasy started I was feeling incredibly guilty about my behaviour. I wasn't sure if my conscience would allow me to continue now that I was aware of Rita's feelings.

'It couldn't work out between us anyway because of the huge age gap,' I said nervously.

Rita thought about this for a few moments.

'The age gap didn't seem to bother you when you were sleeping with me at the hotel,' she said.

Before I could think up a reasonable reply, the words, 'Why would it?' had already left my lips.

There was silence for a few moments as we smoked our cigarettes, during which time there was a loud bang inside of my mind as the fantasy bubble that I had created suddenly burst, allowing the grim reality of my situation to triumph once more.

Three Birthdays; Two Cards

It was now six months since Sarah had been in our lives and Samuel's seventh birthday was approaching and was his first without his mum. Sarah used to organise all of the parties but after his last one, we had agreed to take a few friends to the cinema or to organise a small tea party for future ones. His birthday was three weeks away and his excitement remained on a par with previous years. I decided to book a party at a local indoor activity centre. It was the lazy option as everything, including party bags, would be taken care of. I didn't want Sam thinking that he wasn't getting a party because his mum had died. I would do the same for Olivia on her birthday, which was four weeks after Sam's.

Buying a birthday card was easy, but having to leave out Sarah's name when I wrote inside was difficult and seemed wrong. Just four days after Olivia's birthday, Sarah would have been celebrating her thirty-sixth birthday. I bought Sam far too much for his birthday and started filling my wardrobe with Christmas presents, too. I thought that the nearer we got to Christmas, the further away my enthusiasm for it would be, so I had best stock up on presents early.

Sarah had given birth to our little bundle of a boy who looked like Winston Churchill seven years to the day. Family and friends told us how gorgeous he looked because that is the expected thing to say. The truth is that it took six months before Samuel's body caught up with the size of his head and for him to start looking cute and gorgeous. If he was turning seventy then it would have been quite usual for his mum not to be there. But he wasn't – he was just seven. Only one of us was miserable as I handed over his card and presents. My smile disguised the depression and I closed my eyes really tight as we hugged and I wished him happy birthday.

His party was a triumph and he laughed through most of it. Sweat was dripping from his head after an hour and a half of running around with his friends. I had been staring at him for the whole time but I could only see Sarah, rendering my eyes inactive. I spent the whole party imagining that she was there and therefore missed out once more on the enjoyment taking place right in front of me. I was shattered but I hadn't moved a muscle. Eventually the cake was brought out and everybody sang "Happy Birthday". "Happy Birthday" is one of the most tuneless and embarrassing songs ever to be made up. Singing the whole song out of tune whilst crying went unnoticed in the party room and seven candles were blown out as he made a wish. I hoped that his wish was more realistic than mine.

At bedtime Samuel thanked me for the party. He said that it was a great party but wished that his mummy had been there. I told him that she would have been really pleased and proud of him for enjoying his party and his birthday without her. He asked if we could play the kissing game. This game is simple but I usually end up getting scratched or slapped. Samuel has always been tight with his hugs and kisses and Sarah had to bribe him on many occasions in order to get them. All that is required for the kissing game is a child's face and a parent's lips. Sam gave me a number between one and fifty. He always chose fifty because I would then have to kiss him that many times while he tried half-heartedly to fight me off. For five minutes he would giggle from the onslaught of my kiss frenzy. In return, I got kisses from him by making out it was non-kissing day. I would also pretend to fight him off as he plied me with his kisses. We would both be smiling contentedly as I turned out his light and said goodnight.

I tried to keep Rita in my life. Our early agreement about being honest and only continuing if it remained fun for us both appeared conveniently forgotten. In desperation I booked another Saturday night at a hotel, hoping that it would be as great as the last one. It wasn't! We arrived late and we had hardly said a word to each other in the car.

'Did you sense that there was a bad atmosphere in the car?' Rita asked as we approached the bar after checking in.

I was feeling very tense and a little depressed. 'I am just a bit tired,' I said.

The bar was empty so we had no problem finding a free table to sit at. We had only been sitting for a minute or two when a very familiar song jumped out of the speakers and kicked me in the heart. I hadn't heard "Sarah" since the funeral and I certainly didn't expect to hear it during a night away with a girl who had a different name.

I was distant and preoccupied for most of the night and the following morning. I could feel the reality of my loss in every part of my body. I was missing Sarah so much and I wanted her to be with me. I desperately wanted to be myself again. I didn't like this broken, lost and depressed version of me who was creating more problems by introducing new women into my life. I would have to find the right moment to end my involvement with Rita.

An ideal opportunity arose while we were sitting in the hotel Jacuzzi. Rita asked me if I was feeling okay because of my lack of conversation.

'I don't like myself very much,' I replied hastily as if I had been expecting the question.

I then confessed to the guilt that I had been feeling ever since she had revealed her feelings towards me. I didn't have the strength to end our fun agreement, so I remained silent after my confession. The ideal opportunity passed me by as quickly as it came. Rita reached out and touched my shoulder and made a sound that most people make when they see a new baby or a puppy.

I had no idea that after I'd dropped Rita off at her place she would spend the rest her day crying. We met up during the week and both of us behaved as if our short conversation at the weekend had never taken place. She told me that she was busy on Saturday night and would therefore see me on Sunday at 8.00 p.m.

I had arranged Olivia's birthday party for Saturday afternoon at the same fun factory I had booked for Sam. She was equally as excited as Sam had been and also received some above-average presents as compensation for losing her mum. I spent her fourth birthday party with the same vacant look and singing in the same tearful and tuneless manner as I had at Sam's. As she was blowing her candles out, I was admiring my handiwork. I had finally mastered the art of ponytails and her clothes matched perfectly. She looked beautiful and I was so proud of her. Thank God I had my children in my life to keep me focused and to give me such an obvious purpose.

I was relieved to have got through the children's first birthdays without Sarah and pleased with how successful and enjoyable they had been. But I had to get through Sarah's birthday at the end of the week next and could already sense the sinking feeling. I didn't know what I was going to do to celebrate it. In previous years I would be busy wrapping up earrings and chocolates and planning a night away or a meal out. Wrapping was such a chore, but I would gladly have wrapped up a shark if it could bring her back. Her twenty-first was her first birthday we spent together. I had bought her favourite perfume and collected her favourite Smarties. Sarah really liked orange ones, so I bought about twenty packets and made up a whole tube of her favourites. She thought it was a unique and romantic present and I never did admit to stealing the idea from a friend of mine.

I proposed on her twenty-seventh birthday. I hadn't planned on getting down on one knee during her once-yearly celebration, it was just that the engagement ring I had bought days earlier was burning a hole in my pocket and I couldn't contain my excitement. We were sitting at a table in a local restaurant looking at a menu when I knew that the time was right. I wanted to order my food quickly but I couldn't read any of the words. I was rehearsing what to say in my mind, which is a bit ridiculous considering that all proposals consist of the same words. I put the menu down on the table and dropped to my knees. 'Will you marry me?' I said very quickly, turning it into one word. I almost threw the ring into Sarah's hand and was sitting back in my seat within a few seconds.

'Yes,' she replied, which is always the best answer to this question. Sarah pointed out that the only two people to see me get down on one knee was the waiter and of course herself. 'You were on one knee for the shortest amount of time possible; most people probably thought you were picking up a dropped fork.'

Fortunately, the waiter had seen and brought us a free bottle of champagne. I suggested to Sarah that she should give me the ring back and I could propose again in a different restaurant every week. But the ring was firmly encircled around Sarah's finger and she had no intention of giving it back.

I tried to remember all of her birthdays but kept coming back to her thirty-third and the onset of cancer.

It was Sunday night and the children were asleep. Rita should have arrived an hour ago and I was expecting her at any moment. I kept looking out of the window and checking my phone. Eventually I sent her a message asking of her whereabouts. Another hour passed and there was still no word from her. She had never let me down before and I was getting a little worried. It was dark and she had to catch two buses to get to my house. I sent another message asking if she was okay and tried calling her. Her mobile phone was switched off and her home phone went unanswered. She never got back to me and she never showed up.

I was feeling very lonely on my sofa. The dark clouds of sorrow returned and were thicker than ever before as grief swept over me. The clouds had been building for months and they suddenly descended all at once. The torrential raining of tears that followed would last for some time.

The dark cloud was still upon me when I awoke. There was a message from Rita and an apology for being too drunk to reply. She told me that she couldn't continue to see me as it was too painful for her. She added that she had found someone else.

I was crushed and did not want to face the day. It was the start of half term and Sam would be home for a week. I made a phone call and an emergency appointment with my counsellor for Wednesday. I had purposely avoided Victor because I was sure that he would burst my bubble. I had created a distraction and was living in a fantasy world that I was afraid to give up. Facing the reality in my life was something that Victor wanted me to do but I wasn't ready. Now, I needed him and wanted his help. I was having a breakdown and crying hourly. It appeared as if I was upset over a girl I had only known for a short while. Samuel went to stay at my parents' house for a few days while Olivia went into nursery every day.

My mother told me to get a grip and how pathetic my behaviour was. She thrust a photograph of Sarah in front of my face.

'This is the person who is important, not some silly tart you have known for five minutes. Sarah would be ashamed of you. What happened to that strong man who stood up at Sarah's funeral with such dignity?' she said, without taking a breath and with much emotion.

I assumed that it was a rhetorical question and said nothing.

I recounted the events of the past month to Victor as he sat listening from the leather chair opposite his confessional sofa. I had cried a few times and had to stop talking to reach for a tissue before continuing.

'I told you it would end in pain for you,' he said immediately after I had finished talking. He then explained to me why I was feeling completely crestfallen.

I listened carefully as he told me that Rita was a bandage for my grief wound. My wound was now uncovered and it would take longer to heal.

'You should count your blessings that you had a lucky escape. It could have been disastrous for you if you had a screaming woman beating at your front door for the children and neighbours to witness,' he said.

I was told rather sternly that I would have to face up to my loss and focus on the children. Victor suggested that I get a job to provide me with a healthy distraction. I was already struggling to keep on top of the household chores and cook the dinners. A job would give me less time to do things and make me more stressed. He explained that mass unemployment was the cause for a lot of depression. I was depressed because my wife had died and my job was to look after the children and provide them with what they needed. I considered it to be a full-time job. I certainly had a long way to go before I could provide them with the attention that they required. A job would take up a lot of my time and cause me more anxiety and tiredness, so I chose to ignore his suggestion. The session came to an end and Victor scheduled another appointment to see me in two weeks' time.

At the end of October 2010 there was a message in my Facebook in-box from a lady called Carla. She was a mum from the same school that Sam attended. I had seen her in passing but I didn't know her well enough to stop and chat. She asked me how I was coping and told me about her father. He was in the dying stages of cancer and she had only recently been informed. He lived in a different country, which was only an hour away by plane. She had booked a flight to go and see him but was worried because she didn't know what to say to him. I suggested that she tell him how much she loves him and how much happiness he had brought into her life. I told her not to remain silent or have regrets that would be impossible to reverse and forget. She thanked me and I was feeling proud of myself for being able to help and understand what she was going through.

On Friday, 30 October 2009, I took the children to the beach to celebrate Sarah's birthday. It was the same beach that Sarah and I had taken Samuel to when he was less than a week old. Sarah had stood back and watched as I walked to the water's edge with Samuel in my arms. The sea was blinding because of the bright sun reflecting off the surface and the waves were fierce and loud, causing the light to dance with every rise and fall. Samuel kept his eyes firmly shut and started to cry. His tiny sound was lost against the noise of the ocean, but I got the message and walked back to where Sarah was standing and handed him to her. He was calm and safe in her arms. This was the start of our future as parents. We had a whole new life ahead of us that would take a bit of getting used to, but I was feeling euphoric.

The tide before my eyes had been rising and falling since God created the land and the sea. This natural occurrence was like the rising and falling of my son's chest as he breathed in the air around him, only slower. His breath would come more in an hour than a tide would in a whole year. I was standing next to my wife and child, trying to appreciate the beauty of both creations. The tide would also continue to come long after we took our final breath. How many of us embrace every day and truly enjoy the gift of life? Once the sleep-deprivation stage of parenthood passes, it might just be possible.

I was standing in the same spot now looking out to sea. The tide had come in to greet me. Clouds filled the sky and the beach was almost deserted. We had walked along this beach as a family many times, but Sarah's footprints had long been washed away. I walked as close to the sea as I could without ruining a decent pair of shoes that I shouldn't have worn to the beach. 'Happy birthday, my darling,' I said to the vast sea in front of me. I was feeling a different kind of sadness than previously. I was lonely and I didn't want to be a single dad. I wanted to scream at the sea and demand some answers, but I was too tired.

I thought about Sarah's ashes that were collecting dust at home. A favourite place of ours is Lyme Regis in Dorset. We had visited there a few times and stayed overnight to appreciate it fully both by day and by night. Our first visit there was for Sarah's birthday and her last one as a Miss. We had strolled along the Cobb, which was a large stone walkway that rose out of the sea. It was like a winding cobbled street that comes to an abrupt end, part way out to sea. When we reached the end where Meryl Streep had stood in the film *The French Lieutenant's Woman*, Sarah had said, 'When I die will you scatter my ashes here?' as if she knew that her breath would cease before mine. The waves were splashing against the rocks below, covering us with a fine spray. I didn't think about my own ashes or pay much attention to Sarah's request, because I took it for granted that one day we would part, but not now. We stood holding hands to support each other on the wet stones and we didn't have a care in the world. Our lives were as perfect as the setting of this heavenly place.

I made a decision about the ashes and resolved to visit Lyme Regis on the anniversary of Sarah's death to scatter them at her chosen location. The wind was strong and it was getting cold, so I took my children by their hands and strolled to a place that sold chocolate. If I couldn't make them smile today then a bar of chocolate would do it for me.

My mood remained flat throughout dinner with my parents and continued until my eyes closed for the night.

I started to focus on Christmas next and had bought most of the stocking presents already; though I would have to wrap them all individually to keep up with Sarah's tradition. I was dreading Christmas without Sarah, more than any of the other "first" anniversaries.

I sent occasional messages to Rita accusing her of using me and not caring about me, distracting myself by becoming obsessive towards her. I wanted my bandage back because I was feeling the pain without it. She couldn't understand why I was bothering her when I had rejected her. I had admitted that there could never be any future for us and she had simply found a man who wanted to have one. I had been in control of my involvement with Rita and now I was lost since she had taken control of her own life. Eventually, she told me to leave her alone.

I still needed to grieve properly, but I was scared that once I started to then I might not ever come out of it and that I would remain in its clutches forever. I was still getting angry on a daily basis. And Olivia was still refusing to get dressed by herself on a daily basis. She would argue with me constantly and cry when I dropped her off at nursery. Most of the time she was very happy and responsive but like her mother, she was not a morning person and she was very strong-willed. In desperation I grabbed Poppy, opened the front door and threw her as far up the road as I could. Poppy was a rag doll that Olivia had been given on her first birthday. It went everywhere with her and slept in her hand every night. She had been sewn up dozens of times and smelt of stale spit. I slammed the front door and was confronted by a hyperventilating child.

'Po-o-o-o-o-p-p-y!' sobbed Olivia, trying to get past me to open the front door.

I made her sit in the dining room and have her breakfast, which she found difficult between sobs. While she was eating I had retrieved Poppy from the road and hidden her. I was putting the milk away, when

I noticed a list that was stuck to the fridge door by a magnet. Sarah had made up her own list of Ten Commandments to help Samuel improve his behaviour when he had refused to get dressed at a similar age.

1. No being rude
2. No fighting
3. No shouting
4. Be kind
5. Treat others the way you want to be treated
6. Say please and thank you
7. No pushing
8. Share nicely
9. No snatching
10. Say when you are feeling sad or cross

I brought the list to the table with the same hope that Moses had in his heart when he held the original copy.

Olivia listened with interest when I told her that I was holding her mummy's list of house rules. Number one didn't help my argument much, because I was guilty on a daily basis as far as shouting was concerned. Olivia was quick to point that out, too. My favourite was number ten, which was to speak out when you are feeling sad or cross. I told Olivia that if she was feeling sad then I would give her a big hug. I then made a deal with her that I would try to abide by the rules if she did. I returned her rancid doll to her and she was as happy as a pig standing in something that smelt the same. Sarah was still having a positive influence in our lives eight months since her last breath. I was surprised it had taken me eight months to notice her A4 list of house rules that was right in front of me every time I opened the fridge door.

Victorious Christmas

Christmas was just over a month away and the repeated daily routines were improving with my mood as I became more efficient. I had returned to the world of Facebook and I could now focus whilst reading a book. It was a lovely feeling to be able to read again and enjoy watching films. I bought lots of comedy series to watch in the evening and it was good to hear myself laughing again.

I received another message from Carla informing me that her father had sadly passed away and that she had separated from her husband. She also told me that she was leaving the country with her children to go and live with her mum. She was leaving in a few days and so I asked her if she wanted to meet for a coffee and a chat before she left.

I had been waiting for forty minutes and was beginning to think that I had the wrong day, when Carla finally showed up after having overslept. We chatted for a couple of hours about our losses and I told her about my recent involvements. Unlike my counsellor, she didn't condemn me or judge me but appeared to understand my need for companionship. I thought I could talk, but I had met my match as we both fought to get our words out. I talked far more than I listened, because I was still finding it very difficult to do so with a mind that was full of Sarah. In my mind, Sarah was still very much alive because my love for her had not died. My eyes couldn't see her because she was elsewhere and I couldn't touch or listen to her, but I could feel her with every thought and conversation that she was in.

I thoroughly enjoyed the few hours of non-stop chat with Carla and it was a welcome change from sitting in coffee shops alone. She was leaving the country in the morning and I wished her well as we said goodbye. We agreed to keep in touch through Facebook.

I had met many people since Sarah's death who were suffering as a result of cancer or loss. I met most of them through the support group that I was still attending every month. The group also arranged days out to local attractions for bereaved children and the remaining parent. I had just put our names down for their Christmas party, because I was informed that it was the only party where the real Father Christmas made an appearance.

Although my moods were improving I was still having regular angry outbursts. Driving to school on a Tuesday morning in November I had an angry exchange with another driver. I didn't notice a white van trying to filter into my lane of traffic and we nearly crashed. He wound his window down and screamed some obscenities at me before speeding off. I started shouting as I gave chase and stopped behind him at some traffic lights that I had willed to change red. I unclipped my seat belt and opened the door of my car. I was stepping out onto the road, when Sam asked me where I was going. I was about to leave two children in a car on a main road to have an argument with another driver. I suddenly found my common sense, climbed back into my seat and closed the door. I had an appointment with Victor after dropping Sam off at school. I was looking forward to seeing him but worried that I wouldn't have much to talk about.

At 9.30 a.m. Victor greeted me at his front door with his usual smile and handshake. I led the way up his winding staircase and made myself comfortable in the centre of his leather sofa. I watched him sit down and waited for him to speak first.

'How are things?' Victor asked with a calm, sympathetic voice that made it impossible for me to answer with a lie and say that I was fine.

I started off by telling him about an uncomfortable occurrence at a Salsa lesson earlier in the week. I thought that dance lessons would be a good way to combat my loneliness and keep me out of trouble. The venue was a local school hall. The lessons started at 7.00 p.m. and finished at 10.00 p.m. and were split into two sessions. The first session was to teach the moves that would be put into practice during the second session.

I was assured that all dance requests were honoured. Knowing that it was my first night, one kind lady took pity on me and asked me to dance. We danced for the remainder of a song, by which time I was feeling more relaxed and confident. I immediately approached a very talented lady for a dance. She was of a similar age and very attractive. I explained to Victor how she had managed to crush my confidence in seconds. She kept a safe distance between us and told me very abruptly that I was squeezing her shoulder too hard. She also said that I needed to go and practise some more, before walking away and leaving me standing there all alone in the middle of the dance floor.

I wanted to go and tell her that my wife had died but instead I walked towards the door and never looked back. Victor stared at me with a blank expression on his face and I had no idea as to what his next words would be.

'Maybe she saw something that she didn't like. You probably made her nervous. Why were you there anyway? Were you really there to learn how to dance or looking for another victim to have another no-strings-attached involvement?' he said.

I wanted to give him an answer but I didn't have one. I knew it was pointless to argue with him because he was right.

'I get lonely,' I said rather pathetically, hoping that he would understand why I felt the need for company.

'What is wrong with male friends? You could go for a beer and a chat. If it's company that you are after then that is the best solution,' said Victor rather proudly.

I didn't answer him and after a short pause, changed the subject. I thought back to earlier in the day and mentioned my road rage with the rude van driver. Surely Victor would be on my side and understand my anger.

'The van driver wasn't annoyed at you personally. You have no idea what is going on in his life. He could have had an argument with his wife before setting off to work. Somebody close to him may have died or there could be a number of other reasons. You have to learn to control your anger, especially for the sake of your children,' he said.

I forgot about the van driver and spoke about my anger. I confessed everything about the shouting, screaming and snarling at my children. Victor didn't move or interrupt. He hardly ever moved during our sessions. He would sit there listening to every word, his hands resting on his knees with his unblinking eyes watering. I had finished talking and was looking at the top of his long socks that were visible owing to his considerably short trousers.

'Darren! You must stop shouting at your children. I wouldn't allow any living person to shout at me. It is frightening and unacceptable. If you only ever take one thing away from all of our sessions then let it be this, for I would be happy and feel that I have made a difference. If you stop shouting at your children it will change their lives and I cannot stress this more,' said Victor, sounding more like a headmaster than a counsellor. 'I know that I give you a hard time but I am trying to help you. I think that your story is one of the saddest I have ever heard. I am often on my allotment, thinking of ways that I can help you with your grieving. I don't stop thinking about you after I leave this chair,' he said.

My bottom lip started to quiver as Victor removed his hands from his knees. I started to sob uncontrollably and he was there offering me a tissue from the table beside him. He spent the rest of the session teaching me some breathing techniques that would help me to relax and combat my anger. I smiled as I left and thanked him. He had pointed out the importance of thanking at an earlier session.

'Take care, Darren, and I will see you soon,' he said, waving at me from his front door as I drove away.

In early December I was still filling up bags of presents that would need wrapping, as would all of the stocking presents that had been wrapped up individually and so elegantly the year previously. I thought about Sarah's phone call to her sister and her lack of faith in my wrapping ability. I had listened to the recording on my phone many times over and the world would stop every time I did so. Sarah's voice would penetrate my soul and momentarily confuse my brain for a few seconds, during which I would forget that the voice was from the past. My brain would soon adjust and shake me until I was wide awake. Then grief would ambush me in its usual way, where the reality of my loss became the only focus.

Wrapping up the "bastard" stocking presents had been at the forefront of Sarah's mind as she spoke to Claire. I had heard her tell Claire this dozens of times whilst pressing my phone hard against my ear. I had taken on board the hint and wanted to honour her wishes. I was a slow wrapper and it usually took me about five minutes per present. I calculated that it would take me about five hours. Not only was my first Christmas without Sarah going to be difficult to get through, but I was also going to have to graft as well. My wrapping was so amateurish that every present was as difficult for me to wrap as a

172

bowling ball might be to a modest wrapper. I guessed that the children wouldn't notice all the tears and excess tape.

Being ambushed by my grief didn't just happen whilst viewing photographs or listening to my recordings. I could be driving, shopping or simply walking along a street. There would not always be a trigger or warning before being jumped upon by the reality of my loss. I have never been attacked by a pack of wolves or been caught in the headlights of an oncoming, unavoidable truck. I have never experienced the feeling of being told that I was going to be executed within an hour. I can only guess that the emotional and traumatic force from raw grief is comparable to such obvious terrors.

As Christmas loomed nearer I prayed that it would pass without too many ambushes. I knew that Sarah would want us to enjoy it and participate on a similar level to Christmases in the past. I brought the tree down from the attic and already I knew that it was going to look less attractive than ever before. I opened the box and noticed the star that we had bought in France to go on top of the tree. It had a European plug attached the end of a short piece of cable, so it would require an extension lead and an adaptor for it to work. I placed it in the window of our front room because no matter how hard I tried, I couldn't make an extension lead look like a tree decoration. It looked beautiful lit up in our window. I called it Sarah's star and I decided that we would put it in our window every Christmas until the day I died or until it burned the house down.

There were two weeks to go until Christmas and it was the day of the support group's Christmas party: a four-hour marathon of fun-filled activities. It was held at a local hotel which was surrounded by beautiful woodland. A wedding was also taking place and the happy couple was posing for photographs as I entered. Surely there is nothing better than newly-weds to get me in the mood for a Christmas without my wife! Music was playing as we entered the function room and before I had even taken my coat off, Olivia asked me if I would dance with her. The dance floor was empty and most of the tables that surrounded it were full. I found a spare table, removed my coat and plonked myself down on a chair.

'Daddy, I want to dance!' demanded Olivia.

I didn't feel remotely like dancing but I heard myself saying yes to her. I was feeling a little self-conscious as I stepped onto the dance floor holding Olivia's tiny hands. Within a few moments I had forgotten where I was and delivered the performance of a lifetime. I put all of what I could remember from my wedding dance lessons into practice. We waltzed and jived our way through a couple of songs and I held her up in my arms and spun her round in time with the music. We jumped, skipped, spun and slipped. I was sweating profusely and Olivia was laughing joyfully as we lost ourselves in the moment. It felt like we were the only two people in the room as everything but the dance floor had vanished from my sight and mind. I was dancing for Sarah and I could feel her looking down upon us. I visualised a golden spotlight shining down from a bright golden sky and Sarah's face smiling amongst it. The three of us shared this defining moment until the song stopped and the room was quiet. I half expected to hear a round of applause, but instead I could still feel Sarah smiling down on me. It was the first time I had truly given her something to smile about since the day she had died, or so I thought. Olivia was still smiling too, having enjoyed the attention from her dad that had been elsewhere for some time.

The room was starting to thin out as the party neared its end. Father Christmas had left the building and had been far more generous than I remembered from my own childhood. Sam was finishing off a decorative paper chain that he had obsessively been working on all afternoon. It was far too big for our house and probably Buckingham Palace, too. He insisted on finishing off before we went home. I looked up and saw a lady I didn't recognise. I wanted to speak to her immediately, so I approached her and introduced myself. I don't know why but I was drawn to her. I'd like to think there was more of a reason than her being slim and wearing a pair of very tight jeans but I can't come up with one.

'I'm Mary,' she said through smiling lips that penetrated my heart like Cupid's arrow. 'Your daughter is beautiful,' she said.

I had found a substitute and a worthy replacement. I was going to marry this girl and everything was going to be fine. She thought my daughter was beautiful and she had a beautiful smile. I wanted to thank Sarah for finding her for me. I said goodbye and asked her if she was going to the Christmas pantomime that our support group had got free tickets for. I hardly spoke as I drove home because my mind was busy thinking about Mary and our conversation. I had a whole week to wait before I saw her again. I didn't know if she had a man in her life or if she was even looking for one.

On Tuesday morning I was sitting on the sofa in Victor's house telling him about my weekend.

'I have met a girl who is perfect for me,' I said, hoping that he would be pleased for me.

The shake of his head and the sigh from his lips told me that he wasn't.

'You know nothing about this girl. Stay away from her. She doesn't need you interfering with her life and messing it up,' he said before proceeding to give me a lecture about unhealthy distractions and inappropriate women. 'You are the biggest convincer I have ever met, but you will not convince me that this is a good idea,' he said.

His words went in my left ear and straight out of my right as I had already made my mind up. I had to follow my feelings and find out if Mary was going to be my future. My facial expression was all that Victor needed for him to know that I had already convinced myself.

The car park was full and the theatre lobby was empty when we arrived for the pantomime at the arranged time that I had obviously got wrong. The performance was already under way as we were guided to our seats by an usher. My head was nearly as low as my knees until I sat down because I didn't want to restrict the audience's view. I was removing my coat, when my heart skipped a beat as I saw that I had been seated next to Mary. Fate really was in control of my future. Mary smiled at me and also shook her head in acknowledgement of our late entrance. I interpreted her smile and her body language to suit my own needs and had convinced myself that she was having similar feelings.

During the show I was picked on by the cast and asked to join them on stage. I didn't have a big part to play and was only up there for a few minutes. I had to wave my arms around and make a few noises, but I felt like I was giving my biggest performance. I think it is good for children to see a parent stand up and be seen or heard. I wanted my children to grow up without the shyness and fear that I'd experienced for a large part of my life on such occasions when I was in the limelight.

I was mainly showing off for Mary though, and I wanted her to notice my confident and charming side. I didn't get much of a chance to speak to her that evening, but we spoke briefly during the interlude and as we were leaving at the end of the show.

'Have a lovely Christmas and I will see you at the next meeting in January,' I said as we walked to our cars.

I drove off wondering how I was going to get through my first Christmas without Sarah, which was less than a week away.

Samuel had finished school for the term and Olivia had a couple more days of nursery before Christmas Eve. They were both settling very well and appeared to be happy. Nursery was a godsend for Olivia because she got a lot of attention and cuddles from the girls who worked there, who were like substitute mums. They tied her hair up in an array of styles and they spoke to her about Sarah on a regular basis. Some of them would often babysit, making their relationship with Olivia more personal.

Ruth was a friend of Sarah's and she would also babysit on a regular basis. Ruth had promised Sarah that she would not allow me to be lonely and she knew that babysitting would prevent that from happening. Ruth is a very warm and spiritual person and the children would get very excited when they heard that she was coming over for the evening. The fact that Ruth would let them stay up extremely late and give them their body weight in sweets and chocolate may have been a factor. Ruth would also talk to them about their mum as they all snuggled under a blanket.

Ruth told me that Sarah had always known that she was going to die and that she had deliberately chosen me as her husband and a worthy father for her children. She believed that Sarah was needed elsewhere as an angel because her time here had for some reason come to an end. Maybe that was why Sarah had accepted her death so freely. Sarah had never said to me that she didn't want to die or screamed about it.

I had recently chatted to Gwen, Sarah's grandmother, who loved to talk about Sarah and I loved to listen. She told me that Sarah had called her a few days before she had died. 'Will you miss me, Nan?' was all she said before Gwen told her that she would miss her more than she would ever know. Sarah immediately hung up the phone because she was so upset. I wasn't at the hospital to comfort her as she cried alone. Sarah must have kept a lot of feelings about her death to herself to avoid upsetting others.

One of the select few who would get a hug from Sam was Ruth; although she would have to make the first move and be able to outrun him. Samuel enjoys hugs and kisses, so I don't really know why he is always trying to avoid them. I was still playing games at bedtime to get kisses from him though and was continually finding ways to make him laugh. I even invented a game, where I would put my hands behind my back and get Sam and Olivia to choose a hand. My hands were empty, but I would make up different rewards and forfeits. If they were lucky they might get a kiss frenzy or if unfortunate, they would be fighting off a tickle onslaught.

Olivia liked the giggling throttle. This involved me putting both my hands to her neck and shoulders and bouncing her up and down on her pillow while she giggled and tried to catch her breath. From a distance it might not have looked that great, but she loved it and it became a bedtime ritual. I thought about Sarah and her dislike of having hands anywhere near her throat. I remembered a time when she was deliberately winding me up and I jokingly put my hands close to her throat. She told me sternly that she didn't like hands anywhere near her throat. I joked that she must have been Ruth Ellis in her previous life who, if you are not aware, was the last woman in Britain to be hanged. If not her then possibly a chicken, because they regularly have their necks grabbed. Ruth was one of Sarah's middle names, so there could be something in my theory!

I finished giving Olivia a giggle throttle and told her it was sleeping time. 'I love you, Dad. You're the best daddy I have ever had,' said Olivia as I kissed her goodnight. My smile was wider than it had been for a long time. I was seeing my children laugh more every day and I was getting into the spirit of Christmas.

Tracy had arrived from America and had wrapped up every single stocking present for me. Sarah had been correct when she said that she couldn't see me wrapping them. I couldn't believe that Tracy enjoyed it so much. She seemed to be a little disappointed when she had wrapped up the last one and was looking for more. She had finished inside an hour and I was so grateful.

Every year on Christmas Eve, Sarah and I would go to the same hotel that we had gone to for her thirty-third birthday. We used to meet our friends and have a few drinks while listening to a choir singing Christmas songs. Hotel residents had paid a lot of money for a Christmas package that included canapés and champagne, which was laid out in front of the choir. We always took full advantage of these Christmas treats and were never questioned by the staff. This year I was meeting our friends for the first time without Sarah. There was no free champagne or food sitting on any table. I think this was to do with the recession rather than Sarah not being present. I imagined that she was drinking champagne and eating canapés in her heavenly place.

I ordered a glass of champagne and joined my friends. Then I held my glass up towards the ceiling and made a silent toast to my wife. Dave and Sian had their five-month-old baby with them, whom Sarah never got to meet. I had Samuel and Olivia with me. It wasn't their first time and as with previous years they enjoyed lemonade and numerous rides in the glass lift. The carol singers arrived late just as my friends were leaving, but I decided to stay and listen. I sat directly in front of them with Olivia on my lap and my arm around Samuel. The singing was beautiful and I realised that this was the hardest "first" that I had endured. The moment was bitter-sweet as I listened to the hymns whilst holding my children and I cried for the first time on Christmas Eve. I didn't have a free hand to wipe away the tears and so I let them fall freely, without interference. Samuel had not taken his eyes off the choir, but sensing that I was upset he put both of his arms around me. I was glad of the cold, fresh air of the night as we left the hotel. I raised my head as if to look for Sarah.

'Merry Christmas, darling,' I whispered into the night sky.

I was looking forward to a glass or two of wine as I tried to find all of the presents that I had hidden around the house to surround the tree with them. The children fell asleep quickly and I opened up one of the bottles in the fridge. Then I turned on my computer and logged on to Facebook. I noticed that Carla was online and so I sent her a message asking how she was. We started chatting and continued to chat for five hours. She was the same age as me and I didn't realise how much we had in common when it came to music and comedy. I had finished off two bottles of wine and had laughed and cried my way through them. Carla was very funny and also a good listener. I talked to her a lot about Sarah and our life together and her terminal illness.

At around midnight I proposed a toast to Sarah and to Carla's recently departed father. I couldn't type fast enough for what I wanted to say. I don't know why we didn't pick up the phone and have a proper chat. Carla is a singer/songwriter in her spare time and I have always been quite good at making up lyrics, so I frantically made up parts of songs that would make her laugh, but she thought I had got them all off the Internet. I also made up a song about her and she told me that she nearly choked on her drink from the laughter. I finally got to bed about 3.00 a.m. after placing the children's stockings on their beds. I'd had the best night in ages and without another's physical presence.

The children were kind to me in the morning by not waking up too early. It was so lovely to see them with the same level of excitement as previous years. They were running in and out of each other's rooms showing off their presents. There was no stocking by my bed this year, but I did keep smiling throughout the morning as the unwrapping continued and we left to have a Christmas feast at my parents' house. Mum had got me a stocking though, which was overflowing with overcompensating gifts. My family were keeping me sane and I would surely have fallen apart without them.

The children were spending the night at their house and I said goodbye to them as the evening approached. Mum asked me if I was going to be okay spending the evening in an empty house, but I told her that I was looking forward to the peace and sleeping in late on Boxing Day. I was missing the weekly lie-ins that I used to get in my marriage. Sarah would often get up with the children and let me sleep for a few hours. I would return the favour but she did the lion's share.

I recently had a dream about Sarah getting up and entertaining the children. I dreamed that she was downstairs with the children and then she suddenly woke me up in my dream and reminded me that she was dying of cancer. At first I was racked with guilt and then very clearly I told her how much I missed talking to her before I woke up. I didn't dream very often but when I did, they were very real.

I daydreamed about my Christmas past as I drove home that night. The day had been very different compared to previous years. Being on my own was more obvious at certain times of the day. The children were preoccupied by all of their wrapped stocking presents and the larger ones that filled our living room. This distraction made it an easier day for them than other days. Their day was very similar to other years because Christmas mainly revolves around children. For years I would sit in bed with Sarah and we would open our presents to each other before opening up a bottle of champagne and making Buck's Fizz with the children's orange juice. We would sit and watch as our spoilt little angels tore open their presents and I would enjoy staring at Sarah's happy face as they did so. We would accept the thanks for most of them and only give Santa the credit for the big one.

As soon as the presents were opened we would start the Christmas dinner and finish off the champagne. Preparing a roast dinner always reminds me of planning for a wedding. The preparation always takes about twenty times longer than the actual event. One year as Sarah was serving the dinner, I burnt my hand quite badly. She had asked me to take some food through to the dining room and warned me about the glass dish that contained potatoes that she had just removed from the oven. Knowing me as well as she did, she even warned me every time I stepped into the kitchen. She must have told me about five times, but it didn't stop me from picking it up with my bare hands and trying to carry it to the table. I got as far as the kitchen door when the pain kicked in. My high-pitched scream should have shattered the glass dish. I ran to the worktop, threw it down and heard a slight tear as my skin got left behind on the side of the dish. I spent the whole of dinner with a bowl of water on either side of me and kept my hands submerged. I would release them for a second at a time to feed myself quickly as water dripped onto my plate. Sarah laughed throughout dinner, calling me a complete wally. Maybe it's not such a good idea to drink too much champagne before dinner!

Christmas afternoon would be spent on the sofa. The children would be asleep upstairs and I would be groaning from too much food, and scalded hands on this particular year. I would be content with the peace, the champagne, the remote and my wife next to me. 'Are you OK, Piggy?' she would ask whilst laughing as we watched *The Great Escape* and prayed for at least two hours' respite. The scars on my hands would heal in a couple of weeks and eventually there would be no trace of them. Recollecting these happy memories was painful and these scars weren't healing as easily.

I had no idea how long it would take my mental scar to heal or indeed if it ever would. I imagined my internal scar to be like a photograph. One that was taken at the height of my trauma and possibly at the very moment when Stuart told me that Sarah was gone. The photo will fade with the passing of time and be transformed into a brighter and happier image.

Being at my parents' for dinner had been enjoyable and I was grateful but it also highlighted my loss and my single-father status. I arrived home to an empty house and sprawled out on the sofa with a glass of wine and the remote. I relaxed for over an hour before switching on my computer. Carla was sitting at her computer in a different country and we shared our feelings about our first Christmas as single parents. I didn't notice the silence or emptiness of my house as I chatted, laughed, drank and gave Carla my full attention. We were both merry as we flirted for the remainder of Christmas Day and well into the early hours of Boxing Day. My fears about not getting through the day had been completely forgotten about as my mind engaged with someone who was on the same wavelength. Unexpectedly, we had both had a very good evening without forgetting about our individual grief.

I had spoken in detail about my feelings for Sarah both before and after her death and Carla had spoken about her father. She had also spoken about the death of her marriage, which was unavoidable owing to an incompatibility regarding family commitments. I can't imagine that any lady would choose to be a single parent if they thought for one minute that their marriage could be saved. Some men just never grow up and are unable to take their responsibilities seriously.

A lot of women tell me that I am a remarkable man for doing such a great job of bringing up two children alone. I never tire of the compliments, but I am not doing it alone. I have very supportive parents and friends who take on very important roles in mine and the children's lives. Sarah's influence is still evident. She had laid the foundations for her children and I have learned so much from her that I put into practice on a daily basis. Her house rules and her cooking skills are regularly required for a happy, well-balanced household. But I had failed to keep on at Sam about walking on tiptoe. Sarah had regularly screamed, 'Flat feet!' at him, which would sometimes reduce him to tears. A recent appointment confirmed that his short tendons were a problem and would need operating on. I wasn't ready to face the hospital where Sarah had died just yet, so I asked for it to be delayed and I promised to give more commitment to his daily exercises.

Most evenings while the children slept I would sit at my computer and Carla would do the same. We were still chatting for hours and never ran out of things to say.

I was feeling very sad on New Year's Eve because I didn't want to enter into a new year that Sarah would not see. I wanted to remain in 2009 because she had been part of it. In three months' time I would be scattering Sarah's ashes into the sea. I still had no idea what I was going to tell the children if they asked me about the big green pot that went unnoticed on the shelf above our dining-room table.

Learning to Date Again

In early January, Carla had booked a flight and was planning a few days' visit. I invited her for dinner on the Saturday night of her stay. I had only ever spent three hours in her company before but I felt as if I knew her very well.

I started cooking at lunchtime as Carla was due at 8.00 p.m. I had prepared a three-course meal because I wanted to impress her. Sarah used to compliment me on my culinary skills in recent years and I had come a long way since my blue potato episode.

Listening to music and dancing as I sliced and sautéed had put me in good mood, but it was a welcome relief to sit down and rest my aching legs when Carla arrived thirty minutes late. I didn't understand lateness because I had a kind of autistic obsessiveness about it. I'd wasted many hours of my life standing outside schools waiting for the gates to open after having sat in my car for twenty minutes. I would spend a fortune on sweets in the cinema just to entertain the children while we waited thirty minutes for the doors to open. Nearly every party that the children attended started with a fight owing to them getting bored in the back seat of our car. My timekeeping for every occasion would be as important as catching a flight or getting married.

I greeted Carla with a hug and we ended up having a very pleasant evening. It was lovely to talk to her while she was in the same room and without having to use two fingers and a keyboard to do so. Hours spent in the kitchen, resulting in sore feet, had been worthwhile because the food was as triumphant as the evening, which ended with a kiss. Delicious food and wine had passed through my lips all evening and now my lips were against Carla's. Our lips were silent but the kiss had more meaning than words. If my body had contained an engine then the kiss would have provided the necessary spark to start it first time.

I had mixed emotions as I placed my head on my pillow that night. I had bonded well with Carla but I was a long way from being ready to date again. My previous involvements had been controlled distractions with inappropriate girls with whom I had no desirable future. Sarah had only been gone for ten months and I still had to grieve properly. Victor had warned me that broken people can only attract broken people. Was Carla broken, too? After all, her dad had recently died and at the same time she had left her husband of eleven years.

I met Carla for a coffee a couple of days later before she flew back home to her mum's, at which point we would have to return to chatting with two fingers on the keyboard on Facebook.

I was at the airport two weeks later. The children were staying with my very accommodating parents. I had booked a hotel not far from Carla's mum's. Carla was picking me up from the airport and joining me at the hotel. Sitting on a plane for an hour on a Friday afternoon was quite relaxing, but waiting for forty minutes for Carla to arrive was less so. I had a sneaky cigarette and chewed some minty gum to disguise the smoker in me. Carla abhorred smoking, but I could usually get away with it during our long-distant chats.

The hotel was lovely, as was the company, but it just didn't feel right. Feelings of guilt had crept into my already anxious mind. I had too much respect for Carla to let myself use her in the same way that I had the previous two girls. I didn't know if Carla wanted a relationship or was simply distracting herself and escaping from facing up to her own losses. Meeting her mum worried me some more and having dinner with her brother sent my panic mode to a new level. Was I her new boyfriend? Were they expecting a wedding? These were just two of the questions that plagued my mind and I didn't know what to do. I did the sensible male thing to do and ignored the feelings of anxiety until we were safety back in our hotel room.

On the day I was flying home Carla mentioned my erratic and unusual behaviour.

'How can you be intimate during the confines of a hotel room, yet be so cold and stand-offish outside of it?' she asked.

I just stared at her because I didn't know the correct answer. I hadn't been intimate with anyone apart from Sarah for fifteen years. She had given me the green light for sympathy sex but had never agreed to intimacy that involved holding hands or kissing. She had insisted that I move on and find someone who would make me happy, but not until I had grieved for at least eighteen months. All of these thoughts were going through my mind at the airport as I waited for my return flight.

'Can I kiss you?' asked Carla in the final few minutes before I had to check in.

The whole airport came to a standstill as I stood naked for every passenger to witness. I had never been very good at public displays of affection at the best of times and in the best of circumstances, but thirty seconds of kissing in a public place left me shell-shocked. Feelings of betrayal and guilt swept over me and I imagined that every person witnessing our kiss was ashamed of me for dishonouring my late wife. There was actually nothing wrong with the kiss as far as kisses were concerned. It was just at the wrong time along my path of grieving. Knowing that Carla sensed my uneasiness with the kiss I blurted out, 'Sarah and I never used to kiss in public,' hoping that it would make her feel better.

The kiss was quickly forgotten, because Carla's lateness on my arrival must have been catching and it looked like I was going to miss my flight. Panting and sweating like a fugitive on the run, I made my way down the plane and kept my head dropped to avoid any eye contact with disgruntled passengers. We were in the sky inside of a minute and my heart was still pounding against my chest. The stress caused by being late was far worse than the boredom I usually experience from waiting around for two hours.

Carla knew all about my past involvements and firmly stated that she had no intention of being anything like them. She didn't want to be used and then cast aside. I was confused because I really enjoyed being in her company, but a relationship at this time was impossible. I told her that I wasn't ready and she was very understanding. We still communicated most evenings via the computer.

The first support group meeting of the year was on the last Sunday in January. A lot of the familiar faces were there and it was a bit like a widowed reunion. We kind of understood each other and it was always a great help to discuss any problems with each other, especially ones concerning the children. Mary was there, too, and we exchanged a few words over the coffee pot. She had lost a husband through divorce rather than bereavement. I gave her a scruffy bit of paper with my full name on it so she could look me up on Facebook. I also casually suggested that we should get together so that her two children could play with mine. I still didn't know very much about her, but I thought that she ticked every box on my replacement check list which I had mentally written in a car with Sarah.

On Wednesday mornings I could still be found sitting at a table outside the city centre's most central coffee shop, smoking cigarettes and looking at everyone who passed. The brief moments in the lives of shoppers as they went about their business made more sense than my own life. One lady was pushing a pram and talking to her baby girl. I focused all of my attention on her and my head followed her as she passed. She was ecstatically happy as she continued to talk and walk. I closed my hand over my mouth and cried as I thought about Sarah and how she had lost her own future and that of being with her children.

I was already feeling quite sensitive after passing all the card shops where Valentine's cards decorated the window fronts. I hated Valentine's Day even more now. Every man, woman and child seemed to be part of a different world to mine. My future was as uncertain as the man to my left, sitting on a blanket and asking for spare change. I wanted to shout out, 'Please give me back my wife, can anyone spare my wife?' Instead, I looked at all of the other smokers with contempt. Why would they choose to damage their health and shorten their lives? I knew that I was the biggest hypocrite where smoking was concerned, but my anger needed many outlets.

That same evening I added Mary to my list of Facebook friends. After a brief exchange of questions, I told her that I was a non-smoker and then we arranged to meet up the following Saturday afternoon at a local country park.

The day was not as I had expected it to be. We both spent a lot of the day disciplining our children. Her eldest boy and Samuel were involved in some kind of territorial dispute for most of the day. Mary told me that her youngest had a birthday approaching in March and that she was busy planning a party for him.

'What date is his birthday?' I asked, knowing somehow what the answer was going to be.

I still shook my head in disbelief when she told me that it was March the twentieth.

Mary didn't really say much as we strolled around the wooded park. We didn't appear to have very much in common. As we were driving home I asked the children if they had enjoyed the day.

'I did, but I didn't really like Robert,' said Sam.

I knew from the instant rivalry between them that he was going to say something like that. I had wanted Mary to be a worthy replacement for Sarah but my plan had fallen apart on our first date together. I had to listen to my children because their needs were more important than my own. I was still chatting to Carla most evenings and she was flying over for another visit. I invited her over to my house for dinner on Saturday, 13 February 2010.

I had also exchanged a few messages with Mary during the week, but had ruled out anything intimate between us. On the Friday night Mary asked me if I wanted to meet up on Sunday at another park for a couple of hours in the afternoon. I had nothing planned so I thought I would give it another try to see if the children could get along.

I had cooked another splendid meal and was looking forward to seeing Carla again. I was feeling slightly agitated when she arrived because I didn't know anything about her intentions. I didn't even understand my own. I knew that I enjoyed her company but wondered if I should be spending an evening with her and kissing her if I was adamant that it couldn't go any further at this stage. I avoided mentioning my planned afternoon with Mary because I didn't want to jeopardise our friendship. Since Sarah's death I had spent hardly any time on my own to grieve properly. The thought of sitting on my own feeling depressed and crying until my throat was sore was the less appealing option to the one that involved complicating my life.

Carla stayed until the early hours. While we held hands for a large part of the evening and shared the occasional kiss, our minds had remained separate and disengaged.

In the morning I woke up feeling uneasy and tense, brought on by guilt, which spread throughout my whole body. I received a message from Carla asking me if I was okay, because it was obvious to her that I was not. She reminded me of our recent conversation about not using her and being honest with each other. I told her that I was fine but my short response gave away my true feelings of guilt.

I met up with Mary that afternoon. It was Valentine's Day and I had stopped off on the way to buy six chocolate bars for everyone. The children were devouring theirs and Mary joked about the chocolate bar being the best Valentine's gift she had ever received. We strolled around the park and Mary told me a bit about her ex-husband and her previous failed relationships. I spoke about Sarah and briefly mentioned Alison and Rita, but I couldn't bring myself to tell her about Carla. We spent about three hours at the park and the children got on a lot better than last time.

Just as we were about to get into the car I gave Mary a hug. It was a short one and a bit clumsy, but I was getting better at offering hugs as opposed to waiting for them. Carla is very confident and generous when it comes to hugs and she had helped me feel more comfortable doing so.

I had told Carla truthfully that I wasn't ready for a relationship, so I was confused as to why I was planning a future with Mary as I drove home. I was dreaming of a similar life to the one I had lost, having convinced myself that she was everything on my list of relationship requirements. She ticked all of the ten boxes.

Carla continued to text me and was concerned about my vague responses. She sensed that something was seriously wrong and confronted me about it. I confessed to my date with Mary and in the process caused much upset. I asked Carla if we could be friends and we met up for lunch. I am embarrassed to admit that I spoke to her about Mary for most of our time together. I blurted out that I was going to spend the rest of my life with her and that Sarah had played a big part in our fate.

Carla told me that she didn't want to be my friend and that she didn't want to spend time with someone who could be so insensitive. Later that day she removed me from Facebook and deleted my phone number.

My counsellor had told me that it was too soon for a relationship and he had emphasised the importance of moving slowly and cautiously even when the time was right. I didn't listen to his advice and dived straight into the deepest depths of a relationship. I was even looking at five-bedroom houses on the Internet and dreaming of a "happy ever after". My friends were very concerned about my behaviour.

I took Mary for dinner a week after our first hug. A friend of Sarah's asked me to find out if we shared any interests and to ask Mary what music she liked and what her favourite book was.

We arrived at the restaurant and Mary was wearing a short skirt. I noticed lots of men staring at her as we entered the restaurant and walked up the stairs to our table, making me feel very self-conscious. I was looking at my wedding ring and wondered if Mary was, too. Just after ordering I asked my first question about books. Mary told me that she wasn't very interested in them and that she didn't have much time for reading. I then asked her about music and hoped that I wouldn't get the same response. She thought for a few moments.

'I like Celine Dion,' she said.

Celine bloody Dion was a very disappointing response. Did we have anything in common? I then noticed men staring as they passed by our table to visit the little boys' room. Maybe they had overheard her taste in music and needed to throw up. I had been planning a whole future in my head with someone I didn't know at all. She had a beautiful smile and I'd built a mental future with her based on a pair of lips and some straight white teeth. I would never commit myself to buying a house, having only ever seen it from the outside. The inside is very important and could turn out to be an empty shell. How could I be planning to commit myself to a lady I didn't know very well? Was I basing everything on her exterior? I left the restaurant telling myself that opposites do attract.

Mary and I spoke most evenings on the telephone and mostly about each other's pasts. I learned that she had found love for the first time after her marriage broke up. This had ended a year previously because of her new man being jealous about her children's father.

I invited Mary for dinner on Saturday and spent the whole day preparing a meal that would impress. I would always feel nervous around her as if we were forever on a blind date. I really wanted to be with her and to have a fairy-tale ending, but she made me feel uncomfortable somehow. I was intimidated by her and noticed that there was a hard exterior to her personality. It was quite ironic really that she didn't read books as she was very much a closed book herself. I questioned her about being so secretive and closed and she told me that she didn't trust anyone and I would find out more about her as our relationship progressed.

I was unable to stop the imaginary pen forming crosses instead of ticks in empty boxes as the evening came to an end. I had spent all day cooking dinner and Mary had arrived at my house empty-handed. I used to be guilty of this myself before learning from Sarah that you should always arrive with a bottle of wine or flowers. I was tired and wanted to go to bed as soon as the door closed, but I had piles of washing-up that had been left. On both occasions that Carla had been round to dinner she had brought wine, chocolates and insisted on doing all of the clearing up.

I had enjoyed the closeness with Mary as we held hands on the sofa but there were no sparks between us. I desperately wanted to impress her and to win her over completely, but I was convinced that I was doing a lousy job and I was trying too hard. I was constantly getting no reaction or appreciation for my efforts. I had made her a shepherd's pie once and hand-delivered it to her workplace to save her cooking when she got home. I got a small thank you but later she told me that her two boys had said it looked like poo. I even sent her flowers to make her smile as she worked. Then I had contacted her that afternoon to check that they had arrived and she thanked me and told me that they were lovely. Surely it should have been her ringing me …

Ticks were turning to crosses but I was still telling my friends that she was lovely. I had put her on a pedestal from the outset. I suppose I really wanted her to have all of the qualities that Sarah had and I didn't want the disappointment of being wrong about her. I hoped that she would soon open up to me and prove to me that I was right about choosing her to share my future with.

I was in the process of booking another two-week holiday in America to visit Tracy, so I asked Mary if she wanted to join us with her children. My parents were also going and I was assured that there would be enough room for us all. Mary agreed to it right away and seemed very flattered that I had invited her.

Scattering the Magic Dust

The first anniversary of Sarah's death was two weeks away and it was the last of the "firsts" that I would have to get through on my own. I booked a hotel in Lyme Regis and my brother-in-law volunteered to keep me company while I scattered Sarah's ashes from the Cobb into the sea.

Driving home from school the following day I announced my intentions to the children. I had completely forgotten that I had previously avoided the subject. I still had no idea what I was going to tell them if they wanted details. Sam immediately asked me about the ashes and what they were. I hesitated and said that it was too late in the day for me to explain. I would tell him first thing in the morning, as it was quite a complicated subject.

I lay awake for most of the night trying to think of the best words to explain a cremation. I didn't want to scare the children by telling them Sarah's body had been burned to create a pot of ash. Neither did I want to go into too much detail about her spirit, as I knew it would bring an endless list of questions. I hoped that Sam would forget to ask, but this was unlikely as he had the memory of an elephant when it suited him.

We were halfway through the journey to school when he asked me about the ashes. I was still at a loss as to what to say. I opened my mouth and the words just flowed out. I don't know where they came from or if they would make any sense, but I started by asking him if he had learned about World War I at school. He knew that lots of soldiers had died in the trenches and in no-man's-land, so I told him that the bodies of the men who had died there had turned to dust after their spirits had left them and gone to Heaven. The dust got washed into the soil by the rain and then thousands of poppies grew where the bodies had been. Mummy's body had also turned to dust after her spirit had left and gone to Heaven. I was going to Lyme Regis to scatter her ashes into the sea. This was their mum's favourite place and where she wanted to be scattered. I painted a positive picture for them and said that by scattering Sarah's ashes into the sea she would be everywhere. The wind would take some of her up into the sky and the sea would take her on a journey around the world.

'You just called them ashes,' said Sam, which proved that he was listening carefully.

I pointed out that some people called them ashes and others call them dust. I had slipped up because I wanted to refer to them as dust throughout my explanation. I happened to think that ashes sounded less magical than dust. Both Sam and Olivia had beaming smiles on their faces from the back seat of our car. They were very happy and contented with what I had just told them.

Immediately after telling Mary that I didn't smoke, I gave up completely. It had been five weeks since my last cigarette. Remembering exactly how much time had passed since your last cigarette is never a good sign and usually results in failure. Driving to Lyme Regis I decided that I was in control of my habit and concluded that I would buy a packet of ten for the day because I might be in need of some de-stressing assistance later. This was my first visit without Sarah and I was glad of Stuart's company. Sarah's remains were strapped into the back seat and I was unsure about saying goodbye to them. I had poured some of them into three small boxes before leaving home. I wanted the children to have a box each, to scatter in a place of their choice, when the time was right for them to do so.

The remaining box was for Sarah's mother. She had a bin in her back garden that she had planted a tree in. On many occasions during her illness, Sarah had said, 'Just throw me in the dustbin and be done with me.' I will be holding on to the ashes until Jacqueline is ready to throw them in. I hope she is smiling when she does so and is thinking about Sarah's smile and her happy life as a daughter, wife and a mother. I hope that I will be there too, feeling positive about Sarah's life and not negative about her death.

The rain was falling hard as I stepped out of the car with my overnight bag. We checked into a hotel that looked like it was built and decorated for romance. I had Sarah's remains in a bag and I was sharing a room with a man who was notorious for snoring like a train. I needed a drink and I knew that Stuart would not object. We walked along the seafront in the rain. The sky was grey like the ashes that I held in my hand. The wind appeared to have no direction as it lifted the waves and the spray into the already misty air. I thought about the non-existent grip on the soles of my shoes and whether they would keep me from following Sarah into the sea. The slippery cobbled walkway was in view as we neared the pub and it was empty. Waves were battering into the side and throwing spray over the top. I was sure it would look and feel less treacherous once I was standing on it.

I bought some cigarettes and ordered a couple of pints from the bar. I thought it was best to scatter the ashes soon and before I drank my second beer. My balance wasn't great at the best of times. I was glad of the rain, because it fitted in perfectly with my mood and the drama of the occasion. Having the whole of the Cobb to myself was perfect for an uninterrupted farewell. I finished my drink and held the green pot in my arms as if it was a baby.

I thought of nothing but Sarah as I made my way out to sea and the furthest point possible by foot. I reached the end and looked down to see rocks. Huge boulders were piled on top of each other above the surface of the sea. I didn't want to throw the ashes onto the protruding rocks.

The Cobb is about 20 feet wide and runs at an angle. I walked to the lowest side and peered over the edge. The tide was going out and there was only sand below. I nervously and cautiously walked towards the highest side. I have never been confident with heights and could feel the vertigo as I got within 10 inches of the edge. I glanced over and saw that the sea was below. I wanted to lie on my stomach and crawl to the edge but it was covered in water. The drizzle continued to drench me as I thought about what I was going to do. I walked up and down the Cobb, looking for a more level place to stand. I laughed out loud when I thought about slinging the whole pot into the sea like a message in a bottle.

Finally, I found a flatter spot, which allowed me to stand closer to the edge than I liked. I stared out to sea and opened the lid. Then I held the pot behind my back like a bowling ball but with both hands and thrust it forward, to propel the ashes as far in front of me as possible. Most of them fell below into the sea, but some got caught in the wind. The wind swirled them round and deposited some onto my shoes and the stones beneath me.

'Goodbye, my darling. I love you and I miss you so very much. Thank you for being in my life and for giving me two wonderful children.'

The rain had eased off and a couple passed behind me as I cried into the wind. Did they have any idea how lucky they were? I didn't when I had walked hand in hand with Sarah in the very same place. This was her chosen resting place and I could feel her spirit with every beat of my heart and the love that I held there for her. She opted out of a burial because she didn't want to be a burden. She told me that I would never move on if there was a grave for me to visit. The last thing she wanted was for me to be feeling guilty if I didn't visit often enough.

I stood in silence as I continued to stare at the sea for the next thirty minutes, to appreciate fully how lucky I was to have been loved by a lady whose body and spirit was no longer visible. Sarah was gone but I would never let her die.

I walked back to the pub to find Stuart, placing the green pot into a bin that stood next to a memorial bench on my way there. It wasn't until I was standing in the pub that I noticed how cold I was. My body was numb and I started to shiver. My mind had been so focused on Sarah that it had ignored the temperature of my body.

We drank our way back to the hotel, stopping off in every pub en route. It was 11.00 p.m. when our hotel was in our sights. I threw the empty cigarette box into the bin outside and followed Stuart to our room. My last thoughts before I slept were about Sarah and her perfect choice of location to be scattered.

My first thoughts when I awoke suddenly at 3.00 a.m. were ones of confusion. I was frightened by the loud noises and I tried to remember where I was. At first I thought it was roadworks outside, but as my eyes adjusted I saw Stuart on his back in the bed next to mine. His chest was rising and falling in harmony with his snoring and I wondered if my sister-in-law ever slept.

I had got through my first year without Sarah. The children were enjoying life and appeared to be coping well with having only one parent. It didn't feel like a year had passed. At times I would have to remind myself that her death was longer than a couple of weeks ago.

I would get together with Mary on most evenings and I was still in love with the idea of being in love. Mainly I focused on her smile, because it told me a different story to the actual reality of our incompatibility in a fast-moving relationship. We took a day trip to London by train with the children to meet Mary's mother and visit the Science Museum. Both of our children were playing with their hand-held gaming devices. A couple of minutes into the hour-and-twenty-minute journey, Mary took hers out of her bag and proceeded to play with it. I asked her if she was going to talk to me and have a conversation.

'Why didn't you bring yours?' she asked, without looking up.

I thought about the many train trips to London with Sarah as my companion. We would talk excitedly and laugh from the first station to the last. I closed my eyes and wished that Sarah was travelling with me. The depression was difficult to fight and keep hidden but not impossible. I would need some time alone soon to release the ever-increasing pain.

I was glad of another family holiday a couple of weeks later. I was taking the children back to Cornwall and their favourite hotel. It was my first holiday with them on my own and while I was apprehensive, I was equally looking forward to giving them some quality time with their dad. Giving them my undivided attention was long overdue and I wanted to create our own happy memories. Packing was still a pain in the proverbial, but I was becoming an expert at ticking off my checklist.

The drive down was uneventful and relaxing owing to moving Samuel into the front seat to avoid the back-seat bickering. Olivia slept for most of the way. We were only a mile away from the hotel after driving for four hours without a break, when Olivia blurted out that she was going to be sick. There was a carrier bag in front of Sam, but I didn't even have time to take my hands off the steering wheel. She held her hand up in front of her face to try to catch it, but it came with such force that it bounced back and covered her face completely. It kept coming and landed both on her lap and on the back of the seat in front. I had only valeted the car a day ago. How it got in her hair I will never know. She looked as if she had taken a shower in sick.

Moments later I pulled into the hotel car park. Instead of rushing through the hotel doors in anticipated excitement, I had to start cleaning up a gallon of sick. Anxiety replaced my new-found calmness as I dragged the cases from the boot to look for fresh clothes. A packet of wipes and a bucket of disinfectant later, I had a clean car and a happy daughter.

Jointly, we unpacked the cases and got dressed into our swimwear. The cool water was wonderful for my intensely hot temperature and the chlorine would vanquish the remaining sick aroma from Olivia's hair and my hands. The stress was getting washed away too, until Samuel cut his foot in the pool. He was swimming away from the side when he caught the top of his heel on the underside of the steps. I got them both out of the water and told them to wait while I fetched a plaster from a member of staff. Then I ushered them into the showers to keep them both warm, when Olivia started crying and said that she had cut her foot as well.

'Don't tell lies,' I shouted.

Then I turned around and looked at her feet. She had stubbed her big toe on the edge of a tile and ripped part of her toenail off. I must surely be the unluckiest parent on the planet for both of my children to end up bleeding in a swimming pool. I fetched some more plasters and got them dressed. I was very tired from the drive and already regretting coming away with them on my own. I wanted to go home. I wanted and needed Sarah. I was crying as we left the changing room and I was desperate to tell everyone why.

The remaining few hours until bedtime were trouble-free and I breathed a huge sigh of relief once they were both asleep. I removed the shoebox from the wardrobe and looked at my new purchase. I was saving them for this moment. As an anniversary gift I had bought a pair of Italian handmade shoes that cost me nearly £300. I wanted to wear them to dinner and hoped that they would improve my sombre mood.

Every night I would eat alone and order a glass of champagne. I would hold the glass up high as I had done before and whisper a few words for Sarah. I thought about the body that had housed Sarah's spirit for thirty-five years, which belonged to the sea and moved with the waves. The sea was calm on this night, but I hoped that she had travelled past here on her journey.

Voices from a nearby table broke my concentration. The restaurant was lively and every table was occupied by a couple enjoying the ambience and the sunset. Somewhere out there specks of dust were shimmering in the sunlight. I looked at my hands closely. The freckles, the lines and the hairs were all part of an individual creation that would eventually follow the same path when the spirit moved on. I had eaten most of my dinner without tasting it and wished that I could order again.

I socialised in the bar after dinner, explaining my situation to all who would listen. I discovered that a lot of the parents had booked their children into the kids' club, which ran between breakfast and lunch. I immediately booked my two in for the week and it completely changed my holiday and my life. After breakfast the following morning I led the children to the club and headed for the spa. Sitting in a warm Jacuzzi that had panoramic views of the sea soothed my body and my aching mind. I was smiling within minutes. I became more and more relaxed as the days passed. Towards the end of the week I was enjoying the bubbles and the silence of the Jacuzzi.

On one of the days laughter filled the room as eight bikini-clad girls came into view and passed in front of me. They were in single file and entered the Jacuzzi one at a time, seating themselves directly opposite. Their shoulders were back and their stomachs were flat. I wondered if girls held their stomachs in like a lot of men do.

'Excuse me, but you are blocking my wonderful view,' I said with a cheeky grin on my face.

They all laughed and I felt like a judge in a beauty contest. I decided to go and cool down in the steam room, so I stood up and held my stomach in until I was out of sight.

By the end of the week I was feeling very refreshed, but it was not without sadness. The week had been about Sarah. I had spoken about her to every person whom I engaged in a conversation. I had also spoken to Mary on several occasions but more importantly, I had enjoyed my time alone to face my grief. I was looking forward to seeing her on Saturday night though.

Sarah's List

The children stayed at my parents' the first weekend back and I spent the evening with Mary. My grief had risen to the surface and I was trying hard to contain it. I managed to keep it under control but I knew that it was coming. I could feel it in every cell, just waiting to be released. Mary sent me a message as I was driving to my parents' house with the children the following day. She wanted to spend Sunday afternoon with me and the children. I informed her that I was spending the afternoon with my parents. I wanted to cry on my mum's shoulder because the tears were ready to come.

I was talking to Mum when my phone rang. It was Mary and she was annoyed because I had refused to meet her. She pointed out that I had been away for a week and how much she wanted to spend some more time with me. Much to the annoyance of my mother, I gave in and met up with Mary. We went to the same country park as before, but I was unable to hide my misery. Briefly during the afternoon I cried on Mary's shoulder. What I didn't tell her was that I was crying for my wife. Instead, I told her it was because of the children. This was partly true, because every time I grieved for Sarah I grieved for the children, too.

Most evenings Mary came to my house. She had a lodger, so she was able to leave the children as they slept. I had got used to her coming over nearly every night and indeed expected it, so she took me by surprise one evening when she said that she wouldn't be able to make it. I asked her why and she told me that she was having a drink with a friend. I asked her whom she was meeting, curious because she had not mentioned it previously. It turned out that she was meeting up with an ex-boyfriend. A man who had ended their relationship ten months previous to her meeting me. He was the only man she had ever loved and he had broken her heart by walking away.

My heart sank and I panicked. I made my feelings known and Mary told me that I had nothing to worry about. She said that it was only for one night and that I had been spoilt by having had her company nearly every evening and so I should feel lucky. In reality I was feeling sick, stressed and angry. Jealousy was the cause and it was a feeling that I had not experienced for nearly twenty years.

I knocked on a friendly neighbour's door and asked for some cigarettes. I had not touched one since the anniversary of Sarah's death, but I was still vulnerable and emotionally unstable owing to my need to grieve. I paced the floor for hours and tried to imagine what Mary was saying and doing. I thought that everything had being going smoothly between us and didn't expect a huge crack to divide us instantaneously.

It was later than midnight when I sent Mary a text asking her why she hadn't called me. My phone rang five minutes later and she told me that she had just got home. She assured me that everything was okay and that I shouldn't worry. She said that she was pleased that I was concerned because it showed that I cared.

The next evening Mary was at my house and I could not hide my annoyance or feelings of mistrust. I confronted her about the spontaneous date with her ex.

'I don't get it,' I said a little too loudly.

'I am scared of getting hurt again and letting somebody into my life. I would never ask you to take the photos of Sarah down, but they have started to bother me. I feel that I am involved with a married man,' she ranted before taking another breath.

This was the first time that I had witnessed her snarling and I wondered if I looked as scary when I got that angry. The bubble had burst and I was supposed to be booking our summer holiday in the morning. America and Tracy were three months away. The following morning I was sitting at my computer with all of the passport details and the only names I had not entered were Mary's and her children's. I thought long and hard before finally submitting my details without hers. Later that afternoon, I told Mary about my decision and she asked me if it was over between us. It was not over but it was the start of the end.

'No! Of course not,' I said, which is what I believed to be the truth at the time.

It was over between us three weeks later. The cracks got wider every day, pushing us further apart. One incident that bothered me was when Mary was brushing her hair in my bedroom in front of the mirror. She had accidentally knocked over a photograph of Sarah and it was lying face down. Mary just said, 'Oh dear,' and refused to pick it up. The grand finale came on the same weekend that I was having dinner with Sarah's family. It was a Saturday night and it was Sarah's grandparents' wedding anniversary and the first major gathering since Sarah had been parted from us. I was apprehensive about going because I knew it was going to be tearful and tough.

Mary had stayed at my house on the eve of my departure, but she was not coming with me to the gathering. The tension and upset was already working its way through my body, but I tried to disguise it. The children woke up ridiculously early and I shouted at them in a tired state of fury before going back to bed. I was shaking as I climbed back into bed – all I could think about was that I would be driving to Kent in a few hours and I was going to be the only man there without a wife. In these situations a person's grief is impossible to avoid. Mary remained quiet and I could tell that she was worried about my outburst.

The flood of tears came as we were all seated in the restaurant awaiting our food. Sarah's absence was as obvious as a missing bride on her wedding day or a cloudless blue sky without a sun. There was not one person at the meal who did not have Sarah on their mind, yet they didn't have to mention her name for this fact to be obvious to us all.

I was drinking heavily and I was texting between sips. I wanted Mary to take away my pain and to make me feel better. I wanted her to say something loving to put a smile on my face, but it did not arrive. Instead, she told me to enjoy the party and stop texting her so much. My dream of recreating the past did not look as if it would become a reality. I desperately wanted to feel as loved as I had been for so many years in a secure relationship. The dream was just a dream but the grief was real. It was coming as the dream faded away.

I said goodbye to Sarah's family and drove home on Sunday afternoon. I had a babysitter booked because I was having dinner with Mary at 8.00 p.m. I really wanted to know how she felt about me. She was still very much a closed book and I was desperate to look inside.

Mary was driving and there was silence between us for most of the journey to the hotel where we were having dinner. I was thinking hard about the words that I was about to utter. My palms were sweaty and my body was cold. Mary parked the car and unbuckled her seat belt. Then I told her that I had something that I wanted to say.

'I am falling in love with you,' I said.

I was shaking and the words came out nervously. I was aware that I was trying to get a reaction from her to find out what was going on inside her tough exterior.

'I could really do without this,' she sighed.

She then explained in an angry tone that it wasn't the most romantic place to say what I had said. She continued to lecture me on my inappropriate body language during my confession and asked if we could leave it there and go and eat.

A very uncomfortable evening ensued. I felt somewhere between embarrassed and irate. Even more so after trying to broach the subject again after dinner and being shot down in flames.

Travelling home along the empty roads at the end of the evening brought about a lighter mood with the required amount of small talk to get me to my front door.

I was feeling miserable all day Monday, so I contacted Mary and invited her over for the evening. She had arranged to go to the gym and for a drink afterwards with one of the girls. I told her that it was important and I really wanted to see her. I received a text message telling me that she would call me on her way home from the pub.

The phone rang later that evening, but I was in too much of a bad mood to answer it. Ignoring my grief had allowed it to build up and it was now ready to crash down and smother me. My relationship with Mary was falling apart around me and the only option left was to end it. I impatiently did it by text on Tuesday morning. My phone rang moments later and it was Mary. She asked why I felt the need to throw my dummy out of the pram and whether or not she could come to my house that evening for a chat.

Waiting for Mary to arrive was like waiting to see a headmaster or a manager after doing something that required a fitting punishment. I was feeling nervous and I could feel my heart pounding against my chest. My lungs were not working in the calm and regular manner that they were used to. This was hardly surprising though, having subjected them to the toxins of a cigarette or two.

I opened the door to let Mary in and she walked straight past me and into my living room. Her face of thunder shook me as I followed her into the room. The mood was dark and the next lightning strike was imminent yet hopefully avoidable. I spoke first and explained why I was annoyed about her reaction in the car after my confession of love, albeit a strange and clumsy one. I continued to complain about being ignored while she was at the gym and for an hour afterwards when I had sent five messages requesting to see her.

Before I could utter another word, Mary turned on me. Witnessing her contorted and snarling face as she shouted at me was not the most pleasurable of experiences.

'My phone was in the locker,' she screamed, using her hands to emphasise her annoyance and disdain.

Her hands were in front of her and looked like they were performing an impressive karate chop on either side of her as she moved them up and down with her words. She realised that she had interrupted me with her outburst and muttered an apology. I tried to choose my next words carefully and to say them without stuttering or hyperventilating.

'I am not ready for a relationship and I thought that I could date and grieve at the same time, but it is not possible.' I took a deep breath and continued, 'I am a mess and I need to face my grief. I only have to look at my children and it breaks my heart that they are facing a life without their mum,' I sobbed.

I was expecting Mary to comfort me in some way. Maybe take my hand or put her arm around me, but she did neither.

'Everybody has their own shit to deal with and you just have to get on with your life,' she bellowed without any compassion whatsoever.

Pausing for a moment to let the shock waves settle, I then stood up and turned on her. My shock and disappointment had switched to anger and was more than ready to be released.

'Get the hell out of my house!' I yelled, or words to that effect.

The full force of my anger pushed its way past my lips and filled the room. If anger could really wake the dead, then I would have been smiling. Mary practically ran out of my front room and flinched as she passed me.

'It's not nice to be shouted at, is it,' I asked rhetorically.

The last words before we parted were from Mary.

'You don't deserve to have any friends,' she said as she walked to her car.

My heart rate had returned to normal and my breath was controlled and easy. I walked up the stairs to bed and fell into a deep sleep.

I had made the mistake of wanting Mary to be like Sarah and she obviously fell short with every comparison. Originally I thought that Mary had the same thoughtful and selfless qualities that came naturally to Sarah for many years. It was without doubt that Sarah had set the bar high as far as a suitable replacement was concerned. What I had failed to remember was her warning me about not trying to find another exactly the same. Obviously, it is important if you are looking for love to find someone who makes you happy and has the endearing qualities that you are looking for. But I had made the biggest mistake by having expectations that were impossible for any girl to fulfil. I wanted to get back what I had lost and for my life to return to normal. I realised that the list that I had compiled with Sarah in the car regarding meeting someone else was all about Sarah. Sarah was the selfless, caring and thoughtful, non-smoking girl who didn't have tattoos or a dog on my wish list. Suddenly and shamefully I realised that one of the reasons I had discounted Carla as a replacement back in February was because she was the same age as me. She didn't tick the box that required a girl to be at least five years younger.

I had bumped into Carla two weeks prior to my fallout with Mary at a children's party that Olivia was invited to. Considering my ill treatment of her, she was very pleasant and friendly towards me. I had previously told her that I knew that she wasn't the girl who would walk my path, so I would have completely understood if she had turned her head away and snubbed me. Instead, she asked me how my relationship with Mary was going and I told her that all was well. How could things have gone so wrong in just two weeks? Carla was not the only person I had told about my relationship of the year. I think a lot of people were happy for me and were pleased that they didn't have to worry about me any more. Taking the wrong path and at the wrong time had led me to a place where I didn't want to be. I had pinned all of my hopes on one girl and I was bitterly disappointed that it was over.

Nearly a week had passed since showing Mary the door. My phone would beep but her name would not appear. She was, however, using

Facebook as a cryptic diary. Bitter messages would appear daily, attacking the male species. One message simply said: is no man brave enough to take me on? I became obsessed and annoyed by her messages. I would switch my computer on and check for them about ten times a day.

On Saturday night and after overindulging on alcohol, I gave in and sent Mary a message, admitting that I may have been insensitive and guilty for not understanding her feelings, and asking if we could remain friends. I got a message back and it was direct. First, Mary pointed out that she had a real problem with how I spoke to her and wanted a full apology. The last part of the message surprised me, in that she was unsure if we could be friends because of the risk involved. She was concerned about my anger and the safety of her children and herself based on my recent outbursts. I told her that I had nothing to apologise for except for the four-letter word. Swearing at a girl was something that I had never done before.

My obsession continued and I made an appointment to see Victor. Shamefully, during my obsessiveness I sent Mary a text asking her for sex. I said that the anger between us could make for a very uplifting experience. For some reason, I did not get a reply!

I was not alone with my obsessive behaviour. Olivia's bra obsession was growing. It was impossible to walk through a department store without a visit to the bra section. This was her sweet shop equivalent. She was overwhelmed by the vast array of colours and styles. Olivia would pull me towards them with the same gusto as a dog that drags its owner towards a willing mate. She would squeeze every bra cup and beg me to buy her one. I guess this was better than her grabbing the bras that were attached to the girls at her nursery. She had been grabbing their breasts for weeks.

I took advice on the matter and was given a few ideas, but I didn't like any of them. One suggestion was to buy Olivia a bra as a gift and another was to buy her a childlike bra that she could wear. What kind of person would manufacture any kind of bra for a child to wear before they reached puberty? Maybe I could get a discount if they threw in a pair of high heels and a thong! Olivia was a young child and I wanted her to behave like one. She kept asking me to get her a bra as often as Sam asked me for chocolate. I knew what to do about it after she had asked me if I had any bras of her mum's.

Her obsession was fuelled by the fact that she was in a male environment. I was distraught when I realised that her obsession only existed because Sarah had died. Her curiosity would have naturally been satisfied if her mum was here to wear one every day. I had given most of Sarah's clothes to a charity shop and had discarded all of her bras, so I lied to her about still having some of her mum's bras and told her that I had put them in the loft for safe keeping. A big smile stretched across Olivia's face and she asked if I could get them straight away. It was getting late in the day and I told her I would retrieve them in the morning while she was at nursery.

Instead of climbing up into the loft to get an imaginary bra, I went to Primark to buy a couple of cheap ones. I spent ages choosing two in Sarah's size, in her preferred colour and style. The bras were only in the house for two weeks before Olivia got bored of running around in them. My plan had worked, but not completely.

Stuart pointed out to me that when Olivia grew older and wiser she would think that her dad was a complete cheapskate for buying her mum bras from the cheapest shop in town. I would have to cut the labels out and replace them with designer ones. I needed to go up into the loft two weeks later and as luck would have it, I found a bag of Sarah's clothes up there. She had put them up there without telling me. The bag was full of low-cut tops and bras that she had worn prior to her mastectomy.

I wished that my obsessions could have been dealt with as easily as my daughter's. Maybe I wouldn't have upset as many people in the process, either. I sent Carla a message telling her that my relationship had fallen apart and that she must be pleased because what goes around comes around. She told me that she was very sorry to hear my news and that she wasn't the type of person to gloat.

I hadn't seen Victor since before Christmas and needed to bring him up to date regarding the past five months. First, I told him that I had not listened to his warning about staying away from Mary. He already knew that I would make this mistake.

'I thought that she was perfect for me and I am so disappointed,' I said as I stared at the hands on his knees.

I didn't quite get an "I told you so" reply.

'You will never find a substitute wife or a replacement, so stop looking for one. You are crippling yourself with your unnecessary obsessive behaviour and you need to start looking for a healthy distraction. Get a job and fill your time that way.'

The sofa seemed to increase in size as I got smaller and shrank with shame. In my defence, I accused Victor of not understanding my situation. I asked how he would have fared if his wife had died while his children were young and whether or not he would have coped and dealt with the monumental changes.

He got angry with me and told me that I knew nothing about him. Then he relayed a story to me from his past, in which he and his wife had moved to a different country and they had to do so whilst working and looking after two children.

I didn't see how this compared and I wondered if he really understood my situation at all. He didn't look like the kind of man who would bake a cake or go shopping for bras. Most of the mums I knew practically ran a house single-handedly. They made all the important decisions concerning their children and they came home from work to a tidy house which they had tidied themselves. I not only wanted Victor to recognise that I was doing the work of two people, but I wanted everyone to realise it, too. I left his house for the last time but was feeling more confident about my future.

Some six weeks had gone by since that fateful night with Mary, when we were jointly invited to attend a get-together with our support group friends for a Sunday lunch; the children were invited, too. There happened to be two pubs of the same name and we all managed to arrive at the correct one except for Mary. Nearly everyone had ordered their food by the time my phone rang. It was Mary asking me where everybody had got to. I explained that there were two pubs within a couple of miles of each other with the same name and that we were all at the other one. She asked me if we were all playing a joke on her. I was surprised that she could think that a group of friends, all brought together through bereavement, could play such a joke on her and her children. She asked if there was any point her coming along now because we would have all eaten by the time she arrived. I agreed to wait for five minutes and order our food together, so that she wouldn't have to eat alone.

Mary arrived at the same time as the food and seated herself next to me. We chatted for most of the afternoon and Mary hardly engaged in conversation with anyone else. She was complaining of a migraine for most of it and was clutching her head when it was time to leave. Her children asked innocently if they could come back to my house and play. Mary looked anxious and didn't know what to say. Sam and Olivia asked me if the children could come back with us, too.

In the end I invited them back for dinner and told Mary that she could rest on the sofa while I fed them all. Whilst the children ate I asked Mary if I could talk to her. Her eyes were closed and she told me that it wasn't a good time. I ignored her and started with an apology. I apologised for dealing with the whole situation so badly. I especially wanted to apologise for my language, because swearing didn't quite sit right with me. I had spoken to a lot of friends about the evening in question and I always got embarrassed when I repeated what I had said in anger.

Mary opened her eyes briefly and thanked me through a half-smiling mouth. The children played for an hour after eating while Mary slept. Comparing Sarah and Mary should have been avoided but I couldn't help myself. Sarah had got herself out of bed on the most difficult of days to help me with the chores, even in her final weeks. Mary got up from the sofa and left without even helping me to clear up, saying that she needed to go home to bed. She also left without saying thank you.

I was still obsessing and couldn't understand how Mary could have given up on us so easily and without a fight. I was also suspicious as to whether or not she had started to date her ex-boyfriend again. I wanted some answers, so I asked her if we could meet up for a drink later in the week.

I had a drink waiting for her when she arrived and she joined me on the sofa. I didn't purposely choose a sofa so that she would sit next to me; it was the only seat left in a surprising busy bar for a Tuesday night. I began our conversation by asking her if she was pleased that I had apologised for my behaviour.

'If you could call it an apology, considering I had a migraine and my eyes were closed. Feel free to apologise again properly.'

Calmly and politely I said that I was sorry once more. Mary ended up telling me that she wanted it to work out between us, but there was no point crying over spilt milk. She was a bit vague as to whether or not she was trying again with a man from her past. We hugged in the car park and said goodbye. I was secretly saying goodbye to our relationship and our friendship though, because Mary had very little to offer me on both counts.

Cathy, a friend of Sarah's, had recently told me that friendship is a bit like a bank. You have to put something in to be able to take something out. I had been using up my friendly funds since Sarah had passed away but at some point in my life, I must have put enough in to make it possible. Speaking of friendship funds, Mary was overdrawn as far as I was concerned; she would only get further into the proverbial debt.

Carla sent me a message one day asking me how I was bearing up and before long we were messaging each other on a daily basis. I asked her if she would like to join me for a coffee but she refused my offer. She was reluctant to let me back into her life after the way I had treated her back in February. Though she indicated that there might be a chance of a coffee date at some point in the near future. Most of our text conversations were about Mary. I had confessed to wanting to find a suitable replacement for Sarah and how I had hoped that Mary would be a worthy one. I also told Carla about my list which I had compiled with Sarah and the reason that I had discounted Carla as a result of her age.

Surprisingly, this didn't go down too well, especially as she was younger than me, but I needed to explain further about my recent discovery. I had only been looking for Sarah because she was the only one who could match the list and bring about a happy ending. She was my Cinderella but instead of a shoe to fit, I had a list. Sarah had warned me not to try to find a carbon copy of her or I would end up alone. While it had caused me a lot of emotional pain getting involved with Mary, I had learned a valuable lesson from it. A relationship can only be successful if it develops naturally and should not be a replacement for a lost love. Neither should it be affected by comparisons. In desperation I had made all of these mistakes.

Up until this point I had not considered the children as much as I should have. Cathy had warned me and told me to be careful about female involvement. The children had been used to being part of a loving family unit and I didn't want to damage this by having a long line of angry girls from failed relationships behind me. I wanted my children to grow up and have faith in relationships and know the importance of longevity.

After having confessed to all of my mistakes, Carla agreed to meet me for a coffee three weeks later. We had a very relaxing afternoon and it was lovely to see her again. I was pleased to have her as a friend. I felt very comfortable talking to Carla about Sarah and she was a very good listener. We talked about our time together at the beginning of the year and about my selfish mistreatment of her concerning Mary. There were no secrets, lies or false expectations between us.

We would meet for coffee regularly and chat for hours. I enjoyed making her laugh and being able to laugh again myself, which happened every time we got together. Coffee afternoons progressed to dinners in the evening in restaurants and then at each other's houses. The hugs between us would get longer as the weeks and months passed.

Goodbye Fantasy, Hello Reality

It had been sixteen months since my last conversation with Sarah. She was always at the forefront of my mind but my tears no longer came daily. I still cried most weeks though, as my grief built up over a period of days. Spontaneous sobbing also still occurred, but this was not always brought about by an obvious trigger. The children were also crying a lot less. Obviously they cried, but it was for the same reasons as other children most of the time. Olivia cried more than Sam and was having more tantrums. She was starting school in September and I was desperate for her to start. I was aware of the sadness that the day would bring because of Sarah's last wish about prolonging her life to be present. But at the same time I wanted Olivia to start school because she was not getting enough stimulation from nursery. I remembered that school had improved Samuel's behaviour after he had grown out of nursery and he was now top of his class in nearly all subjects. This was a huge achievement considering the grief he was dealing with concerning his mum. Most of Samuel's tears came at bedtime or first thing after waking up.

He was crying one morning after having a dream about his mum. They were at the funfair together and he was sobbing as he realised it was only a dream and how he desperately wanted it to be real. I understood completely, because I had experienced the same disappointment. I later learned something from one of our bedtime chats about Sarah, when Sam asked me why I didn't tell him that his mum was going to die. He said that we should have told him so he could have enjoyed their time together more and appreciated it. I asked him if he really believed that he could have enjoyed himself if he knew that his mummy was dying. He understood immediately that we had made the right decision and why we had felt the need to hide the truth.

I thought about our first holiday without Sarah in Cornwall. It was supposed to be our last holiday together as a family and I had been so disappointed that it didn't turn out the way I had wanted it to. I had spent the whole week lost in the darkest part of my mind feeling angry that Sarah could not have been spared a little more time. I now realised that we would not have enjoyed the holiday if Sarah had been there. It was selfish of me to want one last week away. I thought about Sarah and how upsetting it would have been for her to see her children playing. She would have been really poorly too and unable to join in with them, which would have frustrated her further. I would have been a wreck and wondering if she was going to make it through each night. I was now pleased that Sarah had been spared this extra suffering just so I could have had her in my life a while longer and it had taken me until now to realise.

Crying in front of the children had been unavoidable and necessary up to a point. I mostly cried in private now and as the children slept. One evening and just before bedtime, Olivia heard me crying in my room. She came into my bedroom clutching a photograph of Sarah. Then she put her arms around me before showing me the photograph.

'Have a look at this picture, Daddy; it will make you feel better,' she said as she held it up to my tear-stained face.

I held her tight against me and I told her how much I loved her. We sat in silence staring at the happy, smiling face of her mum wearing a wedding dress.

Carla encouraged me to put photographs of Sarah on the wall at the side of my staircase so that the children could look at them as they walked up and down the stairs. She also helped me to improve the house. We built furniture together and she would bring her overalls to help me decorate. We would listen to music as we painted and felt comfortable in each other's presence as we worked. As I passed nearby I would squeeze Carla's hand or stroke her back and smile at her. I was enjoying taking this relationship slowly. We had seen a lot of each other over the past three months and I had regained her trust with my honesty and genuine remorse for my recent behaviour.

Cuddling up for hours was now commonplace and I always looked forward to our time together. The kiss between us back in January had been physical and enjoyable, but it had been initiated too quickly. Now, I found myself looking into her eyes as we held each other on my sofa. I noticed how beautiful they were and how they reminded me of a lagoon in paradise. I didn't want to dive in right away. I wanted to hold back and soak up the moment. We moved in slowly for a kiss and I drowned myself in the blue of her eyes before they closed and our lips met. The kiss had feeling and it expressed far more than spoken words ever could. I was feeling relaxed and happy, but I was feeling slightly guilty, too. I think it would have been unnatural not to feel guilt of some kind.

Occasionally I would be cold towards Carla after spending an evening with her. The happiness I had experienced during the evening would turn into sadness and left me feeling depressed for a couple of days afterwards. This was because of the emotions involved and my memory reminding me that I had experienced the feelings before. My present happiness would not let me forget the joys of the past and my grief would return in a different form.

I still spoke to Carla daily, but I would distance myself emotionally until the guilt and the sadness passed. Carla was a very understanding lady, but would understandably question my mood and confront me about my feelings. I didn't understand my feelings too well and would be very vague with my answers. Sometimes I would say unnecessary and hurtful things.

During a conversation about me being stand-offish, I happened to mention a hypothetical scenario. I said that if Sarah was to come back then I would not hesitate to return to my old life, even if it was ten years from now. Carla was very upset by this comment, because it devalued our friendship and our relationship. I explained that I would have no choice in the matter because of the children and their need for a normal family life. Carla said that I should have kept these thoughts to myself, because they were insensitive and unkind.

Sometimes I used my grief as an excuse for irrational behaviour and again Carla would tell me that I was being unreasonable. I liked the fact that she confronted me and continued to be open and honest about her feelings and concerns. I liked her strength, her independence and her thoughtfulness, but it was because of her communication skills that we were able to move forward. Communication was the key to unlocking the hidden problems that occurred without warning but which were not uncommon in dating a widower. We kissed and held each other more often and the guilt became less as our relationship progressed.

I had been used to having a wife and a family life that I considered normal. I had grown up believing that it could never be any different. Now I had to get used to a new kind of normal and I thought about what Victor had told me. It was imperative that I approach a new relationship with caution and to expect difficulties. He'd said that without doubt, I would have to face and overcome obstacles along the way. I had already faced a few and got past them. I could not wave a magic wand and create a new mum for the children. Neither could I recreate the past. But the future would unfold naturally as the three of us grew older and emotionally stronger with every passing day.

Samuel was experiencing guilty feelings of his own. I had come to realise that he would usually get upset after a day of fun and wish that his mummy had been part of it. I would hug him as he cried and he would want some answers about his mum's death.

We met up with Carla and her two boys at the local swimming pool one day and had an hour of fun, which involved chasing and splashing each other. The moment we entered the changing room, Sam started crying. I asked him what was wrong and he finally managed to take a breath in between sobs and speak. 'Mummy,' he said, knowing that I would understand what he meant without needing to add any more words. I knew that he was feeling guilty for having fun with a lady who wasn't his mum and I told him that it was okay to have fun and that it would be his mum's wish for him to do so. In the car on the way home Sam got upset again and said something that had obviously been bothering him for some time.

First, he accused me of forcing him to like people and then he followed this up by telling me that he would always love his mummy a million times more than he ever would anybody else. I explained that it was important for me to have friends and that I would never force him to like someone. I said that it was impossible for anyone to be made to like someone. 'Every person has the right to make up their own mind as far as friends are concerned,' I said.

I was thinking about friendships as I drove home and discovered that we all have to earn the right to be part of each other's lives. There was a few moments' silence before Sam spoke.

'I do like Carla,' he said.

Another five minutes passed before Sam mentioned something else that was really bothering him. Regularly, at bedtime, he would tell me

214

that he was scared and this also happened when he stayed at my parents' house. This was a complete change of direction from our conversation about liking people and feeling guilty about it.

'You and Grandad always tell me that I have nothing to be scared about but you are wrong. I am scared about Mummy. I am scared that she is still ill and suffering in Heaven,' he said.

I had no idea that this was a concern of his and for how long he had kept it quiet. I saw him in my rear-view mirror and his face was full of tears. I wanted to hold him in my arms and never let go. I wanted to know why these two wonderful children sitting behind me had to spend the rest of their lives without their mum. I would never know the answer to that, but I knew that I would always love them and be there for them no matter what occurred.

Love is hard to explain. I had lost so much love in my life as a result of Sarah's death, but there was also so much love that remained and that was to be gained in the future. My love for our children would grow every day and it would always be with me. Without my children, my love would have died, too. Without my children there would have been no colour in my world. I would be breathing but I would be lifeless. I would be suffering in darkness on Earth as Sarah's spirit shone brightly in Heaven.

Samuel listened very carefully as I explained to him about his mum's body, that was separate from her spirit. I don't know how much he understood about a body being destroyed by cancer and not being able to house the spirit any longer. His head was hurting from the crying but he was happy with what I had told him. I really hoped that it would be one less thing for him to worry about now. We were moving forward and we were evolving. Things could only get better.

Olivia was very excited about her first day at school and the day soon came round. I wanted to keep smiling through the obvious emotional upset concerning Sarah's final wish. Olivia looked so beautiful and grown up in her uniform as she walked out of our front door with Sam. I made them pose for photographs before getting into the car. I was happy, sad and relieved at the same time that I had a whole day of peace and quiet after a long six-week break.

We arrived at school and walked into an empty playground. The school was open but not for Reception children. I had got the day wrong and had turned up a day early.

Tuesday morning I tried again and walked into a busy playground. As Olivia joined the line of children to walk into her class, I fought back the tears. I imagined Sarah standing where I now stood showing her proudest smile as she witnessed the simple pleasure of her daughter starting school. Olivia smiled all the way into class and I cried all the way back to my car.

There were tears of happiness mixed in with the sadness because Sarah's smile had seemed very real in the playground. I felt certain that she was there in spirit. During her last conversation with Cathy, Sarah had asked a favour of her. 'Please don't let me die, Cathy,' she said. Sarah wanted Cathy to keep her memory alive for the children and not be forgotten as the years passed. She need not have worried, for she is always here and will always be part of them. Moments after giving birth to her children, Sarah's memory had become immortally ingrained in their minds, regardless of her physical mortality.

Olivia's happy smile as she walked into class turned out to be short-lived. It lasted for one day only. A day at school was all it took for her to realise that she wanted to return to nursery. She didn't get the same level of attention at school and she was already missing the hugs from the nursery girls. She was used to being spoilt and having her hair tied up or her face painted. Now, she was a regular girl in a class of thirty children wanting to be noticed and also craving the attention she had been used to. Every morning she would cry and cling to me as I dropped her off. Olivia was strong-willed like her mother and it became a battle of wills between us. She was hoping that if she cried loud enough and for long enough then she might not have to go to school.

I kept to the same format, which was to tell her firmly that she had no choice in the matter. I would then walk away as she screamed my name. I was very depressed by the time I reached the school gates and wondered if she had stopped crying or was merely out of my hearing range.

Before long Olivia's teacher approached me and asked for my permission to put Olivia into the school nurture group. This meant that Olivia would be taken out of class for an hour every day and be given the special attention that she was craving. I didn't like the fact that she had been singled out because of her bereaved status and I was extremely angry when her teacher labelled her as "needy". I wondered whether some children were called thick for finding the work challenging.

I confronted the class teacher after a good night's sleep and voiced my concerns about Olivia being treated differently and how she would take advantage of any special treatment because she was a very shrewd individual. I also complained about Olivia being classed as needy. Olivia's teacher annoyed me more by telling me that next time, she would look for an equivalent meaning in a dictionary. I was told that the main reason for Olivia going to the nurture group was because she kept putting her hand up and interrupting a lot. All of her teachers were aware that Sarah had died and I wondered whether they were looking for obvious problems that they felt must be apparent after the loss of a parent.

Not long after, there had been a cancellation at the hospital and I was given a week's notice for Samuel's operation. The operation involved cutting through his tight calf muscles to enable his heels to drop for him to be able to walk flat-footed. Both of his legs would be in plaster for six weeks, which worried me and I wasn't sure if I could let him go through with it. He had only been back at school for two weeks, but I was told that he would only be off for a few days. I had the weekend to make a decision and on Friday morning, before the weekend had even started, I had convinced myself that I would cancel the operation. I would inform the hospital on Monday morning.

Samuel's PE teacher approached me as I arrived at school on Friday afternoon. He asked me if I had noticed that Sam walked on his toes. I told him about the planned operation and my plans to cancel. Samuel's teacher joined us and our conversation. They both told me that they would not hesitate if it was their child. Bullying was brought to my attention and the possibility of name-calling as Sam got older and attended senior school. I had two days to make my mind up.

My head hurt for the whole weekend as I tried to decide. I could feel Sarah's anger every time I thought about cancelling. Sarah would have wanted Sam to have the operation and I had to do what was best for Sam and not what was easiest for me. I did not make a phone call on Monday and the operation went ahead on Thursday.

Carla had offered to collect Olivia from school and to drop her off at my parents' house. She had also offered to support me at the hospital while Sam was having surgery. I was feeling nervous and my throat was dry as I entered the hospital where Sarah had died. We were only staying for one night and Sam was showing no signs of nervousness. He was very happy and excited about us having beds next to each other.

A nurse came and spoke to us about the operation and told us about the straightforwardness of it, at the same time assuring us that there was nothing for us to worry about. She then asked if Sam wanted to see the needle that they were going to use. Sam had inherited his mum's needle phobia and I wanted to stick the needle in the nurse's backside. He winced when he saw it and cried when the nurse gave him a dramatic demonstration of what was to come. I promised Sam that the cream on the back of his hand would work this time and why it hadn't on his last stay in hospital for appendicitis. I told him it that it had not been left on his hand long enough. I was worried about him being put to sleep by a general anaesthetic and I was also anxious about him being cut on both legs and being put in plaster.

I walked down to theatre with him and was given a gown. I could only go as far as the recovery room. As soon as we arrived, Sam started shouting about not wanting an injection. The nurse held his arm tight before producing a needle. Sam was strong and was trying to resist. I spoke in my calmest voice and told him that the nurse had already given him the injection and he could now relax. He stopped thrashing about and smiled at me and the nurse then inserted the needle, which thankfully he was unaware of. I watched him drift into unconsciousness to the count of five.

I was traumatised as I thought about Sarah's eyes closing for the last time just a little way down the corridor from where I stood. A nurse was waiting on the other side of the door to collect my gown, and I fell into her arms and cried.

'My wife has died and I am doing all this on my own,' I said.

She hugged me and led me to the main door that opened up onto the corridor that I was familiar with. The same long corridor that I had walked many times with Sarah as we made our way to the chemotherapy ward and where she had walked on her final journey here on Earth.

I was grateful that I was not alone and indebted to Carla for waiting for me as I exited theatre. She hugged me and comforted me before taking me for breakfast in the hospital restaurant. Yummy! Actually, it could have tasted delicious, but I ate it without tasting. I looked up and Carla was still sprinkling pepper onto hers. I had wolfed mine down inside of a minute. Maybe the tightness I was feeling in my chest was more to do with my style of eating rather than the stress of single parenting. I would have to set a good example for the children and not place my lips a sausage length away from the plate. I would make an effort to eat slowly and not to shovel the food down in the same fashion as a rabbit scooping up dirt.

Having Carla to talk to enabled the hour to pass quickly and after breakfast we made our way back to Sam's ward and waited. It was approaching lunchtime and so I asked the nurse if Sam would be able to eat when he returned. She warned me to go easy, because apparently a lot of children are sick if they eat too quickly after an operation. Samuel arrived moments later and he was smiling.

'I am hungry, Dad. Can I have a biscuit?' he said without even muttering a hello first.

I gave him a cheese sandwich first, which was gone before I'd had the chance to warn him about feeling sick. He looked healthy and told me he was feeling good. He then sent me downstairs to the fast-food burger restaurant. Carla joined me and I said goodbye to her and thanked her for being so caring and thoughtful as we walked to the main entrance.

In twenty minutes Sam had consumed a burger with chips, two biscuits, two cream crackers with cheese and a giant mouse-mat sized chocolate bar, which he then washed down with a bottle of Fanta. Sarah would have been appalled by all of the grease and sugar and the amount of calories. But she would have been proud of him too, and pleased that there would be no need to scream the words, 'Flat feet!' any more.

We were only staying in hospital for the night and I enjoyed our conversations as I lay on a bed next to his. It was lovely to see him so happy and relieved that the operation was over. We chatted until about ten o'clock, when his eyes finally closed for the night.

I sent Carla a message asking if Olivia had been good for her while she was dropping her at my mum's. Olivia always seems to be well behaved in the presence of others and saved all of her naughtiness for me. She knew exactly how to wind me up and drive me to distraction. It wouldn't surprise me if I found out that she had been working out new ways to annoy me. I visualised her with a torch at bedtime, drawing up plans in her princess pad and coming up with spectacular ways to get me back for shouting so much.

It was no surprise to learn from Carla that Olivia had been an angel for the whole time and extremely happy. I wasn't looking forward to Monday morning and dropping her off at school, though. She was obviously saving up all of her stubbornness and premature teenage tantrums for then.

Carla was on her way home from a night out and was driving by the hospital so she called in. I met her downstairs in the cafe and we chatted until about midnight. I held her hand and thanked her for being part of my life.

First thing Friday morning and before breakfast, Samuel was sent down to the plaster suite to get his legs set in blue plaster. He was given his first lesson in how to walk with crutches after twenty minutes and after another twenty minutes he was discharged. He took advantage of a free breakfast before we left and then we drove home.

It was comforting to be told that he should be able to walk on his plaster in the morning and would only miss a day of school. He ended up staying at home for a week though, because he didn't want to put any weight on his feet. I took him back to the hospital to the physio specialist and she had him walking across the room within five minutes. These first steps gave Sam the confidence where I had failed. Thankfully, he was walking without a frame by the end of the week and I was relieved that I didn't have to carry him around any more as my sciatica had returned as a result of lifting him in and out of the car.

His walking had improved so much that his plaster came off two weeks early. I hadn't expected it to be removed as we had only attended a routine check-up. I was ill prepared and hadn't packed any shoes for him. His plaster was off and he was now barefoot, so I had to carry him once more. The car was on the top floor of a multi-storey car park about 200 yards away. My sciatica was forgotten about by the time we reached the car, as I was sweating and wheezing from an unwelcome return of asthma, which required more attention than the pain in my butt. I didn't care though, because we had faced and overcome another obstacle and I was proud of Sam once more.

He was walking properly by the end of the month and I could now relax as our second Christmas approached.

Moving On

I was looking forward to Christmas this year and the need to overcompensate had left me. Carla was a big part of my life now and we saw quite a lot of each other and chatted daily.

Christmas would have been lovely had it not been for the criticisms and frank opinions of a male relative, George, and his wife, Selena, who were staying for a few days. All of the presents were wrapped, courtesy of Tracy, and I had enough food for the winter in the unlikely event of being snowed in. An inch of snow covered the ground and Sarah's star shone brightly in the window. A photograph would have turned the view into the perfect Christmas card if the lens managed to avoid the giant inflatable snowman from a neighbouring house.

The inside of my house was not as tranquil. The air was heavy and the children were picking up on the tension that was brought about by our guests. My guests had only been with us for a day and I wanted them to leave. They saw the children about once a year and therefore could only guess or imagine what hardship we had faced since Sarah's death. Everything they had to say I perceived to be negative. I was proud of myself for getting this far and for maintaining a stable home for my children. I wasn't so proud about my angry outbursts, but the good definitely outweighed the bad. I did so many fun things with the children and they were very happy, which in turn made me smile.

Over dinner one night Selena suggested that I buy a book about raising girls; she even offered to send me one. She told me that Olivia would be brilliant in years to come, but only with the correct guidance. I am still unaware if she was joking when she suggested taking Olivia away with her and raising her with her husband. I complained about their negative comments and proceeded to justify my fathering skills.

They told me that they were only trying to help and that their comments were actually positive.

'You are being defensive and therefore failing to see that our comments are positive and helpful,' said George with sincerity.

I still couldn't see this and I was feeling depressed. I wanted them to tell me that I was doing a good job, because I honestly believed that I was. These two were the only ones who made me feel differently.

The next evening during dinner, the mood was greatly relaxed. We had both spoken our minds during last night's meal and the air seemed to thin a little. It didn't last long! Breaking the silence, Selena spoke first and her words attacked me like a virus.

'When are you going to get Olivia tested? You must be aware that she has a 50 per cent chance of carrying the same gene as her mum and is therefore at risk from the same cancer.'

The more she spoke, the further the virus travelled, until it reached every cell. I was frozen in my seat. I had felt this way once before and that was when I was being told that Sarah was terminally ill and going to die. It was five days until Christmas Day and my spirit was crushed. Olivia was five and I wanted to forget about the possibility of her having cancer until she reached a mature age, when the doctors felt it would be necessary to check her over. I also believed that in fifteen years from now, medicine would have advanced greatly and the chances of survival would be much more optimistic. Until such a time when it became imperative to undergo checks, I was happy to put it to the back of my mind. I wanted Olivia to have a childhood first and I wanted to be there, enjoying it with her. I didn't think it was necessary to find out about her genes at this stage, because it would worry me so much that I might fall apart. I had been through so much with her mum and her illness and I wasn't ready to face the possibility of going through the same hell with our daughter.

'Why would you tell me that and suggest that to me?' I said.

Images of my daughter undergoing cancer treatment and a funeral flashed before my eyes.

'I am telling you because it would be ignorant of you not to get her checked out and if she has the same gene you can prepare her for a double mastectomy when she is older,' she said calmly.

I nearly fell off of my chair. She was talking about my precious 5-year-old daughter as if she was a 30-year-old stranger. I managed to stand up and I told them that I was going to bed. I thanked them for coming to stay and for depressing me before I left the room.

I lay awake for most of the night traumatised about our future and depressed about my past and all of the changes that had taken place since Sarah had found a lump in her breast. I couldn't believe how matter-of-fact someone could be about such a serious issue. I had suffered so much emotional pain and I didn't think I would have the strength to deal with any more. I wasn't burying my head in the sand concerning her chances of getting cancer. I had already been told that she has a minimal chance, which was less than 10 per cent. I could live with this fact, because I believe it is a similar amount of risk that we all face where cancer is concerned.

I was wide awake in bed with a clear picture of Olivia in my mind. I had lingered longer tonight as I kissed her goodnight. I had watched her as she slept and I prayed that she would never be taken from me. Olivia was beautiful in every way. From her very dark eyelashes that highlight her naturally curly blonde hair to her radiant smile that is a carbon copy of her mother's. She even tilts her head to one side in the same fashion when posing for photographs. She was certainly hard work at times, but her personality was one to be in awe of. I knew that Olivia would do well in life because she was strong and defiant. She always knew exactly what she wanted and how to go about getting it.

Over time I got a little fed up with a lot of unwelcome comments from people who didn't know us very well. I would be told about reasons for her tears or concerns about her thumb-sucking and would be given suggestions on how to resolve them. I was constantly being scrutinised for being a single dad and I often wondered how the people I hardly knew would feel if I started judging and commenting on their parenting skills. I wasn't that arrogant that I had refused to take on board any suggestions, but it depended on where or whom they were coming from. I always listened to the people who had been involved in our lives and those who had spoken to me regularly about our development as a family of three.

Olivia was doing just fine and displayed no signs of discontentment. She is a survivor and for now I had no room in my delicate mind for thoughts of cancer and real battles for survival. I was feeling very depressed, so I called Carla for a chat. We spoke for an hour and she, too, was outraged about the evening's remarks. She agreed with me about letting Olivia have a normal childhood and forgetting about the cancer for now.

'Olivia will know when the time is right and will make the decision herself, based on her doctor's advice,' said Carla.

I was feeling a lot better after our chat. I was pleased to have Carla in my life, not only because we were on the same wavelength, but also because she was a very good influence. She was caring and thoughtful, which I considered to be important. I had made a list of requirements but at no time did I feel the need either to tick a box or to compare her to Sarah. I liked the fact that she was not threatened by Sarah's spirit and that she understood the need to keep Sarah's memory alive for the children. I liked Carla for the same reasons that she liked me. We understood each other really well and encouraged or comforted each other when necessary.

I was still shell-shocked when I awoke the next morning and I couldn't hide my feelings as I bumped into Selena in the kitchen. 'Good morning,' she said with a smile. Had last night really happened?

'I am not going to pretend to be happy. You were extremely insensitive last night and I want you both to leave,' I said.

She offered an apology but I dismissed it. I left the room with a coffee and retired to my bed. Half an hour later, Olivia ran into my bedroom and told me that our guests had left. They had not even said goodbye to the children. Olivia had heard their car and looked out of the window. She saw them drive away in the snow. The roads were dangerously icy but I was pleased that they were gone and so I put away any feelings of guilt. The children were a lot happier because my mood had changed and I was now relaxed. I wanted to spend some quality time with them and appreciate having them in my life. Christmas was going to be a happy time this year.

I love my children and they are so considerate for waking up after eight o'clock on Christmas Day. Long may this continue and without having to resort to using a cough syrup to make them drowsy. The day was pretty much like the previous year. There was too much food and drink and way too many presents. But although it was obvious that Sarah was missing, I was now taking part. My head wasn't in a cloud and my heart wasn't in a gutter. I was finally living and welcoming the joy that the children brought me.

The children slept over again at my parents' house and I spent Christmas night with Carla. We exchanged presents and talked about our individual days. I spent New Year's Day with her too, and the balance between our family life and our growing relationship was a healthy one. Both her children and mine were still young and needed stability, so we had no plans for the foreseeable future to combine our families and cause possible complications. We were both happy with the way things were between us and with our individual independence.

As I flipped my calendar over to February 2011, I realised that a whole month had passed with very few outbursts of anger or tears. It had been six months since I last held a cigarette and I knew that I would never smoke again. I had established a pretty good routine and my relationship with Carla was moving forward at a good pace. Of course there were complications that required the utmost understanding and communication, but then dating a widower is no easy task. I had also upset quite a lot of people with my inability to empathise owing to me holding the trump card. My trump card meant that my loss was greater than anyone else's problems and I would use my grief as an excuse to win most arguments, failing to consider Carla's and other people's feelings. But I had learned that grief accentuates a person's personality traits. I had anger in my life before my loss but it had been enhanced considerably by the situation in which I found myself. Jealousy, bitterness, low self-esteem and love had all been heightened by the death of my wife.

Carla was always honest about her feelings though and would share them with me. Sometimes she would be left feeling guilty after mentioning something about our relationship that she found upsetting. I would often make her feel worse by not listening to her or by completely disagreeing with her feelings, but Carla wasn't threatened by Sarah's memory. In fact, she had encouraged the hanging of photographs and the writing of my book, although the photographs of Sarah and me as a couple that are displayed around the house confused her at times. I was the only man in her life and the only one that she thought about. Seeing photographs of me with my late wife made her feel as if she wasn't completely with me or as important to me. My wedding ring made her feel this way too, as did the attitude of some long-term acquaintances towards her. Some would behave differently around her and appear to be disapproving of our relationship. Others would ignore her completely. We all have opinions and are quick to judge on certain matters. But I truly believe that unless you are widowed or have dated someone who is then it is impossible to understand the complex feelings that are involved.

I also had my own guilt about some of the raised concerns. I wanted to leave the photographs of Sarah and me as a couple around the place because I had feelings of disloyalty towards Sarah and the children. I didn't ever want them to think that I was ashamed of my relationship with their mum or that I was trying to forget it. I did remove my wedding ring though, placing it in the box with Sarah's. It felt like the right thing to do, as both rings were now together, side by side as they had been once before.

Communication certainly helped our relationship to evolve and I am still learning to listen and to understand Carla's feelings more as we continue to grow. Carla deserves this because she is important to me and the children. We are lucky that she is in our lives.

The second anniversary of Sarah's death had passed when I booked another week at our favourite hotel in Cornwall for Easter. The children would get most of my attention and the spa would get the rest. For two hours every morning I would relax in the Jacuzzi taking a well-deserved rest. Feeling completely relaxed, I would then have fun with the children on the beach or in the outdoor pool. I made a lot of friends at the hotel and this was mainly down to Olivia, who was very sociable and introduced herself to just about everyone staying at the hotel with us.

It was during this holiday that I realised how much I had progressed. I still missed Sarah and thought about her daily, but now I wasn't filled with sadness every time I did so. I was sitting on the grass at the back of the hotel in the glorious sunshine and the sea was spread out in front of me, surrounded by grass-topped cliffs on either side. The tide was out and the smooth sand was vast and inviting. Samuel and Olivia were pretending to be pirates on a wooden ship in the playground to my right, when I noticed an elderly couple holding hands in the distance. They were walking along the clifftop path and were silhouetted by the bright sunshine. I could now understand and feel the love that they had for each other. They had no obvious destination or time restrictions. If the rest of the living world disappeared during their walk, it would have made no difference to them. They had everything they needed in each other.

I am fully aware that Sarah and I would never walk the same path in old our our old age. But envy has now left me and I can smile again. I squinted from the brightness of the sun and sweat filled the lines around my eyes, which was a welcome change from the tears. Although they were half closed from the sun, my eyes were now open and I was aware that the seasons had returned. I had been caught up in winter and dark clouds for such a long time but at long last, summer had arrived. I was looking at the blue sky as if for the first time. When the new seasons arrived, I would be able to enjoy the gold of autumn and the colours of spring in the same uplifting way. The children were now laughing as they played and it was natural and real. It wasn't like the fake laughter that followed a bad joke. I didn't want to miss out on their childhood and have regrets in the future of a past that I cannot reclaim.

I was still learning to accept the fact that they would never be able to ask their mum a question or call out her name to ask for food or to give them a hug. But while some children have no parents, others have two who are unable to love them. Samuel and Olivia are lucky that they have me, because I love them and I have survived our loss because love is far stronger and lasts much longer than death.

'Dad, can you chase us?' shouted Sam, closely followed by Olivia.

'In a minute,' I shouted back, knowing very well that it was going to be at least five.

I am now feeling positive about our future, but I could not have got this far on my own. Mum and Dad have been amazing; they have never once let me or the children down. They have provided a second home for the children and loved them as much as if they were their own. Sarah had told me to listen to Cathy and always to turn to her for advice. She never gave up on me and I am confident that she will always be there for us along our continuing journey. Ruth kept her promise to Sarah regarding my loneliness and she babysits on a regular basis, enabling me to have a social life. She is a great listener too, and always has the time to provide me with words of encouragement when things get too much. My friends and neighbours have also helped me and I sometimes cringe when I think about them hearing me shouting through an open window.

And then there is Carla, who has helped me so much and makes me smile. She becomes more beautiful as the days pass and the seasons change. She is proof that it is possible to find love again. The future is always uncertain, as is a happy ending, but I have learned to embrace every day and to enjoy the here and now. Just like any widow/widower, I am learning to live again and making the transgression towards acceptance. To be truly happy, one has to get the balance right where love is concerned. If your love remains in the past during the present then it is impossible to have a happy, loving future. I will be true to my heart and all of my senses from this day forward as I continue to grow. I finally realise that every beat of my heart is a passing second that I don't want to skip or take for granted.

A large seagull sits on a chimney pot of a nearby house and is also looking in the direction of the sea. Sarah is out there somewhere and she is at peace. She is part of the sea, the flowers, the rain and the sky. And she will keep returning to our minds and our hearts as we live our new lives.

The bird spread its wings and pushed away from the chimney pot and up into the clear blue sky, getting smaller as it flew towards the sea and the horizon. My words follow closely behind as the seagull makes its own journey.

'Farewell, my love.'

Epilogue

Watching the bird flying out to sea was a defining moment, at which point I started to set my grief free and live a new life by moving forward. A year has now passed and we have come a long way as a family. There is routine and structure in our lives again. Feelings of grief still surface occasionally, but it is less frequent once you have reached acceptance.

There is no right or wrong way to grieve and everybody does it differently. I, for one, could never judge a widowed person on their behaviour alone because I have walked in their shoes for more than a day. The months that followed Sarah's death were surrounded by a haze of confusion, which is why the ensuing chapters following her death read like a diary. Now, I can only recollect the more dramatic, significant happenings of each day as at the time I was barely able to function to accomplish even the easiest of my parental duties, in that I was existing from moment to moment. I still get stressed when I am cooking a meal and the children are wrestling in another room, but that is real life. It is the same for all single parents. I no longer think that my life is more difficult than other people's lives, unless I run out of sundry items like milk or toilet rolls when the children are in bed.

I have learnt so much since Sarah's diagnosis in 2006. It has been a very rough ride but love is stronger than grief. Grief doesn't last forever, unlike our memories. When I think of Sarah now I smile. I am honoured to have had fifteen years with her and to have produced two children with her. I will never let them forget what a wonderful woman she was and I will not let her down. Today, this is evidenced by the fact our children are very happy and well balanced. Sarah had faith in my ability as a single dad and I am now strong enough to believe it, too. Sarah wanted me to move on and be happy with somebody else, so I feel lucky and privileged now to have Carla in my life. She is thoughtful, kind and never fails to make me laugh. Samuel and Olivia have accepted Carla into their lives because they, too, can see how genuine and loving she is and they love spending time with her and her two children.

In hindsight I met and started dating Carla too soon, but because of the strong compatibility and honest communication between us, we managed to work through the difficulties of dating after a loss on both sides. It was about getting the balance right between my love for Sarah and my love for Carla. One of the problems with dating again is accepting a new happiness. Every time I reached a pinnacle in our relationship it would be closely followed by a bout of depression, for the feelings of joy I was experiencing would remind me of ones from my past and I would be overwhelmed with guilt, tormenting myself. Letting go of the past isn't easy and cannot be rushed. Getting used to being a family without a mum is a monumental challenge and adjustment.

Having forty photographs of Sarah on the wall in my home and only one of Carla was not a reflection of my true feelings for Carla. Reducing the amount of photographs was difficult at first owing to a loyalty towards my past, Sarah's friends, her family and our children, but nonetheless I decided to take them down and I placed them in a photo album. To have so many photographs on display was holding me back from moving further forward. I didn't have as many pictures up of Sarah when she was alive and I didn't want my house to look like a shrine or mausoleum. Many widows/widowers have trouble removing photographs from display but it is vital that it is their choice when the time is right, because it can be just as difficult as making a decision to move house. I feel that children move on and accept their loss a lot quicker than adults, but it helps if the parent moves on, too. Remaining in a relationship with a ghost for the rest of one's days, especially if you have young children, is a lonely choice as far as I am concerned. One person dying is enough. To have lived the rest of my life in the past would have meant that I had died, too. I could have put my grief on a pedestal and loved only the past, caging any feelings of love for another, but that would not have helped either me or my children.

We all change and grow with every passing day. I will not be the same person tomorrow that I am today because I am constantly evolving and learning to enjoy new pathways in my life. These days, I try to appreciate the people I care about because I understand how devastating it would be to lose them. I hug, kiss and hold hands with all of the people in my circle of love and I am thankful for having them in my life to share the highs and the lows.

Nobody is better than anybody else. We all laugh, cry, love, grieve and die. Unknown celebrities are usually referred to as 'ordinary' people. But there is nothing ordinary about any of us. We are all as unique as our fingerprint, once you get under the shell to the soul. Just because the highest-paid actors are regularly seen on the cover of magazines doesn't mean they have more right to be there than a winner of a reality television show or an unfamiliar face. There is no doubt that some people are more fortunate or attractive than others and some crave the front-line celebrity status. A writer can wander around a shopping centre unnoticed but could very well be responsible for creating a character who made the actor famous for being able to deliver the lines of a script convincingly. Firemen, surgeons, nurses and soldiers, etc., are all celebrities, too. It is these 'unknown celebrities' who make a difference to others' lives on a daily basis, in the same way that Sarah has made a difference to our lives. Just because they are unknown doesn't make them any less of a celebrity in the beholder's eyes.

As I take a break from writing and stare out of the window, I notice three birds flying in the sky. The whole world is behind and in front of them. The direction in which they choose to fly is their choice. I think about my children and how they have a life behind and in front of them, too. They rarely think of tomorrow or yesterday. Like them, I feel happy because I, too, am living in the moment.